The Respectful Parent

The Respectful Parent

A Manual for Moms and Dads

To: Laura and Don

With much respect and love.

Jim and Marcia Deutch

October 2013
Honolulu Hawaii

DR. JAMES A. DEUTCH

AND

FRIENDS

To order additional copies of this book, contact:
Xlibris Corporation
1-888-795-4274
www.Xlibris.com
Orders@Xlibris.com
103821

CONTENTS

Section II. Gifting Your Child

Section III. Role Modeling for Parents

Section IV. Improving Routine Living

Section VI. About Teenagers

Section VII. In Memory

Profit from the sale of this book goes to the Family Education Centers of Hawai'i, a 501(c)(3) nonprofit organization.

To my wife, Marcia, our children, James and Frances, our mentors, Genevieve Painter and Raymond J. Corsini, and to the many parents and children of the Family Education Training Center of Hawai'i.

James A. Deutch

About the Author

Dr. Jim, as his students call him, holds a Doctor of Social Work degree from the Catholic University of America (1969) and a Master of Social Work degree from the University of Southern California (1961). He is a lecturer at the University of Hawai'i in the areas of parenting, marriage and family, and relationships. He also is the Senior Counselor at the Family Education Training Center of Hawai'i, a family-strengthening and counseling program located at the Manoa campus of the University of Hawai'i.

Dr. Deutch is a Hawai'i licensed clinical social worker. He is also a diplomate in clinical social work and clinical hypnosis and is a past president of the American Hypnosis Board for Clinical Social Work.

He began his professional career in 1961 as a clinical social worker in the United States Air Force. After serving as chief of social work services at six major Air Force hospitals, as well as being appointed as a consultant to the Air Force Surgeon General, Dr. Deutch retired in 1985 at the rank of lieutenant colonel. In 1985, he was appointed at the University of Hawai'i School of Social Work as an assistant professor and director of practicum. In 1988, he joined Kaiser Permanente in Hawai'i as a clinical social worker where he remained until his retirement. In 2003, he was asked to return to the University of Hawai'i as a lecturer in the Department of Family and Consumer Sciences.

Dr. Deutch was selected as the Air Force Social Worker of the Year in 1971. In 1975, he was awarded the Air Force Humanitarian Service Medal for his work in helping to rescue three thousand orphaned babies from Vietnam. In 1978, he was appointed as an associate clinical professor of psychiatry at the School of Medicine, Wright State University, Dayton, Ohio. In 2002, Dr. Deutch was voted the Hawai'i Social Worker of the Year for education. He is the coauthor of the Hawai'i social worker licensure law.

He has been married to the former Marcia Ann Ellis for almost fifty years. They have two children, James, an electrical engineer, and Frances, an Air Force colonel.

Dr. Deutch's hobbies include driving and working on his 1951 MG-TD classic car, tennis, family genealogy, and walking his two dogs, Dr. Toby and Ms. Tina.

PREFACE

This book of teaching essays was inspired by the many parents who have attended the Family Education Training Center of Hawai'i (FETCH) over the years, as well as those University of Hawai'i students to whom I have been privileged to teach the subject of Adlerian style of parenting. As I listened, I heard them struggling with particular areas of child rearing. This book is my attempt to address those concerns in a quick and focused manner, using practical stories and solid principles to educate and motivate.

Each chapter essay is self-contained. No one has to read and digest the entire book in order to understand what to do to move toward family harmony. Endnotes lead the reader to sources of information. I have attempted to make the reader aware of the classic Adlerian parenting books. Like other classic books, some copyright dates may not be current, but the wisdom offered in the pages is up-to-date. Each chapter ends with a 𝒩𝑜𝑡𝑒𝑠 page on which the reader can jot down ideas that are important to him or her.

The table of contents clearly shows the focus of every essay. This allows parents to go directly to the essay that will help them deal with their current situation.

I want to thank my wife, Marcia Ann Deutch, MA, who has been my editor and inspiration. She also has been the severest critic of my work, making sure what I produce honors the original Adlerian thinkers, as well as the parents, students, professionals, and interested others who will read this book. I believe that the success we had rearing our two children mostly has been due to her knowledge and application of Adlerian and Dreikursian parenting skills. Our children, who are currently in their forties, are successful in managing life and have always been the best of friends.

I want to thank two good friends and colleagues. Dr. Mary Martini, a full professor at the University of Hawai'i at Manoa, whom I assisted in starting the Family Education Training Center of Hawai'i and who is now its executive director. Thanks also to Fay Rawles-Schock whom I have known for many years and whom I consider to be one of the best Adlerian educators anywhere.

My warmest mahalo also must go to four other friends who read my chapters, made good suggestions, and became part of an encouragement squad. They are Kleo Rigney Corsini, MD, Tom Burke, who became an adoptive father at sixty-five, and Elaine French and her husband Jerry Smith, both caring grandparents.

James A. Deutch
January 2012

The Family Education Training Center of Hawai'i (FETCH) is located on the grounds of the University of Hawai'i at Manoa, 2020 East-West Road, Honolulu, Hawai'i, 96822. FETCH is a shared project of the College of Tropical Agriculture, Department of Family and Consumer Sciences, and the Family Education Centers of Hawai'i (FECH), a private nonprofit organization. For information, go to the FETCH website at *www.efetch.org*, or telephone 808-956-2248.

SECTION I.
Understanding Your Child's Behavior

Deutch family, 1967
Marcia, Frances, James, Jim

Alfred Adler
1870-1937

INTRODUCTION

What Is Adlerian Psychology, and How Does It Strengthen Families?

The Story of the Deutch Family

I was trained as a Freudian, but after having two children, I "converted" and became an Adlerian. As a parent, I soon realized that Freud had not given me the tools to rear my "dynamic duo" the way I knew they should be reared. At the time of my conversion, we were stationed at Hickam Air Force Base in Hawai'i. Our son, James, was eight and our daughter, Frances, was six. To my way of thinking, they were both great children and seldom gave us problems. However, as they grew older, I could see behavior problems beginning to appear on the horizon. My son, James, was beginning to respond to my nagging of "hurry up, hurry up" by becoming slower and slower. The more I nagged "hurry up," the slower he became. I knew the diagnosis to this behavior was "passive-aggressive," but I did not know the solution. Freud had let me down. So I did what every parent does: I nagged more and I nagged louder.

Our sweet little daughter, Frances, had made the decision to yield the academic playing field to her bright brother and became the social child of the family. However, when Frances makes up her mind to achieve a goal, she goes all the way. We soon found that Frances was making good grades in school because she was sweet-talking the teachers and cleaning the blackboard erasers instead of doing her work. More embarrassingly, she was sitting on the lap of every male who came to our home for a social or professional visit. My wife, Marcia, and I knew that the Deutch family was in the early stages of trouble. We didn't know what to do. We thought about going to the Hickam mental health clinic and seeking advice from the child and family social worker, except I *was* the child and family social worker at Hickam.

In the early 1970s, our country was embroiled in the Vietnam War. Our energy at the Hickam Clinic was focused on the troops. We were busy doing mental health evaluations on active duty personnel, psychotherapy with men who had the symptoms of what was to become called post-traumatic stress disorder (PTSD), individual therapy with troops who were suffering from everyday stress, and a smattering of marital counseling with young airmen and their spouses. We were not serving the needs of families with child-rearing challenges. Family strengthening was not one of our duties.

In the fall of 1972, Sandra, a mother of two, knocked on my office door. Sandra was on the board of the Family Education Center of Hawai'i (FECH), a nonprofit organization founded by Dr. Raymond J. Corsini, which focused on family strengthening.[1] The board wanted to open a branch of FECH on Hickam Air Force Base. I knew that our clinic was not serving the psychological needs of military children and their families, and I realized that if anyone was to change that situation, it would have to be me, the base social worker. Sandra told me that a new and wonderful Adlerian psychologist, Dr. Genevieve Painter,[2] was moving to Hawai'i, and we could have her services free of charge if I could arrange for her to do a family education program one night a week. Sandra gave me a book, *Children: The Challenge* by Rudolf Dreikurs,[3] and we agreed to talk again in two weeks.

When I arrived home that evening, I gave the book to my wife, Marcia. She read Dr. Dreikurs's book and subsequently tried several of his techniques on our children with great success. One week later, a smiling Marcia said to me, "I like this book, and it really works. No more yelling and nagging, you've got to read this. It will help you to be a better father, and your patients need to know this material too." I read the book and vigorously agreed with her.

I helped Sandra to create the Family Education Center at Hickam. It met under the counseling leadership of Dr. Genevieve Painter for many years, even after both Sandra and I had left the base. During my sojourn at Hickam, I was privileged to intern with Dr. Painter for three years and became certified as an Adlerian family counselor. Marcia also became certified as an Adlerian family counselor and worked with families in the civilian community.

My becoming an Adlerian has benefitted my family and my practice. We found that when we changed our behavior, the children changed theirs. We put our children into an Adlerian school and both bloomed academically. Adolescence was a breeze for us as parents. Today, James is a successful electrical engineer and has his own family. Frances has chosen to remain single. She is a United States Air Force colonel in the field of intelligence. She is currently working on her doctoral dissertation, successfully having completed her academic coursework. My meeting that day in 1972 with Sandy changed the way I parent, how I handle my relationships with others, and how I practice my profession as a clinical social worker.

Adler and Freud[4]

Many people do not realize that at one time Adler and Freud were friends. The popular story is that in 1902 Adler publically defended Freud's book, *The Interpretation of Dreams*. As a result, Adler was invited to join Freud's psychoanalytically oriented inner circle, which came to be known as the Viennese Psychoanalytic Society. According to the historian Henri Ellenberger, in reality, there is no documentation to validate how these two men actually met. Adler was one of the first four members of Freud's inner circle. He was very active in the early days of the movement, and Freud held him in high esteem. In 1910, Freud nominated Adler to become the president of the society, and he was subsequently elected. Adler also became editor of Freud's newsletter.

At the same time, Adler began disagreeing with Freud's mechanistic and biologically oriented theories. Adler believed the role of the social environment had much to do with how people respond to their circumstances. His was a humanistic and commonsense point of view. For example, Adler disagreed with Freud's concept of "penis envy." Adler believed that it is not the male organ women envy, but the social and economic opportunities men have that women are denied. Historians believe that Adler was the first psychiatrist to advocate for women's rights. Another major difference between the two schools is their view of personality. Freud separated the self into id, ego, and superego while Adler saw the personality as a unified entity.

In 1911, Adler resigned his positions and broke away from Freud and the society and formed his own group of social psychology advocates. Adler labeled his own school of thought Individual Psychology. The name was intended "to express the conviction that the psychological process and their manifestations can be understood only from the individual context and that all psychological insights begin with the individual."[5] Although a number of individuals who had joined with Freud later separated from his inner circle, it is said that Adler's departure caused Freud the greatest degree of hurt and anger from which he never let go.

In 1914, war officially came to Europe. Freud remained in Vienna, writing essays and giving talks. Adler, at age forty-six, was drafted into the Austrian army as a physician and worked in neuropsychiatric settings.

Following the German and Austria-Hungarian Empire's defeat in 1918, Adler returned to Vienna to help rebuild his city and country. There were chaos, famine, epidemics, and shortages of medicine and fuel throughout the land. Crime and juvenile delinquency were on the rise.

Between the years 1920 and 1927, Adler developed approximately thirty child guidance centers in Vienna and assisted in the development of several more in Germany and Holland. The primary focus of these centers was on educating parents as well as training teachers. Adler believed that parent education was the key to building healthy families. He devised a model of "open-forum" counseling wherein families were counseled in "public."[6] He believed that the problems encountered by one family were very similar to problems encountered by all families, and by watching and hearing solutions given to others, people could learn and benefit by being a part of the "audience." Adler's concept was quite different from the Freudian model, which advocates that counseling should be done in private. The private sessions model subtly reinforces the idea that family challenges are "dirty laundry" that should be considered shameful and private. Adler did not believe that family and child-rearing issues were dirty and shameful, but usual and normal.

In 1930, Adler was honored by the City Council of Vienna, receiving the title, "Citizen of Vienna."[7] As the Nazis gained political power, Adler saw the frightening future. Beginning in 1926, Adler had been spending summers teaching in the United States, a country in which he was falling in love.[8] In 1934 his wife, Raisse, with the children, joined him in America, making Chicago their new home.

Rudolf Dreikurs

Rudolf Dreikurs was a successful Vienna-trained psychiatrist who had worked in Adler's child guidance clinics since the early 1920s. In 1927 he began to identify himself as an Adlerian and later became a protégé of Alfred Adler. Adler saw in Dreikurs a man of unusual potential. Dreikurs helped to develop Adler's concepts concerning children and family strengthening. In early 1937, following the Austro-fascist government's closing of Adler's child guidance clinics and experimental school, Dreikurs decided to come to America. The decision to emigrate most likely was enhanced when simultaneously, word reached Dreikurs in Vienna of the sudden death of Adler. Dreikurs was deeply saddened by this loss to the world of a man whom he so deeply admired. I believe that Dreikurs's memorial to Adler is his prolific writing and his success in advancing the theory and cause of Adlerian Individual Psychology in America and throughout the world.[9]

What Do Adlerians Believe?[10]

Adlerian theory is quite broad and comprehensive. However, I have found a number of useful fundamentals to understanding child and adult behavior as it applies to the process of personality development and family strengthening. A familiarity with these fundamentals will serve every mom and dad as they read this book and apply its suggestions to their family.

All behavior is purposeful and goal directed. This means that your child's actions, the way he conducts himself at home, at school, and in public, are not random, but serve the purpose of achieving his desired goal. A child's behavioral goals are usually not conscious, but they affect his behavior nevertheless. Some psychologies believe that one's past is all-powerful in determining behavior. Adlerians believe that while respect for the past is appropriate, behavior is determined by what a person wants for the future. I like the analogy that Freudians drive through life by viewing through the rearview mirror while Adlerians drive looking at traffic through the front car window.

All movement is from a minus to a plus, from inferiority to superiority, from incompetence to competence. Inborn into every child is the desire for competence. Babies on their backs desire to turn onto their stomachs and back again. A baby lying in a crib desires to stand. A crawling child desires to walk, and a walking child desires to run. We go to school to become smarter and wiser. Each of us desires to work and become more competent than we were a moment before. "This drive—to become smarter, more attractive, more competent—is the basic force that pushes people into action. It is an inherent motivation, the urge to move from minus to plus."[11]

Children learn by trial and error. A child's intellectual ability to reason, abstract, and plan is limited by his lack of experience and the immaturity of his developing brain. Children do, and by doing, they learn. When a piece of behavior offers some kind of a payoff, the child repeats that behavior, reinforcing what has been learned. When a piece of behavior does not offer a desired payoff, the child tries something else until another payoff is at hand. Many parents believe their child is out to get them by practicing aberrant behaviors at their expense. In reality, children merely do what they believe rewards them in terms of some kind of a payoff. Children's behavior can appear to the parent to be useful or useless. To the child, useful and useless have very little meaning. For him, it is his desired payoff, his goal, that really counts.[12]

The family constellation is the child's primary crucible for personality develoment.[13] Each child has a special position within the family. From this view, he observes and interprets the world and makes decisions on how he is going to interact with it. The family usually begins with a couple. When the first child is born, he is seen as "king baby" or she as "the princess." This child receives much, and nothing is expected in return. With the birth of the second child, the first child loses his position as the "only child," now becoming the first child, but in reality, he has been dethroned. Mother's attention is no longer solely on him, and for a while, it may be lost completely. When a third child is born, the first child is usually given more responsibility and even less attention. The second child now becomes the middle or squeezed child, being dethroned from his former position as the baby. The youngest child now holds the title of "baby" with all the rights and privileges thereof. The shifts in the family's constellation as it grows larger cause the dynamics to become more complex and provide for a wider range of interactions and learning experiences. The family is the child's center of the world and prepares him to meet the complexities of everyday life.

Social interest.[14] Social interest is a sense one has of belonging to the greater community, having a caring concern for its welfare and the welfare of others. It also connotes a sincere desire to contribute to society and having good feelings about oneself. While social interest is innate, it must be developed, usually by the caretaking mother. Often, it is seen as a measure of mental health.

The major goal of a child is to belong to the family with significance. Unique to the human infant is the necessity of having nurturing others surrounding and caring for him in order to survive and prosper. This need for human contact seems to be hardwired into every human at birth. There is a basic need on the part of every child to be a part of a family, a group, a community, to belong with significance.

The best way to belong to the family with significance is through cooperation and contribution. Cooperation means doing what is appropriate for the situation. However, due to their immaturity, children solve the age-old question of "How do I belong to this family with significance?" by using their immature and inexperienced belief system. A child's belief system is not necessarily based on "reality" but on his *interpretation* of what he perceives and experiences. For the human, there is no such thing as "reality," only one's *interpretation* of what is real.

The quality and quantity of a child's contribution is dependent on many factors, such as age, experience, abilities, and innate talents.

Rudolf Dreikurs, MD
1897-1972

Dreikurs's Principles for Child Rearing[15]

Adlerian psychology, as formulated by Rudolf Dreikurs, offers thirty-five principles that parents can use to rear happy and healthy children.

1. ***Encourage your child.*** I like the way Dr. Dreikurs begins his chapter on encouragement in his ground breaking book, *Children: The Challenge.* To me, this quote speaks volumes.

   "Encouragement is more important than any other aspect of child-raising. It is so important that the lack of it can be considered the basic cause of misbehavior. *A misbehaving child is a discouraged child.* Each child needs continuing encouragement just as a plant needs water.

He cannot grow and develop and gain a sense of belonging without encouragement."[16]

2. *Avoid the use of punishment and reward.* Punishment and reward have been handed down to us from the autocratic and social systems of the past and totalitarian regimes of the present. Punishment and reward do not have a viable place within a loving, democratic family of the twenty-first century. Researchers consistently find that while punishment can be effective in the short-term, it does nothing to teach a child how to behave on the useful side of life in the future. Researchers also find that children who are punished for rule breaking in the home often demonstrate higher levels of rule breaking when away from home.[17]

   Children who grow up in the reward system, in actuality, are being trained to believe that nothing is worth doing unless there is an external reward, positive or negative, awaiting them. Adlerians believe that internally derived motivation is far stronger and longer lasting than externally derived motivation.

3. **Use natural and logical consequences.** Adlerians train their children using a more powerful discipline than punishment and reward: one that has none of their inherent side effects. Natural and logical consequences are disciplinary methods that are in harmony with the way nature and society teaches behavior, not only to our children, but to adults as well.

   Think of the word *nature* while using the word *natural*. A surfer who does not tie his surfboard to his ankle may lose his board when toppled by a large wave. When the temperature is freezing, anyone out of doors who is not wearing earmuffs will chance frozen ears.

   Logical consequences are what parents do when nature is too dangerous or would take too long to teach its lesson. "If you act goofy at the restaurant, I immediately will take you home." "If you don't pick up your clothes in the living room before supper, you can't eat until the cleanup is done." Logical consequences must never be a punishment in disguise.[18]

4. ***Be firm without dominating.*** Children want parents who are firm, set limits, and consistently do what they say they are going to do, thus establishing credibility. Without limits, children test to see just how far they can go, which sets the stage for parental outrage and overreaction.[19] Parents who dominate and show similar behaviors that are disrespectful often find themselves in unnecessary power contests. In its authoritarian way, dominance shows the child that the parent is striving to be their boss, which is very disrespectful to the child and to the adult. Parents need to listen more, talk less, and understand better.

5. ***Respect your child.*** "Democratic living is based on mutual respect. If only one person in the relationship is granted respect, there is no equality."[20] One shows respect by listening to the other, asking their opinion and input, being considerate of the other's feelings, being encouraging rather than discouraging, never being physically or mentally cruel, and never proffering putdowns to show one's superiority. Respect also means keeping one's expectations of the child to what is age appropriate and reasonable.

   For five decades, parents have been telling me that when they began respecting their children, treating them the way they as parents would want to be treated, the quality of the parent-child relationship bloomed and disharmony within the family faded away.

6. ***Induce a respect for order.*** Order is the way of the universe. Planets revolve around the sun and have a special relationship with each other. The universe tends to be predictable. However, it is when asteroids, the missiles of unpredictability, appear that trouble begins. Imagine driving your car down the freeway without other drivers having a respect for common agreements that make driving orderly and safe. Traffic would not move and one's life would be in constant peril.

   People who live in groups, such as families, also need a respect for order. To live happily, group members need to cooperate regarding tasks. Who gets up first in the morning? How is the morning meal created? When do children leave for school and parents for work?

At school or at work, in what order are the necessary tasks to be accomplished? By what processes do parents and children return to the home? How does supper get made? How does the house get cleaned? How does homework get accomplished? What is the order in which one does things to get ready for sleep? Order is a necessary and valuable commodity in family living that must be respected by all participants.

7. ***Induce a respect for the rights of others.*** In a democratic family, parents have the same rights as children. Children are not our superiors, nor are they our inferiors. Parents have a right to dignity, privacy, and self-respect. Children have a right to the same. By parents modeling a respect for the rights of others, children will watch and learn how to be respectful too.

8. ***Eliminate criticism and minimize mistakes.*** When I was a little boy, I wrote a letter to my "Ant" Betty. I remember my mother correcting my spelling. It was then that I learned the pain of "constructive criticism." There is no such thing as constructive criticism; there is only criticism. It took another twenty years before I wrote my next letter. Dreikurs strongly believed that focusing on mistakes can be disastrous. When parents center their attention on the error, they direct the child's attention from the positive to the negative. Children easily become afraid of making mistakes, and the more mistakes are pointed out, the more discouraged the child becomes. Parents should never attempt to build on weakness, only on strength. Weaknesses have a way of resolving themselves in strong children.

9. ***Maintain family routine.*** "Routine is to a child what walls are to a house; it gives boundaries and dimensions to his life."[21] Children feel safer when they know what is to come next. When parents establish order in the home, their children become more relaxed and cooperative. It is up to the parent to create a family schedule.[22]

10. ***Take time for training.*** Children need hands-on training. Being told or even observing another in action is not always the level of training a child needs. Learning to tie shoes, determining which clothes to wear, learning table manners, knowing how to behave at the restaurant, and

how to act at the grocery store are all behaviors that need practice. Teaching your child what to do while you are in a hurry is ineffective and leads to bad conduct on the part of all participants. Take time for training and enjoy watching your child learn in a relaxed and pleasant atmosphere. Times like these make parenting fun.

11. ***Win cooperation.*** In authoritarian and totalitarian environments, cooperation means doing what one is told. In our increasingly democratic social atmosphere, cooperation means working together to meet the demands of the situation. Parents need to learn how to stimulate cooperation. Demanding cooperation by saying such things as "You do it or else" is a sure way of setting up a power contest, which can lead to situations of revenge by both parent and child. It is far easier and more productive to win cooperation than by demanding it. I believe that having individual special time,[23] having a family council,[24] implementing listening skills,[25] and showing respect and deference for the child are all ways for parents to win cooperation and achieve family harmony. Parents who win children's cooperation are light years ahead of parents who are stuck in the demanding mode.

12. ***Avoid giving undue attention.*** The Deutch family was living in a Hickam Air Force Base sixplex base housing unit when I, as a new Adlerian, came to understand the meaning of undue attention. The eleven-year-old boy next door was a bright young man with an annoying high-pitched voice and a nonstop one-word vocabulary of "Why?" Whenever one of his parents said something to him, be it a fact or sometimes an order, he would reply with a "Why?" His parents told me that they were very proud of their boy's high intellect and that they were happy to supply his intellect with information. Unfortunately, this kid had learned to get undue attention from his parents by keeping them busy with him through uttering a word that he had found did the trick. He was not interested in learning, only getting parental attention.

Undue attention is the first of the four misguided goals of children found by Dreikurs.[26] As you read the many case examples of undue attention in this book, you will get a deeper understanding of how children use this "annoying" method to gain their misguided goal.

13. ***Sidestep the struggle for power.*** As your once darling child repeatedly ignores your requests and chronically argues with you, do you find yourself saying, "I would never have acted that way toward my parents"? Do you get the message that she is saying, "I'm going to be the boss and do what I want, not what you want me to do."? Do you ever feel angry about the way she behaves? When these things happen, know that your child is into a power struggle. Believe it or not, most parents are threatened by this kind of behavior. Their goal then is to beat the child at her own game by overpowering her. In the long run, unless you want to become Attila the Hun, this is exactly the wrong strategy to use. "Children sense the democratic atmosphere of our times and resent our attempt at authority over them. They show their resentment by retaliation. They resist our attempts to overpower them and show us their power instead."[27] By engaging in power struggles with your children, you teach them to become power mad, and your family life loses quality.

Undue power is the second of the four misguided goals of children found by Dreikurs. If you are constantly being challenged by your child and feeling angry about the process, you have a child who is into power. The best solution, as Dreikurs believes, is to sidestep the struggle for power.

14. ***Withdraw from the conflict.*** When you find yourself, and you will, in a conflict with your child, withdraw. The field of battle is always represented by two opposing forces. When the parent strategically withdraws, there is no one left for the child to fight. She is left in a vacuum with no audience or opponent to defeat. As we Adlerians say, "Take your sails out of your child's wind." Be sure to read the essay chapters on other parent-proven methods of withdrawing from conflict.[28]

15. ***Action, not words.*** Learn to keep your mouth shut. Parents talk too much and as a result, children become "parent deaf." Reasoning with young children usually does not work nor do words work in a conflictual situation. When parents want to change the behavior of their child, they must act; words are futile. While one cannot decide

for the child what to do, a parent can always decide what he or she will do. By acting wisely, a parent can teach their child how to behave.[29]

16. *Use quiet insistence, not indiscriminant admonitions.* Before becoming an Adlerian parent, I was a nag. "Hurry up, James, hurry up, James" was my badger. I was allowing myself to be provoked into an irritated reaction that Dreikurs describes as "shooing flies." Other parents use indiscriminate admonitions to correct their children's disturbing behavior with a series of words such as "don't," "stop that," "move it," and "be quiet." Our words are said as we would wave away a bothersome fly. A friend of mine and father of six daughters told me the story of how embarrassed he felt when one of his little girls replied to an inquiry about her name, saying, "My name is Betsy No No." Rather than shoo flies around a behavior we find irritatingly inappropriate, it is best to attend to the matter and follow through with quiet insistence until the child willingly complies. Otherwise we are training our children that they do not have to comply until we become demanding.

17. *Use care in pleasing—have the courage to say no.* Parents who lack the courage to say no usually feel obligated to please the child as much as possible. Such parents may feel guilty because of a divorce, a child's physical or mental handicap, an attempt to balance the harshness of the other parent, a fear that their child might think they are not loved, and any of a hundred other reasons related to the private logic of the parent. Whenever indulging an offspring, a parent runs the risk of being shortsighted and disrespectful to the real needs of the child.

18. *Avoid the first impulse—do the unexpected.* Often, children purposely misbehave in order to get a "rise" out of their parent. The parent is then tempted to react on impulse and swat, yell, curse, or talk cross in return. Guess what! That is the exact behavior your child wants from you. When you fall into the child's trap, there is nothing good to be learned, and no lesson for life's success comes from it. Rather than responding on your first impulse, think for a moment and do the unexpected. During a heavy discussion with your child, try saying something like, "You have a good point there. Let me think about that." If a child is

talking of her frustration about which clothes to wear for what event, try an unexpected, "When would you like me to help you clean up and sort your closet?" If your children are fighting, silently get up and walk away. Making a positive learning experience out of any situation is great parenting.

19. ***Refrain from overprotection.*** It seems mothers, more than fathers, are guilty of overprotecting their children. Rather than training our children for courage and strength, overprotecting them does just the opposite: it makes them weak and unprepared for the ordinary stresses of life. This is especially true of a child with a disability. Children with handicaps, from juvenile diabetes to spina bifida, need extra coping skills that are best developed in a courageous environment. Dreikurs warns us that many parents, under the pretext of concern with their children's welfare, keep their children helpless and dependent. This lets them appear powerful and protective to their children as well as to themselves. This behavior places the parent in a superior dominant position and keeps their children submissive. Behind our overprotective efforts, Dreikurs believes, are our own doubts as parents that we have the ability to tackle our own problems. Children who are coddled, spoiled, and pampered can easily grow up with a rage against a seemingly unfair world that doesn't quickly meet their wants or needs.[30]

20. ***Stimulate independence***. Children who do for themselves feel the pride of accomplishment. Feelings of accomplishment lead to further accomplishments and a belief in themselves that they are up to any challenge. Children that receive service from a parent are vulnerable to developing feelings of inferiority, which teach them that they are useless, helpless, dependent, and inadequate human beings. To avoid this undesirable state, parents need only follow this one rule, "Never do for a child what he can do for himself."[31]

21. ***Stay out of fights.*** Much parental energy goes into settling fights between siblings and teaching them fairness. Parents need to remember that all behavior is purposeful and goal directed. Most parents believe that what children fight about is the real issue. This very rarely is true. While children do have disagreements, the rule of thumb is, *children*

fight for parents' attention. The goal of children when they fight is not always obvious to their parents. When parents interfere, they are giving a payoff to the misguided behavior and denying their children a chance to work and grow their sibling relationship. If fighting is harsh and chronic, parents also need to look at the quantity and quality of individual time they are giving each child, as well as the level of encouragement. The responsibility to deal with the conflict belongs to the children; the parents need do nothing. Parents need to think, "This fight is none of my business, and they are only trying to sucker me in." Once parents realize this and apply Adlerian corrective actions, fighting and rivalry will become significantly less.[32]

22. ***Be unimpressed by fears.*** I was a teenager driving home from a date in the family car when the auto in front of me was hit head-on by another vehicle. I stopped and rendered aid to the two unconscious men, one whose head had penetrated the front windshield. What I learned that night was that fear was a luxury I could not afford if I were to be useful during a life-threatening situation. In later years when I had children, I realized in order to have courageous children, I must not give into fatherly fears. When my children were sick or hurt, while being empathetic, I chose not to be emotional. When our son, James, became afraid to take a bath after watching the movie *Jaws*, I gave him assurance that a shark was far too big to swim up the tub's drain and kindly gave him the choice of whether or not to take his bath that evening. He chose to bathe, and in several days, his shark fear was no longer an issue. I realized that his fear reaction, if somehow reinforced, would become a deficit to his self-esteem. I also wondered if his fearful behavior was somehow a misguided bid for my attention. What I gave my boy was far greater than an immediate payoff for his fears; it was a lesson in courage.

23. ***Mind your own business. Keep out of others' relationships.*** All people, including children, have a right to their own relationships, free from the interference of others. The child has a right to his relationship with his father even if the mother does not agree with the father's manner of discipline. Criticism of him in front of the child is inappropriate. If

Mother needs to talk with her husband, it should be done in private away from the ears of the child. At times, parents may not like the way the grandparents spoil their child. Here again, parents might want to talk with the grandparents about the way they are "spoiling" their child. However, interfering with the grandparent-grandchild relationship should be avoided. While children love to be spoiled, they understand the difference between what they can get away with at Grandma's house and what they can get away with at home.

When multigenerational families live together, the lines of parenting responsibility often become blurred. Oftentimes the child is placed in the care of grandparents whose child-rearing philosophy is in conflict with that of the parents'. In such situations, it is doubly important that the parents and grandparents have strong and open lines of communication.

24. *Avoid the pitfall of pity.* When parents assume that disappointments are too much for their child to take, they are showing great disrespect for their offspring. When children are pitied, they lose courage and the strength to accept the reality of what is. Such a belief can prevail throughout a person's life, permanently relieving that person of the chance to be all that he or she can be. As Dreikurs says, "Pity is damaging, even when justifiable and understandable."[33]

25. *Make requests reasonable and sparse.* Micromanaging your children because you think you know best, not trusting their judgment, or wanting to show your authority, is a very poor way to develop your child's abilities to think, feel, and act responsibly. A child who feels imposed upon will act disobediently. Nagging parents cause children to act parent deaf and passive-aggressive. Wise parents make reasonable requests few in number while speaking to their children in a kind and respectful manner.

26. *Follow through—be consistent, gain credibility.* Parents need to follow through on their word and become credible in the eyes of their children. Do what you say you are going to do. A parent's word needs to be his or her bond.[34]

When our children were preschoolers, we would take them to midlevel restaurants and allow them to choose from the menu and give their order directly to the server. Our son, James, would always order a hamburger even though he knew he could order anything he wanted. Daughter Frances was more adventurous. One day, she ordered lobster. Looking at the price, I about died, but I managed to keep my mouth shut and my credibility intact. Much later, we had a family discussion and modified the rules to exclude the overpriced dishes on the menu, except on designated occasions. Today, my daughter still loves lobster, and when I visit her, she always takes me out and we enjoy lobster together.

27. ***Put all your kids in the same boat.*** Multiple kids in a family have a way of working together as a team to "beat" the parents. When an infraction occurs such as "Who did the artwork on the wall?" or "Who started the argument?" more often than not, it is difficult to know who did what and for what reason. Since consciously or unconsciously children conspire, Adlerian parents play it smart and put all the children in the same boat. If a wall is crayoned, all the children clean it up. If all the children are loudly arguing and you decide to boot them out doors, send them all out. When you put your children in the same boat, it keeps you from trapping your children into roles such as "the good child," "the bad child," or even "the deficient child." Be pleased that your children work as a team, but respond so that the team works toward contributing to the welfare of the family as a whole.

28. ***Listen liberally, speak sparingly—LL-SS.*** Children learn best by *doing* and little by hearing the orders and commands of an unhappy parent. As children speak, they are involved in the "doing process"; they are learning as they speak. Parents often assume that they know what the child is going to say and therefore guess without listening. That kind of behavior is disrespectful and teaches a child how to disrespect in kind. The family council is an excellent place for parents to learn to listen. All must remember that just because a parent is listening does not mean that they are agreeing with the child. Adlerians believe that every child should have its say, but not necessarily get its way.

29. ***Watch your tone of voice.*** One's tone of voice is a tool as is one's words. Your tone of voice can say many things. Listen to the tone used by parents when they are upset by their child's behavior. "Do it now or else!" or "You are a disappointment to me." Also, listen to the tone of voice when a parent is encouraging. "I know you can do it" and "I have faith in you." Have you ever heard someone talk baby talk to an infant? "Wouldums like to goums with me?" Such language is condescending and disrespectful as it signifies our superiority and the little one's inferiority. In any case, baby talk does not teach the child the proper use of the English language so needed to succeed in school. Talk to your child in the voice and tone as you would talk to a respected and intelligent friend.

30. ***Take it easy; it's impossible to treat every child the same.*** Over concern with fairness and trying not to show favoritism, while laudable, is nearly impossible. Some families prefer girls to boys, others, boys to girls. Some parents like best the child of the opposite sex while others prefer the child of the same sex. Among some parents, the older child is preferred while in other families the baby is preferred. Unless the preference is too biased, little harm will be done.

   There are some things parents can do to ensure fairness. For special occasions, a parent can ask each child what gift they want. Allow each child to pick his or her own present from among a group of gift possibilities. When buying the same item for each child, allow each child to pick their favorite color. When serving cake, allow one child to slice and the other to have the first choice. Rather than using up parental energy to do the impossible, it is far better to treat each child according to his or her needs. Children respond to a parent's attitude, and respectfully loving your child is the best behavior a parent can offer.

31. ***Downgrade the importance of "bad habits."*** When you pay attention to a child's behavior, you are reinforcing it and upping the probability you will see it again. If you ignore it, you are giving it no energy and increasing the probability that it will extinguish. If the behavior is important enough that a lesson should come from it, at a later and

neutral time, you can talk with your child about the issue. Otherwise, as a rule of thumb, let go of the incident and let it disappear. The choice is yours.

32. ***Have family fun.*** For years, I have been asking students and parents to recall their childhood's happiest memories. In one way or another, all have revealed their happiest times as being with loving family members while having fun. What parents and students say is that family fun must never be competitive. There should be no winner or loser, fun comes from participating in family games. Fun parents are always encouraging and never critical.

33. ***Talk with your children, not at them.*** As parents, we are far too busy trying to shape our children as if they were soft clay and we were the master potter. It really doesn't work that way. As parents, we are far better off finding out what the child is thinking rather than telling her what to think. Parents become aware of what their children are thinking by listening to them with both ears and a closed mouth. If a parent knows his child's private logic and misguided goal, a parent has a better chance to be of help. I suggest from early on, you become your child's consultant. As you both enter his teen years, as a consultant rather than the boss, you will have a greater voice in determining his future conduct.[35]

34. ***Establish a weekly family council.*** A family council is "a meeting of all members of the family in which problems are discussed and solutions sought."[36] "The secret of its success," says Dreikurs, "lies in the willingness of all members of the family to approach a problem as being a *family* problem."[37]

35. **Establish individual special time with each child**.[38] I suggest that parents schedule ten minutes a day of individual special time with each child. At our family education center, I guarantee each parent that special time will become the lubricant that makes the wheels and cogs of family life run more smoothly. As parents, we want much for our children, yet we are neglectful in giving them the greatest gift of all, our time and ourselves.

Spelled out by Dreikurs, the above thirty-five principles have been a guide for counselors, family educators, and parents who advocate the Adlerian methodology of family strengthening. These principles have been a boon to me as a practitioner, teacher, and family man. I believe they will be of great benefit to you as you make your journey through this book as well as your journey as a parent.

Endnotes

[1]   Dr. Raymond Corsini, a prolific writer and Adlerian psychologist, worked with Dr. Rudolf Dreikurs in Chicago, Ill. prior to moving to Hawai'i in 1965. The following year, he started the Family Education Center of Hawai'i. Dr. Corsini passed away in 2008 at the age of ninety-four.

[2]   Dr. Genevieve Painter first met Dr. Rudolf Dreikurs when a single parent needing help rearing her two boys. Later, she finished her doctor's degree and was invited to train with Dr. Dreikurs, becoming an Adlerian counselor and author.

[3]   Dreikurs and Soltz, *Children: The Challenge.* p. 36.

[4]   Much of the information in this section is found in Ellenberger, *Discovery of the Unconscious.*

[5]   Furtmuller, referenced in Hooper and Holford, *Adler for Beginners.* Also see *Adlerian Group Counseling and Therapy.* "[The term Individual Psychology] was meant to denote the indivisibility of the person." p.98.

[6]   Adler interviewed children and their parents in front of teachers and concerned school officials, all of whom he considered and referred to as his students. "Adler's basic orientation to child guidance differed from that of others in that he was primarily concerned not only with helping the child but also with conveying his knowledge and skills to others." Adler had great faith in teachers and believed they were the right people to help train troubled children. Adler's teaching model was in great contrast to the prevailing Freudian model of counseling in a closed clinic. The above information comes from Terner and Pew, *Courage to be Imperfect*, p. 63. It is suggested that readers interested in Adler's child guidance clinics read pages 60-69.

[7]   "Following a decision of the City of Vienna of July 11, 1930, Alfred Adler received the title, Citizen of Vienna, 'in acknowledgement of the great merits that he acquired in science and on the occasion of his sixtieth birthday.'" Ellenberger, *Discovery of the Unconscious*, p. 590.

[8]   Adler came to believe that in America "lay the hope of humanity at large: there liberty could be preserved and reasonable freedom practiced. Man could become a 'whole human being' in America better than anywhere else." Bottome, *Alfred Adler*, quoted in Turner and Pew, *Courage to be Imperfect*, p. 92.

[9] In 1977, Sadie "Tee" Dreikurs was staying at our house at Wright-Patterson Air Force Base in Ohio when I had the occasion to ask her the following question. "Was Rudolf Dreikurs Adler's best student?" She thought for a moment and then replied, "No, but he was Adler's most prolific student." Dreikurs's most popular and circulated writing is the 1964 book *Children: The Challenge,* which is still readily available.

Dreikurs's biography is extremely interesting and gives much insight into the mind, struggles, and courage of this extraordinary man. Terner and Pew, *Courage to be Imperfect.* A bibliography of Rudolf Dreikurs's writings is found on pp. 377-92.

[10] Much of the following information pertaining to the principles of Adlerian psychology as related to human behavior and family strengthening can be found in Painter and Corsini, *Effective Discipline,* and in Dreikurs and Soltz, *Children: The Challenge.*

[11] Painter, G. & Corsini, R. (1990). p. 11.

[12] Read "How Parents Train Their Children without Knowing It."

[13] Read "The Importance of Birth Order in Determining Behavior."

[14] Social interest is also known by the terms community interest and *gemeinschaftsgefuhl*, the latter word being German.

[15] The following 35 principles of child rearing were taken from *Dreikurs and Soltz, Children: The Challenge.* They have been modified for presentation and clarification. Principal 35 was added by the writer in the tradition of Dreikursian growth of Adlerian theory.

[16] Ibid., p. 36. Read "Words of Encouragement."

[17] Kohn, *Unconditional Parenting*, pp. 63-73.

[18] Read "Natural and Logical Consequences in a Nutshell."

[19] Read "The Incredibly Credible Parent."

[20] Dreikurs and Soltz, *Children: The Challenge*, p. 91.

[21] Ibid., p. 116.

[22] Read "Create Order: Make a Daily Schedule."

[23] Read "The Gift of Individual Special Time."

[24] Read "The Family Council in Brief."

[25] The classic book on the subject of parent-child communication is from Gordon, *P.E.T.: Parent Effectiveness Training*. The book was somewhat

rewritten by Gordon and his daughter, Judith Gordon Sands, and is now referenced as *P.E.T. in Action.*

[26] Dreikurs and Soltz, *Children: The Challenge*, chapter 4.

[27] Ibid., p. 146.

[28] The withdrawal methods that Adlerian family counselors seem to utilize most are referred to as the three Bs: beat it, bear it, or boot it.

"Beat it" means the parent quickly and quietly leaves the scene of conflict. "Bear it" means the parent ignores the conflict, pretending not to notice. "Boot it" means asking the conflicting children to go outside and return after their conflict has been resolved, or the noise is no more.

Dreikurs is famous for suggesting the "bathroom technique" wherein a mother can lock herself in and enjoy a relaxing bath until the conflict settles or the child's misguided behavior ceases. Withdrawal as a training method must be done preferably in silence, without rancor, and without rejection. We are not withdrawing or ignoring the child, only from his or her misguided behavior. Painter and Corsini, *Effective Discipline*, pp. 31-33, 152-53.

[29] Read "Teaching Cooperation to Parent-Deaf Children."

[30] Dreikurs and Soltz, *Children: The Challenge,* pp. 187-92.

[31] Ibid., p. 193.

[32] Ibid., pp. 201-14. Read "Adam and Eve: The First Dysfunctional Family."

[33] Dreikurs and Soltz, *Children: The Challenge,* p. 236.

[34] Reread "The Incredibly Credible Parent."

[35] Reread "Parent as Consultant."

[36] Dreikurs and Soltz, *Children: The Challenge,* p. 301.

[37] Ibid., p. 305. Read "The Family Council in Brief."

[38] Read "The Gift of Individual Special Time."

Notes

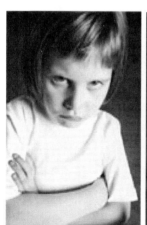 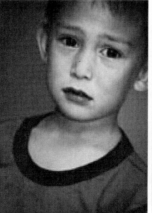 

WHY CHILDREN MISBEHAVE

Many parents seem to believe that their child's misbehavior is the result of a long thought-out process of revenge and reprisal. Nothing could be further from the truth. The chances are good that your little one does not lie awake at night plotting against you. In actuality, his or her errant behavior is based on just the opposite—a need to belong to the family with significance.[1]

Basic Adlerian Principles

Here are a few basic Adlerian principles about your child's personality development and behavior. All children come to us with certain propensities. They grow up in an environment that we call the family. Within this family, each child has a special position, known as a birth order, which plays a significant part in how he sees the world and how he believes the world sees him. For example, the firstborn child usually gets a great deal of attention and most often becomes the responsible child. The second child often strives to surpass the first, but usually in a differing area of competency. The middle child often feels squeezed and left out; he is neither the oldest nor the youngest. By the time the youngest child is born, the parents are more relaxed and less demanding. The youngest child is often seen and treated as the baby of the family. A child's lifestyle, the way he sees and responds to the world, is determined by his *interpretations* of his life experiences.

Parents need to know that all of their child's behavior is *purposeful* and *goal directed*. This means that whatever your child does is for a reason, and that reason is focused on obtaining his goal. As a parent, you may not immediately know what your child's goal is, but be assured, there is a wanted goal in his quick young mind.

Within the child is an innate and nature-driven desire for *competence*. Your child wants to be the best he or she can be. All behavior is a *movement* from a minus to a plus, from *incompetence* to *competence*. Many parents believe the only way to motivate their child toward competence is to nag, punish, or reward. Little do they realize that they are not trusting the power of Mother Nature and the natural order of things. Nagging, punishing, rewarding, or the like do not motivate the child for the long run. They only set the stage for a poor parent-child relationship. *Encouragement*[2] is the key to enhancing nature's push toward the goal of competence.

By the time your child is six years old, his personality has been formed. While time and therapy do help a person to change, the core of who your child is has been irrevocably determined during this brief window of time.

A basic need of your child is *to belong to the family with significance*. All children everywhere have this need. There is absolutely no question about this. To your child, it ranks up there with air, water, food, and shelter.

The best way to belong to the family with significance is by cooperation, and making a significant contribution to the family's welfare. Unfortunately, this is usually not what a misbehaving child has learned or practiced. Remember, to a child or anyone, there is no such thing as reality, only *interpretation*. The interpretation a child gives to an event becomes the meaning of that event. What a child thinks and believes becomes his *private logic* (his unconscious reasons for his behaviors) that guides his actions and behaviors usually for the rest of his life.

The Answer to Why Children Misbehave

A child's misbehavior is his *solution* to the very basic and compelling question, "How do I belong to this family with significance?"

Dr. Rudolf Dreikurs found that when children misbehave, their behavior falls into one of four categories that he called misguided goals.[3] Each category represents a greater degree of discouragement on the part of the child.

Misguided goal no. 1: "I am significant only when I keep you busy with me" (*undue attention*).

Misguided goal no. 2: "I am significant when I make you do what I want," or when "I do what I want" (*power*).

Misguided goal no. 3: "I feel hurt and I want to hurt back" (*revenge*).

Misguided goal no. 4: "I am significant only when I act completely inadequate" (*inadequacy*).

The Four Misguided Goals of Children

Misguided Goal	Child Says (Private logic)	Parent Feels (Gut response)	Solution Strategy
1. (Undue) Attention	"I'm going to keep you busy with me."	Annoyed	Ignore.
2. Power	"I'm going to be the boss and make you do what I want."	Angry	Keep out of the power struggle.
3. Revenge	"I feel hurt, and I want to hurt back."	Hurt	Make friends.
4. Inadequacy	"I give up."	Defeated	Massive encouragement.

Modified from "Children's Mistaken Goals" in Soltz, V. *Articles of Supplementary Reading for Parents*. Chicago: Alfred Adler Institute of Chicago, 1975.

The problem with punishments like yelling, hitting, and depriving is while they may work in the short term, they do not work in the long run. Research has found that the side effects of punishment can be quite harmful.[4] Punishing a child for his misguided solution to a problem situation, does not work because it attacks the misguided behavior at a low level of cognition. Children under the age of two are best corrected by the use of redirection. Since it is difficult to reason with children under the ages of five or six, it is best to use the Adlerian commonsense solutions of natural and logical consequences.[5] As your child matures, talk with—not at—him and help him to understand why his private logic is flawed. Talking in a kind manner as a consultant, not a boss, deals with problematic behavior at a high level of intellect.[6] By first using the Adlerian technique of logical consequences, then later the more cognitive technique of active listening,[7] your child's thinking, feelings, and actions will change for the better. Misbehavior will become a problem of the past.

Parents also need to be aware that in certain cases and situations, there may be other causes for disobedience. They include, but are not limited to, (1) an inconsistency in the way a parent gives an order, (2) an indecisiveness in the tone of the order giver, (3) a violent approach or expression on the part of the parent, (4) the child's fear of being humiliated by the approach of the parent, (5) impatience on the part of the parent who does not wait a reasonable time for compliance, (6) repetition of an order, often interpreted as nagging, (7) parents arguing with each other or with the child about an order, and (8) an overly tired child.[8]

Endnotes

[1] For purposes of this paper, I am excluding children with significant brain dysfunctions.

[2] Encouragement focuses on the deed. Praise focuses on the person. Read "Words of Encouragement" and "The Gift of Individual Special Time."
See Painter and Corsini, *Effective Discipline*, pp. 34-39, 315-49.
See Dreikurs and Soltz, *Children: The Challenge*, chapter 3.

[3] Dreikurs, *Challenge of Parenthood*. Dreikurs and Soltz, *Children: The Challenge*.

[4] Read "To Spank or Not to Spank: That is the Question." A section of "Further Reading" is provided at the end of the essay for those wanting to read direct research on the subject of corporal punishment.
See Kohn, *Unconditional Parenting*, pp. 63-73. Dr. Kohn has done an excellent job of researching the literature on various aspects of parent-child relationships.

[5] Read "Natural and Logical Consequences in a Nutshell." See Painter and Corsini, *Effective Discipline*, pp. 27-33.

[6] Read "Parent as Consultant."

[7] Gordon and Sands, *P.E.T. in Action*. Active listening is the technique parents should use when communicating with their children. It allows the parents to understand and confirm what their child is saying while the child simultaneously feels he is being listened to and understood.

[8] Suggested by Cater, "Parent Work Book for use with The Practical Parent in a Parent Study Group," unpublished manuscript.

Notes

TO SPANK OR NOT TO SPANK: THAT IS THE QUESTION

How many times have you been in a situation where your child whines and whimpers in her most annoying nasal tones? As you stand there, the whining and whimpering escalates into an irritating cry. You find yourself annoyed and becoming angry and, if you are in public, perhaps a bit embarrassed. From your point of view, this behavior is totally unnecessary. For a moment you feel helpless to make her stop. Then an impulse comes over you. You want to yell at your cherub and give her the old-fashioned threat: "If you're going to cry, I'll give you something to cry about!" You have a growing desire to smack the little brat on the side of her head, but you settle for a hard smack or two on the kid's bottom just to make her shut up. Even though normally you are a calm and collected person, you know that right now you have to control your temper; otherwise things easily could get out of hand.

Does this scenario remind you of anything? If it does, read on. If it doesn't, you possibly are in denial, have a perfect child, or are an authoritative (not authoritarian) parent who successfully uses the techniques I will suggest shortly. If you are a parent whom I have just described, you need not feel guilty, embarrassed, or shamed. Your feelings are not unusual. Your child has learned ways to push your buttons. It is time you learn to dodge kiddy bullets with grace and poise.

Maybe your child has had a long day. She has been up and on the go since the crack of dawn. Now she is overly tired, is beginning to whine, and acts like the tired child she is. In this situation, sleep is the best antidote for her annoying behavior. Spanking, a smack to her body, or yelling doesn't work.

Sometimes a child's motivation for acting horrid may not be so clear as sleep deprivation. Children want to belong to the family with significance. The problem is that their annoying misguided behavior is their solution to achieving this goal. There are four misguided goals that children can put into play: undue attention, power, revenge, and inadequacy.

1. Your little Suzy could be acting up in order to get your attention and keep you busy with her.
2. It could be that Suzy is into power, and she is letting you know that she is the boss and that she is going to do what she wants to do or make you do what she demands.
3. Possibly, your cherub is into revenge, somehow feeling hurt and wanting to hurt back.
4. A fourth possibility as to why your child is acting out is that she feels helpless and doesn't know what else to do. In any case, you don't have to be a master diagnostician to deal with the problem; just read on.

Recently, at one of our Family Education Training Center of Hawai'i parenting classes, a young mother asked me a set of very important and insightful questions. "Why do so many parents spank and use other forms of physical and mental punishment? If it works so well, why do parents have to spank over and over again? Is it true that spanking leads to long-term harm?"

Parents spank their children for a number of reasons. It quickly stops children from doing what they are doing. Parents do not have to think too hard about dealing with the behavior in a more sophisticated way. Some parents do not know what else to do, so they punish in a manner similar to the way they were punished by their own parents. Some parents spank because it makes them feel powerful. These people have problems with self-esteem and rarely admit to their true motivation. Other parents spank for "religious reasons." Personally, I find it impossible to imagine a loving God hurting little children "to teach them a lesson."

The reality is, spanking does work—but only in the short term. Spanking is best at getting a child to stop whatever he or she is doing in the immediate situation. It teaches a child what not to do rather than what to do. Its lesson teaches in the here and now, not in the future. Think of the (many) times you were spanked. What lessons for managing life did you learn that you can articulate now?

There has been much research on the effects of spanking and other forms of corporal punishment. Research shows the long-term effects of spanking can be harmful. Even those occasional "innocent" swats on your child's behind may be injurious. Here are some of the long-term effects of which you may not be aware. Children who are spanked, when compared to those who are not, display a higher level of aggression at home and in school, have more emotional, social, and learning problems, earn lower academic scores, as well as lower IQ scores, have impaired child/parent relationships, display significantly more antisocial behavior, are more angry, are more at risk for drug and alcohol problems, and later in life, commit more acts of domestic abuse and have more sexual problems when they become teens and adults.

Other recent research shows that spanking on the buttocks can be injurious to the sciatic and pudendal nerve bundles, which have to do with having a robust physical life and, when an adult, a healthy sex life. If you don't think that spanking and the buttocks are related to human sexuality, just go to http://www.google.com/ and type "spanking." On the day I researched it, of the first twenty results, thirteen (65 percent) were very sexual in nature, and seven were educational.

While not all adults who received spankings and corporal punishment as children have all of these problems, what is the benefit of taking a chance of harming your child? I am not aware of any scientific research that shows any benefit that cannot be achieved from other nonviolent forms of discipline. I have provided the reader with a list of research references used in developing this article that can be found at the end of this paper.

If I Can't Spank, What Can I Do?

There are better solutions to child discipline than spanking, smacking, threatening, yelling, or harsher forms of corporal punishment. These solutions definitely work and do not have any of the negative long-term effects.

Let's take another look at our little Suzy scenario. You are home when Suzy begins to whine and continues to whine in that annoying nasal and infantile tone that you hate so much. As you stand there, the whining escalates into a whimpering cry, and you find yourself annoyed and becoming angry. At that moment, you have three choices: beat it, bear it, or boot it. "Beat it" has nothing to do with whacking your little cherub. It means you immediately leave the situation. "Bear it" means you stay in the area and, like an award-winning actor, pretend that nothing is happening. "Boot it" means you calmly tell Suzy that it is okay to make a fuss, but please do it outside as you do not want to be disturbed. Parents using this last technique need to be very careful not to turn it into a power contest which is all too easy to do, especially with teens.

In this example, the parent finds herself becoming angry with her child. The best solution is to immediately walk away and go to another room. By withdrawing from the conflict, the parent disallows the child an audience to play to and gives herself or himself time to regain self-control. Dr. Rudolf Dreikurs suggested that mothers lock themselves in the bathroom until the whimpering sounds disappear. He called this the "bathroom technique." It is absurdly simple and extremely effective. The younger the child, the more often she will follow Mother and pound and whimper on the bathroom door. For nervous mothers, I suggest they install a miniature spyglass into the door so they can look out without being seen. Some fathers who are combat oriented may think that leaving the room is equivalent to losing the battle. In reality, you are giving the child a message in a logical consequence term: "If you whine and act annoyingly, I will leave because I refuse to put up with your shenanigans." Later, at a neutral time, ask the child what she was wanting and ask her to use her words when she has needs. Help her to talk rather than cry for her wants and needs. Remember, talking to a child (or anyone) at the moment of crisis is useless. She is not listening, and your talking only serves to reinforce the unwanted behavior. If you are not at home, I suggest you accompany the child to the car and stay with her, or better yet, drive home. On your drive home, say nothing, and keep a neutral demeanor.

There are several major long-term solutions to dealing with children's unwanted behavior. They take a bit of time, but I guarantee you, these activities will enrich you and your child's life.

The Family Council

The family council, or family meeting, is a structured event that allows everyone in the family to have a voice in family matters. Discussing and working out family problems and planning family fun are just two examples of what this structure can achieve. Remember, the family council is not a place for parents to manipulate their children. It is a place for honest talk and listening to each other. For an in-depth understanding of how the council works, parents should read the chapter titled "The Family Council."

Individual Special Time

Individual special time is a guaranteed allotment of ten minutes a day, every day, which a parent cheerfully gives to his or her child, no matter what the interfering distractions of life may be. Children who have this special time with their parents become more cooperative and display less negative behaviors both at home and at school. Special time, as it is also called, is the psychological oil that smoothes the relationship and decreases the friction between parent and child. When a parent "forgets" to do special time with his or her child, the child will complain and remind the parent. Parents also have told me that when they terminate individual special time for whatever reason, they can feel the child returning to many of his or her old negative ways. When they start again, the misbehaviors dramatically disappear. For an in-depth understanding of how to employ special time, parents should read the chapter titled "The Gift of Individual Special Time."

Respectful Communication

Talk with your children and not at them. Listen to what they have to say without interruption. Let them know what you heard them saying so as to double-check their message and make sure you got it right. Avoid communication roadblocks such as preaching, nagging, shaming, and even shouting. Role model respectful communication and teach your children how to successfully use their words. These are a few of the verbal techniques parents can use to rear happy and cooperative children. For a better understanding of communication techniques, parents should read the chapter titled "Teaching Respect by Example: Using the I-Message."

Encouragement

Encouragement is one of the most important aspects of child raising. It is a conscious process that inspires courage, self-respect, spirit, confidence, hope, and cooperation in our children. Encouragement is any act or gesture that leaves our children feeling better about themselves or their situation. Parents need to realize that no child ever felt encouraged as a result of being spanked, scolded, or harshly punished. Resentment, anger, revenge, inadequacy, and discouragement are the usual feelings that follow these kinds of parental acts.

Sophisticated parents know the difference between encouragement and praise. Praise focuses on the child and aims at her integrity and worth. While seemingly innocent, it is often manipulative. "You are such a wonderful girl for drawing me that lovely picture." Encouragement focuses on the deed and conveys to children that they are great just as they are. Encouraging words show acceptance, confidence, trust, and a faith that the child will do the right thing by herself and her family. "It looks to me like you had fun drawing this picture. Thank you for sharing it with me." To become excellent encouragers, parents should read the chapter "Words of Encouragement."

Using Natural and Logical Consequences

More powerful than punishment and with none of the side effects are natural and logical consequences. Natural consequences are the most powerful technique I know to teach lessons to a child without being directly involved in the event. Natural consequences occur out of the child's own actions. A child who chooses to play rather than eat will soon find him or herself very hungry. Going outside on a rainy day without proper rain gear will get one "soaked to the bone" and feeling quite miserable. These are examples of nature's consequences to unintelligent behavior. When nature does its thing, who is your child going to be angry at? She only can blame herself.

Logical consequences are consequences preferably agreed upon by both parent and child. "We agreed at the family meeting that if you act whiney and cry at a restaurant, we will have to leave. We have to go home now." If the child is too young to participate in agreement making, he or she should be given a choice. "If you keep on bothering Mommy, you will have to leave the room, or you can sit here quietly and draw your pictures. The choice is yours." If the child is too young to understand choices, I suggest she be distracted, or, as in the situation above, be gently put into a playpen or another safe place with boundaries in the house. To be truly a logical consequence and not a punishment, a logical consequence must meet all four of the following criteria. It must be related, reasonable, respectful, and restorative. Spanking and other forms of corporal punishment do not come close to meeting these criteria. Parents need to read the chapter "Natural and Logical Consequences in a Nutshell" to fully understand and use this powerful concept.

In Summary

Children have a way of driving their parents up the proverbial wall by doing what their parents define as misbehavior. At these moments, parents have to make a choice as to how they are going to react. Far too many mothers and fathers respond to their feelings by striking physically or verbally at their child, believing that it will teach them a lesson in good behavior. Spanking or other corporal punishments usually do stop a child from acting out their annoying behaviors. The problem lies in the fact that parents seeing this short-term result mistakenly believe they have found the solution to all the child's undesirable acts. Parents fail to realize that spanking has been demonstrated to have undesirable long-term effects such as increased aggression at home and at school and antisocial behaviors as preteens, teens, and adults. By talking and listening to your children, having a family council meeting once a week, enjoying individual special time, being encouraging, and using natural and logical consequences—including walking away and ignoring unwanted behavior—your child will grow up to be a respectful and healthy adult. Isn't this what we all want for our children?

Further Reading

American Psychological Association (2002 June 26). Is Corporal Punishment an Effective Means of Discipline? *American Psychological Association.* Retrieved June 21, 2011, from http://www.apa.org/news/press/releases/2002/06/spanking.aspx.

Bahr, S. J., Hoffman, J. P. Parenting (2010). Style, Religiosity, Peers, and Adolescent Heavy Drinking. Journal of Studies on Alcohol and Drugs, 71(4), 539-543.

Bakan, D. (1971). *Slaughter of the Innocents.* San Francisco. Jossey-Bass Publishers.

Barber, Jim. (2004 February 6). Does Spanking Work? *Toronto Star.* Retrieved from *www.nospank.net*

Berlin et al. (2009). Correlates and Consequences of Spanking and Verbal Punishment for Low-Income White, African American, and Mexican American Toddlers. *Child Development, 2009; 80(5):1403DOI: 10.1111/j1467-8624.2009.01341.x*

Boyle, L. (2006 April 11). Corporal Punishment in American Schools—Teaching Tough Terror? *Huffingpost.com.* Retrieved June 24, 2011 from http://nospank.net/n-u53.htm.

Bradshaw, J. (1996 November 22). *The Bradshaw Connection.* Broadcast on November 22, 1996, WOR-TV. Retrieved June 22, 2011, from www.nospand.net/bradshaw.htm.

Brigham Young University (2011 June 13). Fathers Still Matter to Kids Who Have Moved Out. *ScienceDaily.* Retrieved June 22, 2011, from http://www.sciencedaily.com /release/2011/06/110613122529.htm.

Child Trends Databank (2008). Attitudes towards Spanking. *Child Trends.* Retrieved June 28, 2011, from *http://www.childhoodtrendsdatabamk. org/?q=node/187.*

Child Welfare Information Gateway (2008). Long-Term Consequences of Child Abuse and Neglect. *U.S. Department of Health & Human Services.* Retrieved July 11, 2011, from http://www.childwelfare.gov/ pubs/factsheets/long_term_consequences.cfm.

Coghlan, A., Le Page, M. (2001 June 16). Babies Might Be Killed by Even Mild Shaking. *New Scientist.* Retrieved June 25, 2011, from http:// nospank.net /shake .htm.

Collins, R. (2009 October). James Dobson Just Has to Be Responsible for Many Psychopaths in America. *End Heredity Religion.com.* Retrieved June 23, 2011, from http://www.endheredityreligion.com/2009/10/ james-dobson-just-has-to-be-responsible-f . . .

Dreikurs, R. and Soltz, V. (1964). *Children: The Challenge.* New York. Hawthorn Books.

Everyday Health (Undated). Shaken Baby Syndrome Causes, Symptoms, and Treatment. *Everyday Health.* Retrieved June 25, 2011, from http:// www.everydayhealth.com/health-center/shaken-baby-syndrome.aspx.

Gershoff, E. (2002). Corporal Punishment by Parents and Associated Child Behaviors and Experiences: A Meta-Analysis and Theoretical Review. *Psychological Bulletin.* 128: 539-74.

Gershoff, E. (2008). *Report on Physical Punishment in the United States: What Research Tells Us about Its Effects on Children.* Columbus, Ohio: Center for Effective Discipline.

Glueck, S. and Glueck, E. (1940) *Juvenile Delinquents Grown Up.* New York: Commonwealth Fund.

Glueck, Sheldon and Eleanor (2011). In *Encyclopedia Britannica.* Retrieved June 23, 2011, from http://www.britannica.com/EBchecked/topic/1353094/ Glueck-Sheldon-and-Blueck-Eleanor

Goodmama, Tammy (2005 August 30). The Statistics on Spanking. Retrieved June 16, 2011, from http://www.epinions.com/content 4499546244

Guthrow, J. (2002 December). Correlation between High Rates of Corporal Punishment in Public Schools and Social Pathologies. *Parents and*

Teachers against Violence in Education. Retrieved June 25, 2011, from *http://nospank.net.*

Holden, G. W. (2002). Perspectives on the Effects of Corporal Punishment: Comment on Gershoff (2002). *Psychological Bulletin*, 128(4), 590-595. http://www.childwelfare.gov/pubs/factsheets/long_term_consequences.cfm.

Kobayashi, K. (2011 June 20). Judges Split on Ruling on Parental Discipline. *Star Advertiser* (Honolulu, Hawai'i). Retrieved June 23, 2011, from http://www.staradvertiser.com/news/20110620.

Kohn, Alfie. (2005). *Unconditional Parenting: Moving from Rewards and Punishments to Love and Reason.* New Lehigh University (February 1, 2001). New York: Astoria Books.

Legacy.com (2011 March). Dr. Benjamin Spock: Child Care and Controversy. The Obit Report. *Legacy.com.* Retrieved June 20, 2011, from http://www.legacy.com/ns/news-story.aspx?t=dr-benjamin-spock-child-care-and-controversy&id=278.

Lehigh University (2001 February 1). Lehigh Researchers Examine Link between Abusive Child-Rearing, Overly Aggressive Behavior. *Lehigh University.* Retrieved from http://www.eurekalert.org/pub_releases/2001-01/LU-Lrel-3101101.php—8.1KB—Public Press Releases. Also found on http://www.nospank.net.

Lombardo, L. (2002 November 17). Our Child Don't Deserve to Be Beaten. Retrieved June 23, 2011, from nospank.net/lombardo.htm.

Miller, A. (1988). *Truth or Illusion? Afterwards to the Second Edition (1984) of For Your Own Good.* Retrieved June 23, 2011, from NoSpank.net.

Miller, A. (1998). *Paths of Life.* New York: Pantheon.

Miller, A. (1998). Every Smack Is a Humiliation. Written for *Project NoSpank.* Retrieved June 23, 2011, from http://nospank.net/miller3.htm.

Miller, A. (1999 June). Spanking Is Counterproductive and Dangerous. *Parents and Teachers against Violence in Education.* Retrieved June 23, 2011, from *http://www.nospank.net/miller10.htm.*

Miller, A. (2001). *The Truth Will Set You Free.* New York: Basic Books.

Miller, A. (2002, 4th Edition). *For Your Own Good.* New York: Farrar-Straus-Geroux. Retrieved June 23, 2011, from NoSpank.net. [Free download.]

Miller, A. (2008 September) *The Roots of Violence Are Not Unknown: The Misled Brain and the Banned Emotions.* Retrieved June 23, 2011, from www.nospank.net/miller33pdf.

MyDr.com (Undated). Sciatica: Symptoms, Causes, and Diagnosis. *MyDr.com.* Retrieved June 28, 2011, from *http://www.mydr.com.au/ sports-fitness/sciatica-symptoms-causes-and-diagnosis.*

Newman, D. (2009). *Families: A Sociological Perspective.* New York: McGraw-Hill.

NoSpank.net (Undated). *Spanking Can be Sexual Abuse (Section 7).* Retrieved July 16, 2011, from http://www.nospank.net.

NoSpank.net (Undated). Psychological Evaluation of a Child Abused at School.

NoSpan.net. Retrieved June 25, 2011, from http://www.nospank.net.

NoSpank.net (2009 April). Corporal Punishment to Children's Hands: A Statement by Medical Authorities as to the Risks. Retrieved June 25, 2011, from http://nospank.net/hands.htm.

Ohio State University (2009 August 12). Mothers, but Not Fathers, Follow Their Own Moms' Parenting Practices. *Science Daily.* Retrieved June 21, 2011, from http://www.sciencedaily.com / releases/2009/08/090810024827.htm.

Olson, D., DeFrain, J., and Skogrand, L. (2011). *Marriages and Families: Intimacy, Diversity, and Strengths, Seventh Edition.* New York, McGraw-Hill.

Parents and Teachers against Violence in Education. (2002 October 9). *Violated School Children: Corporal Punishment-Induced Trauma.* Retrieved July 12, 2011, from www.nospank.net/violatn.htm. [Editor's note. The images attached can be upsetting to some viewers.]

Parents and Teachers against Violence in Education. Quintilian's Observation on the Smacking of Children. Institutes of Oratory, Rome, circa 88 CE. Retrieved June 28, 2011, from *http://www.nospank.net/quint.htm.*

Patten-Hitt, E. (2000 December 29). Child Abuse Changes in Developing Brain. *Reuters Health*, Yahoo! News. Retrieved June 27, 2011, from *http://www.nospank.net/teicher.htm.*

Physorg.com (2010 August 9). Corporal Punishment of Children Remains Common Worldwide, UNC Studies Find. *Physorg*. Retrieved June 19, 2011, from Physorg.com.

Physorg.com (2008 February 18). Children's IQ Go Up When Parents Learn [Parenting Techniques]. *United Press International*. Retrieved June 20, 2011, from http://www.physorg.com/news122545602.html.

Pitten-Hitt, E. (2000 December 29.) Childhood Abuse Changes the Developing Brain. *Yahoo News*, December 29, 2000. Retrieved June 23, 2011, from http://nospank.net/tericher.htm.

Reuters (1998 August 3). Want Smarter Kids? Don't Spank Them. *Reuters*. Retrieved June 21, 2011, from http://www.nospank.net/straus4.htm.

Riak, J. (2006 April). Ask Ten Spankers. N*ospank.net*. Retrieved June 16, 2011, from http://nospank.net/askten.htm.

Riak, J. (2011 Edition). *Plain Talk About Spanking*. Parents and Teachers against Violence in Education. Retrieved July 12, 2011, from *www.nospank.net/pt2011.htm*. Free download.

Sagan, G. (2010 July 6). Spanking Can Turn Easily into Abuse. Retrieved June 22, 2011, from http://nospank.net/sagan-1.htm.

Society for Research in Child Development (2009, September 15) Spanking Found to Have Negative Effects on Low-Income Toddlers. *ScienceDaily*. Retrieved June 21, 2011, from http://www.sciencedaily.com/releases/2009/09/090915/100941.htm

Spock, B., Needleman, R. (2004). Baby and Child Care. 8th edition. New York: Pocket Books.

St. Joseph's Hospital and Medical Center. Pudendal Neuralgia. Retrieved June 18, 2011, from http:www.stjosephs-phx.org/Medical Services/Center for Women's Health/196316.

Straus, M. (1997 August 13). Spanking Makes Children Violent, Antisocial: Effects Same Regardless of Parenting Style, Socioeconomic Status, Sex of Child or Ethnic Background. *American Medical Association News, Update*. Retrieved June 22, 2011, from http://nospank.net/straus.htmthe American Medical Association News, Update.

Straus, M. (1999 July 24). Spanking Teaches Short-Term Lessons, but Long-Term Violence. *Forkidsake.org*. Retrieved June 21, 2011, from http://forkidsake.org/spanking.html.

Straus, M. (2001). 2nd Edition. *Beating the Devil Out of Them: Corporal Punishment in American Families and Its Effects on Children*. New Jersey: Transaction Publishers.

Straus, M. and Paschall, M. (2009). Corporal Punishment by Mothers and Development of Children's Cognitive Ability: A Longitudinal Study of Two Nationally Representative Age Cohorts. *Journal of Aggression Maltreatment & Trauma*, 2009; 18 (5): 459 DOI: *10.1080/10926770903035168*

Teicher, M. (2002, March). The Neurobiology of Child Abuse. *Scientific American*, pp.68-75. Retrieved June 23, 2011, from http://nospank.net/teicher2.htm.

Teicher, M. (2010 October 18). *The Pierre Janet Memorial Lecture: Does Child Abuse Permanently Alter the Human Brain?* Retrieved June 27, 2011, from *https://www.softconference.com/isstd/itin.asp*.

University of Chicago (2011 June 19). Fathers Benefit from Seeking Help as Parents. *ScientificDaily*. Retrieved June 22, 2011, from http://www.sciencedaily.com/releases/ 2011/06110615103222htm.

University of Illinois at Urbana-Champaign (2009, August 13). Parental Influences Differ in Determining Later Latter Academic Success. *ScienceDaily*. Retrieved June 22, 2011, from http://sciencedaily.com/releases/2009/08/0908111443htm.

University of Michigan Health System (2011 March 18). Sad Dads Spank More, Read Less, Study Finds. *ScientificDaily*. Retrieved June 22, 2011, from http:// scientificdaily.com/releases/2011/03/110318121905.htm.

University of New Hampshire (2008 March 2). Spanking Kids Increases Risk of Sexual Problems as Adult. *ScienceDaily*. Retrieved June 21, 2011, from http://www.sciencedaily.com /release/2008/08/080228220451.htm.

Weber, G. (Undated). Grooming Children for Sexual Molestation. *The Zero 5.Olaf-The official website of Andrew Vachss*. Retrieved June 25, 2011, from http://www.vachss.com/guest_dispatches/grooming.html.

WebMD (Undated) Results for: Sacrum. *WebMD*. Retrieved June 28, 2011, from *http://www.webmd.com/search/search_results/default.aspx?query=sacrum&sourceType=undefined*.

Whitehurst, T., Haskins, D., Crowell, Al. (Undated). *The Nonviolent Christian Parent*. Christian Nonviolent Parenting. (Read online at http://nospank.net/cnpindex.htm).

Wikipedia (Undated). Child Grooming. Retrieved June 25, 2011, from http://ne.wikipedia.org/wiki/child grooming.

Wikipedia (undated). Corporal Punishment in the Home. Retrieved June 21, 2011, from http://en.wikipedia.org/wiki/Domestic_corporal_punishment.

Notes

A TEACHER'S LESSON
By Jordan Riak*

At my last teaching job, I conducted this little experiment with each new class. This is what I said to my students.

> Listen very closely to what I am going to describe, and if my description matches your childhood experience, please raise your hand. Now listen closely. Your childhood environment was an absolutely safe environment. You always knew that nobody—not parents, grandparents, babysitters, big brothers, big sisters, family friends, schoolteachers, neighbors, *nobody*—had the right to hit you. You knew, without a doubt, that you were safe, that your body was your own personal, private property. If that description accurately fits your childhood experience, please raise your hand.

I scanned the students' faces while they pondered my question, and waited. They looked at me and waited. We all waited. Not one hand went up. The results were always the same. I did that experiment with each new group of approximately thirty men who were enrolled in the prerelease program at California's Folsom State Prison.

*Jordan Riak is the the executive director of Parents and Teachers Against Violence in Education, Inc., a 501(c)(3) organization located in Alamo, California. He is an author and advocate for children's rights. He originated and maintains an educational website dedicated to the well-being and rights of children. View at http://www.nospank.net/. Jordan is a much-loved husband, father, and grandfather. The above correspondence is used by permission.

HOW PARENTS TRAIN CHILDREN
WITHOUT KNOWING IT

By acting on our first impulse, we tend to intensify the child's
misbehavior patterns rather than to correct them.

—Rudolf Dreikurs, MD

Fifty-five years ago as an undergraduate college student, I gave serious thought to becoming an animal psychologist. In addition to my studies in psychology, I found a job at the college's animal laboratory. I fed and cared for a colony of rats, and I cleaned up after two monkeys that I named Freud and Jung because they always were squabbling. I also assisted my professor training small animals to behave in predetermined ways. One day, I realized that I was not destined for the world of experimental animal psychology when I found I could not bring myself to drown a couple of old rodents who had lost their usefulness to science. My inability to take the life of geriatric rodents made my professor somewhat unhappy. Even though I was not destined to become the world's next Pavlov,[1] I did learn a few valuable concepts that year, which I have been able to apply to my life's choice of a profession, that of parent education and family counseling. Specifically, I discovered how animals learn and how to train them to behave in predetermined ways. It was only after I became a parent that I realized children and animals learn in much the same manner. During my professional observations of parents and children, it became clear to me that parents train their children without ever being aware that training is taking place.

Examples of the Training Process in Action

Little Jerry, aged two, is served his meal and responds to his food by dawdling, playing with his veggies, and otherwise not eating. Mother, wanting Jerry to eat, decides to help Jerry by playing "spoon airplane." Initially, this is fun for both mother and child, but after a few meals and a busy schedule, "spoon airplane" becomes tedious, and Mother finds herself irritated with dawdling Jerry.

What did Mother teach Jerry? The real question is what did Jerry learn from Mother? Jerry learned, "If I eat slowly, Mother will play with me." This, of course, was exactly the opposite of Mother's intentions. Mother eventually became angry and frustrated with Jerry for being a very good learner. Mother never took credit for being a good teacher because she did not realize her part in Jerry's learning.

Kalena, a toddler, falls down while walking. She whines and looks up at her parents for guidance on how to act next. Mother becomes upset, quickly runs to Kalena, and gives her a hug to make her feel better. The hug feels good to Kalena, and she stores the knowledge of this event in her developing mind. Did Kalena just learn that walking leads to falling and this is dangerous? Did she just learn that being hurt has a payoff of a warm hug? Does Kalena lose courage?

A little later Kalena falls again. This time there is no looking at her parents for guidance. She knows exactly what to do to get that loving huggy feeling and all that marvelous attention. Kalena whimpers, cries, and then signals a pathetic look toward Mother who quickly runs to her and gives her a hug to make her once more feel better. Yes, Mother has taught Kalena that walking and falling is dangerous, and being hurt and whining has a payoff of a warm hug. Kalena has lost courage. Mother eventually becomes angry and frustrated with Kalena for being a very good learner. Mother never takes credit for being a good teacher because she does not realize her part in the teacher-learner process. Is this really the behavior Mother wants to teach her daughter?

Maika, a preschooler, is having a "bad day." He has been pouting, whining, acting moody, looking and behaving unhappy, and Mother cannot figure out the cause. Father comes home from work and experiences Maika's low mood. Wanting to be a hero to his son and to show his wife how good a dad he really is, Father picks up Maika, swings him around, hugs and gives him a lot of attention in order to distract him from his moody behavior.

What has Maika learned from his father's training? Maika has learned that when he acts pouty, moody, whines, and looks unhappy, Father will give this behavior a payoff of plenty of attention and lots of fun. Meanwhile, Father thinks he is a hero until he gets tired of a whiny kid. Is this the lesson Father wants to teach his son?

Bobbi and Sandi are ten-year-old twin girls. There has always been a great deal of competition between the two that seemingly ends in loud arguments and bickering. Mother has tried to be an impartial referee but always ends up greatly annoyed and playing the role of judge, jury, and hangman.

What is going on with the girls that they continually argue? Is this the kind of household in which Mother is doomed to live? What have the girls learned from Mother that they chronically behave badly?

How Do Parents Unknowingly Train Their Children?

To help parents understand how they unknowingly train their children, we need to turn to an uncomplicated, well-known, and studied theory of "Stimulus-Response-Reinforcement." Simply put, first there is a *stimulus* or triggering event to which the animal *responds*. This is followed by a *reinforcement* of some kind, which ups the probability that the animal's response will be repeated. The *outcome* can be thought of as what the animal has learned and, most likely, how it will now respond in the future. Translating this into parenting language, we can say, first there is an *event* to which the child responds with a particular *behavior* or pattern of behaviors.[2] When this is followed by some type of reinforcer or payoff, there is a high probability that this behavior or behavior pattern will be repeated. The more reinforcements or payoffs that are given, the higher is the probability the behavior will be adopted by the child. The *outcome* is how the child behaves after a like or similar triggering event.

Adlerians believe that a child's response is purposeful in that it gives him or her a desired payoff. For children, the desired payoff can be on the useful or useless side. A useful response teaches a child behaviors that are useful like cooperation and courage. A useless response teaches undesirable behaviors such as the misbehaviors categorized in the four misguided goals.[3]

The focus of this essay is to help parents understand how they reinforce their child's behaviors, no matter what purpose or goal it serves for the child. By seeing how they, through reinforcement, cause the behavior to recur, parents have a better chance to allow useless behavior to extinguish and useful behavior to repeat. Let us look at the above four situations and tailor healthier outcomes.

In the case of two-year-old Jerry, he is served his meal, which becomes the *event*. His *response* or behavior to his food is dawdling. Mother then attempts to motivate him to eat by playing "spoon airplane." Mother thinks she is motivating Jerry to eat, but in reality, she is *reinforcing* his response of dawdling. The *outcome* will be a child who chronically dawdles and a mother who becomes annoyed and irritated.

The simple solution to this problem is for Mother to tell Jerry that if he chooses not to eat his food at the table during the family meal, she will remove his plate and he can eat again at the next meal.[4] Mother must not say another word on the subject. A few minutes after everyone has finished his or her meal and if the child has continued to dawdle, Mother should, without saying a word and with a pleasant look on her face, quietly and politely remove Jerry's plate. Continuing with a kind voice, she then might say to her son, "It's okay to get down." If Mother becomes annoyed or angry, or starts talking, her response will become a *reinforcement* to the child's misguided behavior. As a result, the dawdling will continue. Mother should not worry about Jerry's health as he will eat heartily at the next meal because he will be hungry.

Kalena is a bright child and, like most toddlers, learns quickly from her parents' cues. In the original situation, falling was the *event*; looking for her parents' guidance was her *response* to falling; Mother's doting of her child by giving hugs to make her feel better was the payoff *reinforcement*. When Kalena fell again, Mother's doting *response* continued the cycle. The *outcome* is a child who has learned not to take chances, believes that walking is dangerous, and that the lack of courage has significant positive rewards. Meanwhile, Mother becomes discouraged about Kalena's lack of walking skills. She wonders if there is anything wrong with her child, and if she, the mother, is somehow at fault.

The healthy solution to a toddler falling is paying little attention to the *event*. As parents, we all want to make sure that our toddlers do no damage to their muscular-skeletal structure. Nature and a thick diaper have given toddlers the needed padding for falling. Unfortunately, too many parents interfere with Mother Nature's consequences by cueing children with discouraging prompts. It is best to ignore the fall, or as one parent told me, "When my toddler falls, I cheer and clap my hands happily, saying, 'Yeah, Joey is learning to walk.' To that cheering sound, a smiling Joey gets up each time and toddles away."

Maika, the preschooler who was having a bad day, learned how to behave when he thinks and then feels in a certain way. Whatever the reason, this was the *event*. Acting pouty, whiney, moody, and looking and behaving unhappy is his *response* to whatever is going on inside of him. Father, picking Maika up, trying to distract him out of his low mood, is actually coupling the low mood to a wonderful payoff of daddy-centered fun and attention. To say it another way, Father's behavior is *reinforcing* the idea that low mood behaviors lead to high levels of attention. The *outcome* may very well lead to the idea by Maika that to get all of this wonderful daddy-centered attention, I need first to feel miserable, then act miserable, then wait for the fun that will come from my daddy. Very soon, Mother finds that she does not enjoy being around moping Maika, and Father soon gets tired of coming home to an unhappy wife and moody child. Father tires of being Maika's rescuer and never realizes that he is the cause of the family's misery.

What is Maika's father to do? The first thing Father might do is to get down on one knee to Maika's level, look him in the eye, and caringly recognize Maika's feelings. "You don't look very happy today," Father might say. To have his feelings understood and not judged for having them is a very important happening for this preschooler or any other child for that matter. If Father wants to go further, he can say, "Will you tell me about your feelings?" Father need say no more. If Maika talks, Father should listen empathetically. If Maika chooses to say nothing, after a little while, Father should get up and, without saying a word, go to another part of the house. Saying or doing more will be reinforcement for unwanted behavior. Father is not ignoring Maika; he is choosing not to reinforce Maika's unwanted behavior. Later, when appropriate, Father can invite his son to have his usual individual special time.[5]

Bobbi and Sandi have been arguing and bickering since early childhood. Now that they are ten years old, their confrontations have become louder and more intense. Mother no longer wants to be the "impartial referee" and just wishes her daughters would shut up and be quiet. Mother needs to realize that the day she decided to be the impartial referee was the day she lost control of this dynamic duo. Note the following sequences. There is an *event* to which the girls decide to *respond* by arguing and squabbling. Mother then becomes the referee, which is a *reinforcing* payoff of attention to the girls' behavior. The more Mother talks the greater the *reinforcement*, the greater the chances that she will see the arguing and bickering behaviors repeated. Mother has failed to realize what Adlerians have known for years. Although children can have disagreements, they do not fight and bicker over what seems to be the obvious; they fight to get their parent's attention. In other words, children fight to keep Mommy and Daddy busy and involved with them.

What should Mother do? The answer is quite simple and can be thought of as the three Bs solution: beat it, bear it, or boot it.[6] "Beat it" means that Mother leaves the scene of the commotion and goes to another room. She must walk away as if nothing annoying is happening. If she stomps or mutters as she leaves, the girls will see Mother's actions as a *reinforcing* payoff, and mother will have accomplished nothing by her noisy departure. "Bear it" means that Mother must behave as though nothing is happening. To respond in any manner, verbal, facial gestures, or body language, will serve only to give the girls the undue attention they want, thus *reinforce* the undesirable behavior. "Boot it" means the girls are allowed to fight if they want, but they must go outside to do it. Mother can say, "You may fight but not inside the house. You can come back when you have finished."

When they have finished arguing and come back into the house, Mother is to say nothing as though the event never happened. To do anything else would be a *reinforcement* of unwanted behavior. Parents must be careful not to turn "boot it" into a power contest or a punishment.

Where should Mother go? In this case, anywhere she wants, in or out of the house or into any room she thinks appropriate. Rudolf Dreikurs suggested mothers go to the bathroom when it is time to withdraw. This is Dreikurs's famous bathroom technique, and it really does work.[7] If the girls end up fighting outside the bathroom door, this tells Mother that she has hit the jackpot in strategy: the girls are fighting for Mother's attention. In any case, Mother should stay in the bathroom until there has been silence for at least five minutes. Sometimes children's behavior gets worse before it gets better. If the girls' arguing and bickering becomes worse after Mother withdraws, that is always a good sign as the girls now sense that their old behavior is not working, thus they are trying harder. Mother is on the right track by not giving *reinforcement* to the children, thus allowing their annoying behavior to extinguish.

In Summary

Parents frequently become upset with their children's behavior. They often see their children as miniature adults who "just don't get it" or who are out to get them. They wonder why their kids repeat seemingly useless and unwarranted behaviors, especially when warned not to do so. Mothers and fathers become upset when their children do not seem to use reason and logic. What parents do not understand is that they have trained their child how to act. Whatever the purpose of a child's behavior, parents have reinforced and trained the child to repeat it. It makes no difference whether or not the parents realize what they are doing. The younger the child, the easier it is to shape behavior by reinforcing it. As children grow and mature, their ability to reason, solve a problem, and make rationally based decisions grow too, eventually maturing when the person reaches their twenties.[8] Jerry, Kalena, Maika, Bobbi, and Sandi are all students of their parents' training through the simple process of behavioral reinforcement.

Endnotes

1. Ivan Pavlov was a Russian physiologist whose classic work on the digestion of dogs and the psychological consequences of classical association ushered in tens of thousands of experiments on animal and human learning.

2. Strictly speaking, Adlerians believe that a human's response is determined by his interpretation of the stimulus.

3. Read "Why Children Misbehave."

4. Read "Eating Should Be the Child's Business." See Painter and Corsini, *Effective Discipline*, chapter 10. The best time and place to discuss logical consequences is at a family council meeting. Children should never be surprised by a parent's method of discipline but should always have a choice in deciding whether or not to cooperate. Read "The Family Council." Dreikurs, Gould, and Corsini, *Family Council: The Dreikurs Techniques*. Painter and Corsini, *Effective Discipline*, chapter 33, pp. 238-47. Rigney and Corsini, *The Family Council*.

5. Read "The Gift of Individual Special Time."

6. See Painter and Corsini, chapter 19, "Fighting in the Home," pp. 151-56.

7. Dreikurs and Soltz, *Children: The Challenge, pp. 158-59.*

8. Parker, "Longitudinal Brain Scan Study."

Notes

STUPID IS AS STUPID DOES

Forrest Gump is one of my favorite movies. In it, Forrest makes a statement that has managed to stay glued in my mind. "Mama says stupid is as stupid does." I guess I like this statement because it reflects my own Adlerian view of life. Adlerian psychology is a "psychology of use." That is, it is not what we are endowed with but how we use it. One can be born a genius, but what is important is how that person chooses to use his or her intelligence. Some people are born with athletic ability; to them, movement comes naturally. What counts is not that they are born gifted but how they choose to use their athletic talent. As adults, we all have the ability to make new choices. If what we learned as children does not look, feel, taste, or seem right, then we may use our talents to change and make better decisions than we were taught. The ability to make choices is one of the fun things about being grown-up.

A while back, a father came to the Family Education Training Center of Hawai'i (FETCH) and announced at our first meeting that he believed in spanking although his wimpy wife did not. "Dr. Jim, do you know why I spank my three-year-old? Because my father spanked me. Do you know why I yell at him? Because my mother yelled at me. And I turned out all right," he said angrily.

That remains to be seen, I thought to myself. However, out loud I politely said the following, "Let me see if I have this right. You discipline your three-year-old son by hitting him and yelling. Your wife doesn't believe in hitting or yelling. She is very unhappy with you and the way you treat your boy. This is having a negative effect on your marital life. You're wife wants you both to learn a better way." The man smiled and agreed with my summation. "At this moment I have just one question for you. Would you like to hear it?" I asked, knowing that he was dying to hear my reaction to his stubbornness and alleged great insight.

He smiled and answered, "Yes."

My question was short and direct. "Would you rather be right or happy?"

He looked at me, then at his wife, paused another moment, and answered. "I'd rather be happy."

"Thank you," I said. "During the next twelve weeks, I promise I will show you better and more effective ways to get cooperation from your son. Are you with me?"

As humans, we have the power to make choices. For some people, choosing to parent differently from the way they were parented is frightening and unthinkable. To walk a new and unknown path brings fear to their very core and, for some, a feeling of disloyalty to the people that reared them. It takes courage to rear your children differently, even when you know that it would be "stupid," as Forrest might say, to commit the same errors as your parents.

Many parents spank, hit, and yell at their children because in the short term it has worked. However, as a long-term solution to child rearing, violence in whatever form does not work well to make cooperative kids.

When my children were young, we had a miniature poodle named Bon Bon. He was raised as our third child. One day, I came home from work and found that six-month-old Bon Bon had made a bowel movement on the stairs leading to the second floor. Following a procedure that my father had taught me, I called the dog to me, stuck his nose in the poop, slapped him on the behind, yelled "Bad dog," and then proceeded to clean up the mess, all the time acting stern and angry. The next day, I arrived home to find another poop on the stairs. Since my father had told me what to do, I acted out his teaching. I called the dog to me, stuck his nose in the poop, slapped him on the behind, yelled "Bad dog," and then proceeded to clean up the mess, all the time acting stern and angry. On the third day, I came home and—would you know it? A poop awaited me on the stairs. By this time, I had decided that maybe my father wasn't so right; in any case, his solution wasn't working for me. Being new to Adlerian psychology, I wondered out loud to my wife, "Since what we are doing to gain cooperation from the children is working so well, I wonder if Adlerian psychology will work on Bon Bon too?" So an hour later, at a neutral time (when the poodle wasn't looking), I very quietly cleaned up the poop and said nothing. No negative payoff was given to the perpetrating pooch, and all was done in silence.

The next day, when I came home from work, the stairs were clean. At that moment, I recognized that I had learned three lessons. First, that Adlerian psychology sometimes can work on dogs as powerfully as it works on children. Second, that what my father taught me was not necessarily correct; at least, it wasn't working for me in this situation. Third, it is up to me to find solutions to life's problems and not blindly follow others' prescriptions, even my father's. For those interested, never again in his sixteen years of life did Bon Bon poop in our home.

If there is a lesson to be learned by reading this essay, it is that we, as twenty-first-century parents, are never tied to our past nor the past of our parents. They used reward and punishment as disciplinary methods that they learned from their parents, who learned it from their parents, and up the genealogical line. As humans, we have the ability to make choices that may be different from those who reared us. If you know that your family needs a change in your leadership methodology, be courageous and make that change. Do things differently. Hiding behind the face-saving phrase, "And I turned out all right," may be bogus. Perhaps you are just being, as Forrest would say, stupid about your behavior. It's something to think about. Start your change by being more respectful toward your children, be encouraging, give more individual special time, start a family council. Your family will benefit from your newfound wisdom. Follow up by reading all of this book, then taking a class in family management from your local family education center.

Notes

THE THINK-FEEL-ACT CYCLE

Many parents believe they have no control over the way they react when they respond to their children's misbehavior. The following is a "desperate-gram" I received from one such mother.

> Dear Dr. Deutch,
>
> When my husband and I are upset and angry with our kids, we shout, yell, and talk them to death, way beyond the misbehaviors and issues at hand. We angrily add unnecessary criticisms like, "How many times have I told you . . ." "We always have to pick up your toys." "Why can't you follow directions?" And I am ashamed to add, "Why are you so damn stupid?" Our mouths are creating kids with low self-confidence, poor self-esteem, and there is a feeling of tension throughout the household. Our children are fighting with each other, now more than ever. We want to change. Dr. Jim, any insights into what behaviors parents like us should adopt when we are angry?

This mother knows that her husband's and her behaviors are resulting in damaged children. Yet like so many parents, they think they have no control of their actions once a feeling has been triggered; they are slaves to whatever they feel.

Like most "good"[1] parents, this mother rationalizes that yelling, scolding, commanding, threatening, and angry put-downs will have a positive influence on her children in the days and years to come. On the other hand, she realizes that their harmful parental behaviors are damaging their children.

Are we really in control of our feelings, and do we, in truth, have thoughts before we feel? Are our feelings a biologically predetermined response that we are preordained to follow?

What Do Social Scientists and Philosophers Say about Our Feelings and Behaviors?

Contemporary social scientists as well as philosophers of old have given us the answer that seems to be counterintuitive for many. Adlerians believe that our intellect and interpretation of our life experiences directly control our feelings, thus our behavior. Dr. Alfred Adler often wrote that one's emotions are at the service of the intellect and that our emotions serve the intellect's purpose.[2] Dr. Albert Ellis, in all his books, writes that an event's emotional consequence is created by the individual's belief system.[3] Dr. Wayne Dyer writes, "If you change the way you look at things, the things you look at change."[4] My mentor in psychodrama, Dr. Dorothy Satten, in her book *Real Is Better Than Perfect*,[5] writes, "Be your own detective. If you tend to get angry first, try to find out what you are afraid of. If you're often fearful, try to discover what you're angry about." Dr. Satten often spoke about being in control of one's own life through practicing healthy thinking.

The great Greek philosopher, Epictetus, wrote, "Men are not disturbed by things, but by the view they take of things."[6] Shakespeare scribed, "There is nothing either good or bad, but thinking makes it so."[7] And the Buddha said, "What we are today comes from our thoughts of yesterday, and our present thoughts build our life of tomorrow: Our life is the creation of our mind."[8]

What is the lesson to be learned from these researchers and great thinkers? It is that people learn their emotions from their interpretation of their life's experiences. From these events come their perceptions, beliefs, and assumptions about how life is or should be.

Parents' Anger toward Children

All behavior is purposeful, learned, and chosen as a response to the event. Disjunctive emotions like anger are not mysterious. They serve the purpose of bringing about a change in the situation in favor of the parent. Anger is an intensified emotion that an individual feels only when she or he no longer believes that there is any other possibility of asserting herself or himself. An important aspect of this emotion is a feeling of inferiority or inadequacy that forces the parent to put together all her or his strength to carry out a power movement greater than usual in order to become victorious. There is no rage without an enemy. In an outburst of temper, the angry parent wishes to overcome her imperfections as quickly as possible. To hit (spank), accuse, or attack the child often seems at that moment to be the best solution to correct the situation.[9]

What Can Parents Do about Their Angry Mouths and Hands?

Each of us must realize that we can learn to be better parents and people. We are not stuck with unwanted emotional responses. We can choose to behave the way we want. For some, this journey will be quick; for others it will be longer and more difficult. For those parents who choose to begin their journey now, I suggest the following steps.

1. Realize that you are a person of beliefs, attitudes, and values. You obtained these characteristics by living life. Some of your experiences were positive and enhanced your social development while others were negative and stunted your growth. Realize that you are not biologically commanded; you always make choices.
2. Alter your thoughts, if necessary, by challenging and disputing them. Do not let your old parenting ways get in the way of practicing, learning, and mastering new ones.

I suggest you use the simple but powerful technique developed by Noah Blumenthal.[10] Blumenthal, a master storyteller, points out that every person tells himself or herself stories about an event. He points out that it is the story you tell yourself that determines how you subsequently think and feel. Your story will feature you as a hero or a victim. The hero tells the self stories that are respectful, encouraging, and bring a heroic state of mind. The victim focuses attention on blaming, being angry, frustrated, helpless, hopeless, vulnerable while concurrently losing the ability to face challenges.

It is your choice which story you choose to tell yourself. In the case of the mother who was quoted above, the parents tell themselves a story about being victims of their children's misbehavior. They respond to their story's victimization theme by becoming upset, angry, shouting, yelling, and nagging.

Parents need to recognize that a child's misbehavior is really the child's solution to the perplexing question, "How do I behave in order to belong to this family with significance?"[11] That's really the story the parents ought to be hearing and telling themselves in order to be and act like a hero, not a victim. Whether or not the story you tell yourself is completely true and accurate makes no difference. "If two stories are equally likely to be true or untrue, the hero chooses the one that makes him happier and more effective. The victim chooses the one that makes him angry and frustrated."[12] Thus at the moment of crisis, a parent might as well choose to be positive rather than negative toward the child's behavior. All parents need the practice of thinking like a hero.

3. Modify who you are by practicing your new way of thinking like a hero. If you learned parenting from a spanker, you don't have to spank. If you learned parenting from a yeller, you don't have to yell. You can become the parent and person you want to be; you will grow by changing your thoughts from victim to hero. Becoming a hero in no way implies becoming permissive. Democratic parenting, as demonstrated throughout this book, means rearing children without the strong-arm tactics of an autocrat, nor the laissez-faire attitude of a permissive parent.[13]

Here is a small hint for parents. The next time you are confronted by an unpleasant situation, casually, quietly, and without a fuss, walk away in silence. This will give you time to think and prepare your hero story and your parenting responses. Be armed with the knowledge you have gained from reading this book. Keep coming to FETCH or your family education center. As you learn new ways of thinking and parenting, you will become more comfortable and proud of your new self. Have the courage to be imperfect. Realize that perfection is a direction, not a goal.

Endnotes

1   My mentor, Dr. Genevieve Painter, used to differentiate between the "good" parent and the "responsible" parent. She would say what the world needs are more "responsible" parents.

2   Ansbacher and Ansbacher, *Individual Psychology.*

3   Ellis and Dryden, *Rational-Emotive Behavior Therapy.*

4   Dyer, "Wayne Dyer Quotes."

5   Satten, *Real is Better Than Perfect.*

6   *Epictetus.* (Undated). Retrieved July 26, 2011 from http://www.brainyquote. com /quotes/authors/e/ epictetus_2 .html Epictetus also wrote, "It's not what happens to you, but how you react to it that matters."

7   Shakespeare.

8   Buddha.

9   The scholarly reader will be interested in Adler's words on "Feelings and Emotions." See Ansbacher and Ansbacher, pp. 226-28.

10 Blumenthal, *Be the Hero.*

11 Read "Why Do Children Misbehave?"

12 Blumenthal, p. 84.

13 The following nine features of democratic parenting are presented by Mary Martini, PhD, in her University of Hawai'i parenting course syllabus. (Unpublished document.)

    1. Parents focus on their children's strengths and assume they are sensible, competent, and well-intentioned;

    2. Family members are equal in their rights for dignity and autonomy;

    3. All family members focus on the family good and contribute to the family unit in proportion to their skills;

    4. The family functions in an orderly way, established through democratic discussion involving all members;

    5. Certain rights are inviolable (respect, dignity, privacy, self-determination);

6. Dealings are straight, honest, and devoid of hierarchical power maneuvers (no forcing of one person's will on another, no harsh punishments, no manipulations, no violence);

7. Family relationships are based on logic, reason, and mutual respect;

8. Logical and natural consequences are the major training methods;

9. Parents are friendly but firm.

Notes

WORDS OF ENCOURAGEMENT

As an Adlerian-oriented family educator, I receive a great deal of satisfaction when given the opportunity to strengthen families. My advice is tailored to the needs of the family and its specific situation. Some families feel confident and creative. At those times, giving information and tools is all that is required, as in this letter.

Dear Dr. Deutch,

I am new to the FETCH program. Although I have taken other parenting courses, what you said last night about encouragement being more useful and powerful than praise with none of the drawbacks, caught my attention. I was a coach working with children many years before I became a dad. Coaches seem to come from the same mold, using praise and punishment to motivate their kids. When I became a dad, I just transferred the words I knew to my son. I heard what you said, and I would like to be a better dad and even a better coach. Please give me a few rules and a pocketful of encouraging words, and I promise to use them at home and on the playing field.

Coach

Dear Coach,

According to the grapevine, you are one of the most sought-after coaches in our area. The kids love and respect you, and their parents want their children on your teams. You teach children to enjoy sports by having fun and respecting the rules. You teach the concept of team effort: everyone belongs, and all are significant. Your word is law, but you never punish. When your team takes laps, you run with them. You are an Adlerian at heart, and training you in the Adlerian method will be a joy.

The information I am about to give to you is basic and to the point. It comes from the experiences of the old mentors in the Adlerian movement.[1] There are other sources available for your inspection in our Family Education Training Center library.

What Is Encouragement and Why Is It Important?

I see encouragement as a conscious process to inspire courage, spirit, confidence, and hope in fellow human beings. I also like the Bettner and Lew definition: "Encouragement is anything that leaves the other person feeling better about themself or the situation."[2]

Encouragement may be the most important aspect of child rearing. It is "the nourishment of the soul just as food is the nourishment of the body."[3] According to Dr. Rudolf Dreikurs, "It is so important that the lack of it can be considered the basic cause of misbehavior . . . . A child needs encouragement like a plant needs water."[4]

The major difference between encouragement and praise is that encouragement focuses on the deed, what the child actually does; praise focuses on the doer and aims at the integrity and worth of the child. Encouragement conveys to the child the idea that he is good enough just the way he is. Encouraging words show acceptance, confidence, trust, and appreciation for the child's contribution. It implies a parent's faith, a belief that vigorously says, "I know you can do it; I believe in your abilities." Children respond joyfully when a parent is friendly and more so when the parent shows affection. They feel good when their parents talk with them and not at them. Encouragement focuses on effort and improvement. No child achieves competence immediately. Children who do not believe they will be successful may give up. When parents focus on effort and improvement, they make it clear to the child what is important. Encouragement is what every child needs when he believes he has failed. Encouragement infuses the discouraged child with courage, confidence, and hope.

Unfortunately for their children, many parents have a knack for seeing their child's inadequacies and all too often focus on these. Parents need to look for and support their child's strengths. The wise parent catches his child doing something right and reinforces it by pointing it out. "Thank you, Tommy, for putting your toys in the box. You have made my vacuuming easier." I guarantee parents will see an immediate positive change in their child's attitude and behaviors when they focus on encouraging his strengths and ignoring his weaknesses.

The Dangers of Praise

As said earlier, praise focuses on the doer and aims at the integrity and worth of the child. Because praise focuses on what the child already does well, it may lead the child to the impression that only success counts. This could lead to a fear of new tasks as new tasks do not guarantee success.

Praise as a means of encouragement can be very dangerous as the child can easily begin to identify what he does with what he is. Dr. Rudolf Dreikurs points out the problems praise generates.

"If the child sees praise as a reward, then the lack of it becomes scorn. If he is not praised for everything he does, the child feels he has failed. Such a child does things in the hope of winning a reward rather than doing them for the satisfaction of contribution. Therefore, praise could easily lead to discouragement since it would fortify the child's mistaken concept that unless he is praised he has no value."[5]

There are other faults in using praise as a means of encouragement. Praise often sounds phony and insincere. "You are such a great child for drawing me that wonderful picture." While praise is given for work well done, what does a parent say to his child when work is subpar or done poorly? Praise implies a demand for continued high performance that can be very overwhelming as a child looks into the future and wonders if he can keep up the pace.

To an already very discouraged child, praise can be devastating. Discouraged children have problems believing in themselves and in their abilities. When a parent or coach makes a devaluating remark or statement, very little remains to prop up the already discouraged youngster. By default, he may go deeper into depths of discouragement. Unfortunately, children who need encouragement the most often get it the least. This is because their behavior drives potential supporters away, which further pushes them into discouragement, inadequacy, and rebellion.

Even positive words, when used as praise, can be harmful. What about the girl who is praised for her beauty? Soon her belief system becomes, "It's not what I do, it's how I look." Her belief system also could take on the logic, "If I'm not beautiful, then I must be ugly." "If I can't be a winner, then I must be a loser." Often, such women never make the transition from "beauty equals worth," to "what I do makes me a winner."

There is no guarantee that praise will increase a child's self-esteem; usually it does not. There is, however, a guarantee that encouragement will never do harm, not even to the most discouraged child. If you want to be on solid ground as a parent or coach, be wise and always choose encouragement.

I am now going to give you the "pocketful of encouraging words" you requested. I like Ken Marlin's presentation found in Margaret Cater's *Parent Work Book*.[6] It is simple and makes good sense.

Words that encourage and stimulate cooperation

Good work	Really	I like that
I agree	Groovy	You don't say
I see	I understand	I'm happy
Oh	Thank you	How considerate
Please	Good idea	I'm glad
Fine	Very clever	Would you help me?
Okay	That's right	Fine job
Great effort	I'll buy that	

Conversation door openers

Tell me about it.
I'd like to hear about it.
Tell me more, please.
Want to talk about it?
Let's discuss it.

Let's hear your side.
Shoot—I'm listening.
Sounds like you've got troubles.
Seems pretty important to you.
Tell me the whole story.

Facial expressions that tell the other person she/he is okay

Smiling
Winking
Nodding head
Laughing

Giggling
Looking interested
Grinning in a friendly fashion

Nearness that tells the other person she/he is okay

Walking together
Sitting down beside him
Talking/listening
Just visiting

Eating together
Playing games together
Solving a problem together
Going to a movie together

Physical contacts that tell the other person she/he is okay

Sitting (holding) on lap
Patting back, shoulder
Shaking hands

Hugging
Touching
Stroking arm

Holding hands
Smooching
Kissing

Vicki Soltz, RN, who coauthored with Dr. Rudolf Dreikurs, the landmark book, *Children: The Challenge*, edited an excellent and useful publication, *Articles of Supplementary Reading for Parents.*[7] From her article, "Why Not Praise?," the following "encouragement" statements are presented.

Isn't that nice that you can help?

We appreciate your help.

Don't the dishes shine? (After wiping)

Isn't the carpet pretty now? (After vacuuming)

How nice your room looks.

Thanks for watching the baby. It was a big help.

I like your drawing. The colors are so pretty together.

How much neater your room looks now that your toys are put away.

How nice that you could figure that out for yourself. Your skill is growing!

I'm so glad that you enjoy learning.

We all enjoyed being together in the restaurant.

It is so good to see that you enjoy playing.

We all appreciate the job you did.

I have to give you credit for working hard.

The last "pocketful of encouraging words" I am going to give you is based on an excellent article by Clint Reimer, titled *Some Encouraging Words*.[8] For my purposes, I extensively have edited his work.

Some More Words of Encouragement

As parents we want to see growth and improvement in our children. When we point out their progress, children are encouraged to do better.

"You have improved in . . ."

Children should be encouraged when they are not expecting it. Catch your child doing something right and give a verbal payoff. You will happily see the behavior repeated.

"You do a good job of . . ."

Children often feel that they are not liked because they have made a mistake or have misbehaved. A child should never be made to believe or feel that he, the person, is not liked. Parents need to distinguish between the deed and the doer, the act and the actor.

"We like you, but we don't like what you do."

Parents need to give children an opportunity to make a contribution to the family welfare by encouraging their innate need to feel useful and helpful.

"You can help me by . . ."

Children who think they have to do things perfectly are often afraid to attempt something new for fear of making a mistake or failing.

"Let's try it together."

Mistakes are for learning. Children must never be made to feel inadequate or embarrassed for having made a mistake. It detracts from their courage.

"So you made a mistake, now what can you learn from what happened?"

When your child whines or conveys a message of inadequacy, that she/he thinks a task is too hard or that she/he is afraid to try, a parent might say this:

"You would like us to think you can't do it, but we think you can."

When a child is attempting a task but not meeting with success, a comment like this is often helpful.

"I like the way you keep at a problem and don't give up. You have determination."

Parents need to have confidence in children's ability resolve conflicts.

"I'm sure you can solve this problem. But if you need any help you know where to find me."

Sympathizing with another person, no less your child, is seldom helpful. It conveys the idea that life has been unfair, and she or he has been inadequate to the task at hand. Understanding the situation and believing in the child's ability to adjust to it is of much greater help. With empathy, not sympathy, say, "I can understand how you feel, but I'm sure you can handle it."

Coach, I hope these ideas and words do as much for you as they have done for me. Please feel free to contact me at any time and ask any questions. Thank you for your enthusiastic participation in FETCH.

Respectfully,

Dr. Jim

Endnotes

[1] Dreikurs and Soltz, *Children: The Challenge*. Soltz, *Supplementary Reading for Parents*. (1975). Painter and Corsini, *Effective Discipline*. Cater, *Parent Workbook for Use*, unpublished manuscript.

[2] Bettner and Lew, *Leader's Guide*.

[3] Painter and Corsini, *Effective Discipline,* p. 34.

[4] Dreikurs and Soltz, *Children: The Challenge,* p. 36.

[5] Ibid., p.55.

[6] Marlin (edited for current use) in Cater, *Parent Workbook for Use.* p. 45

[7] Soltz, *Supplementary Reading for Parents.*

[8] Reimer in ibid. p. 18.

Notes

NATURAL AND LOGICAL CONSEQUENCES IN A NUTSHELL

What would you say if I offered you a magic bullet that is more powerful than punishment and has none of its drawbacks? Would you take it?

This is not a theoretical question. I *can* give you that power. The magic is embedded in the Adlerian concepts of *natural* and *logical consequences*. These methods are in harmony with the way nature and society teaches behavior, not only to our children, but to adults as well.

Natural Consequences

The use of natural consequences is the most powerful technique I know that teaches children appropriate behaviors. Its beauty allows children to learn from their own behavior without parental interference or discouragement. When you think natural, think of the word "nature." It's futile to be angry at nature.

A story that describes the concept and spirit of natural consequences is told by my friend and Adlerian psychologist, Dr. Malia Thompson-Ginoza, daughter of long-time Adlerian psychologist and teacher, Dr. Vernon Thompson.

> We had just spent an enjoyable family day at the beach, and it was time to pack up and go home. While sorting out who wanted to carry what, my four-year-old son, Micah, announced

that he wanted to take home his pail of wet sand. I had visions of the beach spilled over the back of our car and all over his room that he shares with his twin brother. I realized that I could shout "No," but that would shatter his desire to continue the fun day with its joyous memories. Remembering what my father had taught me, I merely said, "You can take the sand home, but because my hands and arms are full, you will have to carry it yourself." Fortunately for me, the car was parked at least a football field away, and I remembered how heavy a child's pail of wet sand can be. About a third of the way to the car, my son stopped, dumped the wet sand out of his pail, and then continued without saying a word or uttering a whimper or whine. When we got to the car, the mother in me had to ask, "Where is your sand?" Micah looked at me and said, "It got too heavy, so I decided I didn't want to take it home." Relieved of my disaster fantasies, we all got into the car, buckled up, and quietly drove home. Natural consequences had saved the day. I said to myself, "I'll have to tell my dad about this, he'll enjoy the story."

The natural consequence in this situation was the stress of a too-heavy-to-carry pail of wet sand that Micah decided was not worth the effort to carry to the car and home. The child realized his limitations and made a conscious decision that satisfied the needs of the situation. At age four, Micah learned a valuable lesson in decision making that will benefit him for the rest of his life and without Mother uttering a word of advice.

The two caveats I give to all parents is that natural consequences as a teaching tool have their limitations. First, the time frame involved may be too extensive for immediate learning to take place. For example, telling a child that if he does not brush his teeth, he will get cavities. Since cavities can take years develop, that consequence will not be a helpful teaching tool in this current situation. Second, never allow your child to do anything that would be dangerous or harmful to him or anyone else. As I always say to parents and students, "Do not allow your child to drink poison, play on the freeway, or jump out of a second-story widow with a towel wrapped around his neck while pretending to be a super hero."[1]

Logical Consequences

In real life, natural consequences alone are not enough to train children. Parents need something more. Logical consequences are the best answer. A logical consequence is a consequence that is applied to the child when agreed-upon behaviors are not met.

There are three requirements that must be met for a logical consequence to be truly a logical consequence. Otherwise, the technique is just another punishment with a fancy name.[2]

First, logical consequences, if at all possible, should require a well-discussed and well-informed agreement between parent and child as to what behavior is to be expected and when it is to occur. The agreement must be an authentic buy-in by both parties, not another forced proclamation on the part of the parent. How many times have we seen a parent wanting to get an agreement by repeatedly saying, "Okay? Okay? Okay?" Children who are forced or passively agree to a so-called agreement usually do not follow through with parent-stipulated agreements.

I suggest that all family agreements[3] and related consequences be discussed at a family council meeting prior to their adoption. Discussions should be centered on finding solutions to family challenges. Children who participate and have a say in a solution-finding process will not feel punished should the consequence be on them. By taking the time to understand and discuss issues and consequences, buy-ins by all concerned are much more likely to happen. Parents need to remember that any behavior that needs a consequence must be applied to them and their children alike. For example, a family agreement that any articles of clothing left lying in the family's common area should not be returned to the owner until the next family meeting, also must apply to the parents' garments, not just to the clothing belonging to the children.

I also suggest that all new family agreements and related consequences be tried for one week and then reevaluated at the next family council meeting. If an agreement and consequence is working, it should be kept. If there is some difficulty, it should be reworked, tried again, then reevaluated by the family at the following council meeting.

Second, any logical consequence must meet all the requirements of the four Rs: *related, reasonable, respectful, and restorative.*

> ***Related.*** *Related* means exactly that. There must be an obvious logical tie between the misbehavior and the consequence assigned to it.
>
> ***Reasonable.*** Whatever the consequence, it cannot be obtuse or absurd. A consequence for a six-year-old that lasts thirty days does not pass the test for what is reasonable.
>
> ***Respectful.*** We teach our children respect by modeling it. Spanking, yelling, threatening, and cursing at a child is disrespectful and teaches disrespect. Doing for a child what a child can do for himself or herself also is disrespectful. It prevents the child from learning a life task or allows the child to put the parent into service. For example, putting on a five-year-old's shoes in the morning because he "always" puts them on the wrong foot. Adding humiliation or shame to the consequence is not only disrespectful but also is very destructive to the child. Saying "Shut up" or "I'll really give you something to cry about" is inappropriate. Parents do not have to make their children feel worse in order to make them do better.
>
> ***Reparative.*** A new R that was put forth at our Family Education Training Center of Hawai'i seeks to repair any harm done

by the misbehavior. We believe that a family needs to be
made whole, and if possible, the logical consequence needs
to reestablish family resources lost or damaged by the
misbehavior.

Mother picks up Matt after school every day at 4:00 PM. Today, Mother
had to wait forty-five minutes for Matt to show up. "Since you made me
wait forty-five minutes," Mother said, "I need you to do forty-five minutes
of work around the house that I would have done had you been on time."
Matt agreed and Mother designated the tasks needed to be done.

Third is what I call the "six caveats." (1) The child is always given a
choice. He may behave any way he wishes but knows the consequence that
will be applied to his behavior. (2) The parent must not show anger. Angry
parental behavior can be a payoff to cause more misbehavior. (3) The
parent must follow through. Credibility, doing what you say you are going
to do, is a necessity for successful parenting.[4] (4) A logical consequence
works best when the child is seeking undue attention, that is, annoyingly
keeping his parent busy with him. It should never be imposed when a
child is angry or having a temper tantrum as it easily could be seen as a
punishment. The best solution is for the parent calmly to walk away. (5)
Logical consequences should not be imposed on teens as it easily can be
interpreted by the adolescent as punishment. In these cases, discussion and
otherwise treating the adolescent as an adult is the best solution.[5] (6) A
logical consequence may not work the first or even the second or third
time it is attempted, no matter how well executed it may be. This can be
caused by a number of factors but is usually caused by the misbehavior
being strongly ingrained in the child's behavior patterns. It is as though
the child says to herself, "It worked before, it will work again. All I have to
do is to do it harder." In these situations, the parent must follow exactly
any directions given by their counselor and be consistent in the direction's
execution.[6] Many times, such behaviors such as bickering and fighting
among siblings,[7] bedtime antics,[8] and eating,[9] can take several days or even
weeks to change.

James and the Family Garbage

My personal favorite example of a logical consequence is the true story of James and the family garbage.

Nine-year-old James wanted the chore of taking out the garbage each evening after the supper dishes were done. At the weekly family council meeting, his father asked him the following question. "James, if you forget to take out the garbage, may I remind you at my convenience?" James answered yes, as he had every intention to do his chosen chore. One week later, James went to bed without doing his chore. When deeply asleep, his father went into his room and awakened him with a gentle touch and the words, "James, you're not ready for sleep yet." James grumbled but did not attempt to get up. Ten minutes later, Father reappeared and again gently touched his son and said, "James, you're not ready for sleep yet." James grumbled but this time got out of bed and completed his chore. James did not forget again. I know this story is true because I am James's father.

The reader is invited to inspect this story and see how it meets the three requirements of a logical consequence. Was there a well-informed agreement between parent and child as to what behavior is to be expected and when? Did it meet all the requirements of the four Rs: related, reasonable, respectful, and restorative? Was the child given a choice, did the parent show anger, and did the parent follow through?

School Is Tim's Responsibility

Ten-year-old Tim, a bright young man, was not turning in his homework, even though both parents were spending hours with him each evening "helping" him with his studies. Many times the "helping" sessions turned into arguments and bad feelings.

As new parents at the Family Education Training Center of Hawai'i, Tim's parents had begun to have weekly family council meetings. At midsemester, Tim's parents received a letter from his teacher informing them that Tim would fail the fourth grade if he did not do his assignments. At the weekly family council meeting, Mom and Dad informed Tim of the letter and its contents. They asked if there was anything they could do to help him pass the fourth grade. Tim meekly answered, "No." His parents then apologized for the arguments they had during their "helping" sessions. Then Father said kindly:

> From now on, school and homework is your responsibility. We will not interfere. If you want help on any specific problem, let us know. If you need any special items to make school work more productive, tell us, and we will purchase them. If you need a tutor, we will get one for you. If you choose not to pass the fourth grade, we will still love you because you are our son. Is this an okay way for us to be good parents and help you to be what you want to be?

Tim smiled and answered an enthusiastic yes. He continued by saying, "I want to be in charge of my own life. I don't like it when you nag me. I know what to do." Tim's parents believed that they had meaningful agreement with their son. It was now their turn to carry out their half of the agreement.

Tim's parents then arranged for the three of them to meet with Tim's teacher.[10] At the meeting, Mom and Dad explained their new Adlerian philosophy and that Tim was now solely responsible for his education. They also told the teacher that she had their backing to do whatever she thought necessary, short of corporal punishment, to help Tim do better at school. Tim's teacher, like most teachers, understood what they were attempting and said she would take care of the situation and keep them informed of Tim's progress.

Once Tim found that school was truly his responsibility and that he would have to repeat the fourth grade if he kept his goal of failure, he buckled down and did the required work. At the end of the school year, Tim was promoted to the fifth grade.[11]

Lei and Dinnertime

At dinnertime, five-year-old Lei played more with her food than she ate. She also kept her parents busy with her by goofy antics. At the third session of their newly begun family council meetings, Mom and Dad told Lei of their unhappiness with her eating habits and what they were going to do starting with the next dinner meal. "If you keep on playing with your food at dinnertime rather than eating it, we will clear your plate when we clear ours. You no longer will have to stay at the table until you finish, and we promise not to yell at you anymore. You can eat again at the next meal. Does that seem fair to you?" Lei seemed to understand, and she agreed. Her parents noticed a smile across her lips when they mentioned that they would no longer yell at her.

At the next dinner, Lei continued her antics as if no discussion had taken place. Mom and Dad bit their lips but ignored her antics. A few minutes after everyone had finished eating, Mother calmly and silently took away Lei's plate, throwing its contents into the garbage, as she had promised. Lei was then respectfully excused from the table.

Mother and Dad later reported that after the meal, Lei begged for more food, saying that she was hungry. "My heart was breaking," Mother stated, "but I calmly said, 'You can eat tomorrow at breakfast.'" Lei tried her eating misbehavior at the next family dinner, and her parents repeated their calm, nonverbal consequence. After that, Lei ceased to play with her food and to otherwise keep her parents busy with her. Mother and Father reported that within two weeks, it had become a pleasure to eat all meals with Lei.[12]

A Bedtime Story

Three-year-old Ryan and his five-year-old sister, Carolynn, were driving their parents crazy at bedtime by being wild, loud, and jumping in and out of bed. Their parents learned about "room time" and its one major imperative that the children must remain in their room.[13] After a fun discussion at family council, the children agreed to this new procedure. That night, they stayed up to midnight and needed to be returned to their room on two occasions.[14] The next night, they stayed in their room, were reasonably quiet, and were in their beds and asleep by 10:00 PM. After that, the parents lost track of what time the children went to bed as bedtime, now room time, was no longer a struggle.

Acting Without Consensual Agreements

There are times when a parent must act without the desired consensual agreements brought about by a discussion at the family council. Parents need to remember that their unilateral decisions must carry the same requirements as any logical consequence in order to avoid becoming a punishment.

For use at those rare times, I am presenting a few logical consequence-oriented statements a parent can apply. The wise parent will bring the related issue up at the very next family council meeting for clarification among all family members. For fun and learning, the reader is challenged to figure out how each statement below meets the four major requirements to be a logical consequence and not a punishment. Earlier in caveat number 6, it was pointed out that a logical consequence, no matter how good or well executed, may not always work. I suggest that if a parent's spontaneous logical consequence works well, it may not need to be discussed further. However, if a spontaneous logical consequence goes poorly, it needs to be discussed by all family members at the next family council meeting.

"If you don't behave at the restaurant I will take you home."

"Unless you agree to act properly at the supermarket, I will not take you there."

"If you lose your money, I will not give you any more."

"If you do not eat at lunchtime, I will not serve you food until supper."

"If you are not ready to leave for school on time, I will take you in your pajamas."

Adlerians have found that a logical consequence when performed correctly by the parent is the most powerful technique a parent can apply to carry out discipline and without any of the side effects or by-products inherent in punishment.[15]

Endnotes

[1] My older sister, Florence, claims that she stopped me when I was a tyke from jumping out of a window while pretending to be Superman. I have no memory of this event, but if she did stop me, I now, in writing, officially thank her.

[2] Read "The Family Council." The book on the family council I like best is Dreikurs, Gould, and Corsini, *Family Council: The Dreikurs Technique.* Other suggested books that discuss the family council are the following:
Dreikurs and Soltz, *Children: The Challenge,* chapter 39.
Painter and Corsini, *Effective Discipline,* chapter 38.
Rigney and Corsini, *Family Council.*

[3] A rule is an authoritarian demand set forth by a superior to direct the behavior or action of an inferior. An agreement is a consensus of opinion, a situation in which everyone accepts the same terms or has the same opinion. A wise parent comes to agreements with children and, with the buy-in, gains tremendous cooperation and family harmony.

[4] Read "The Incredibly Credible Parent."

[5] Read "Peer Power in Teen Life."

[6] Read "Do or Do Not. There Is No 'Try.'"

[7] Read "Adam and Eve: The First Dysfunctional Family."

[8] Read "Bedtime Made Easy" and "The Art of the Wrist."

[9] Read "Eating Should be the Child's Business."

[10] Adlerians believe that parent-teacher conferences always must include the child. All parties need to be up front about the child's performance and their expectations. The child needs to hear when he or she does well and needs to have a say about the failures and challenge he or she is experiencing. Without the child's buy-in of the process, his motivation to do better is diminished.

[11] Read "School Homework: Who Owns the Problem?"

[12] Read "Eating Should Be the Child's Business."

[13] Reread "Bedtime Made Easy."

> Some parents and counselors would like to add a second imperative that the children must be quiet. How is such a request enforceable? It isn't without the parent becoming

authoritarian. I suggest that computers, televisions, and other entertainment centers not be housed in the child's room. I also recommend that the computer used by the child be housed in a common area amenable to good parent supervision and not available at room time.

14   Read "The Art of the Wrist."

15   Other sources for studying logical and natural consequences are the following:
Dreikurs, *Challenge of Parenthood*, pages 65-78.
Dreikurs and Soltz, *Children: The Challenge*, pages 76-85.
Nelson, *Positive Discipline*, pages 80-102.
Painter and Corsini, *Effective Discipline*, pages 27-33.

Notes

CHILDREN ARE GREAT OBSERVERS BUT POOR INTERPRETERS

I have often said that children are great observers but poor interpreters. By this I mean that children study us from the moment of birth, measuring our ways and figuring out how they can get what they want and need. I also believe that our children know us better than we know them. They work us every which way they can. How many men have been worked by a daughter who soon becomes known as "daddy's little girl"? Sons, too, know how to get Mother's attention by becoming "Mommy's little man." Children learn by trial and error; thus they do what seems to them to work. It is only when they mature both in brain physiology and through life experiences that they have the ability to use in-depth reasoning.[1]

I once had a reliable patient who told me the following story. She babysat for a family whose six-month-old son would make horrible choking sounds so as to quickly get picked up and held by its parents. My patient, who often had heard me preach Adlerian psychology, told me that when she sat for this child, she ignored his choking sounds but secretly kept an eye on him. Soon he stopped feigning choking for her.

However, he continued this behavior for the quest of his parent's immediate attention, and why not, it worked well for him.

The "children are great observers" part of the equation is good; we want our children to see clearly the world in which they live. The problem lies in their poor interpretation of what they observe. When children make interpretations about the cause of family catastrophes such as divorce, separation, and death, they more often than not blame themselves, believing that their omnipotence and a lifetime of being corrected for wrongdoings must be at the cause.

Six-year-old Sam had a change in personality soon after his parents divorced. Once a happy kid, he looked and acted depressed, his grades had fallen, and his teacher said that he lacked the energy and concentration he once had. When I talked with Sam, he shared with me the following. Sam believed that he was the cause of his parent's divorce. "If only I would have kept my room cleaner," he said, "maybe my parents wouldn't have fought so much and gotten a divorce." There were many "if onlys" in Sam's misinterpreted belief system. If only he had gotten better grades, minded his parents more, not have been so jealous of the attention given to his little sister, not asked for money or an allowance, and even had he played better soccer so his father would have been proud of him, were among his thoughts. Sam was looking for the answer to his parent's divorce, and these were his interpretations of their behavior. Sam needed his interpretation of his part in adults' behavior reinterpreted. It took a while, but Sam did correct his misinterpretations. Today, Sam is a licensed psychotherapist working with children of divorce.

The above two cases are examples of misinterpretations being related to survival needs and the perplexing sequelae of a family tragedy. The following case examples are misguided interpretations of what a child believes she or he needs to do in order to belong to the family with significance. The reader might want to refer to the chart, "The Four Misguided Goals of Children," located at the end of this essay.

Alicia, a toddler, was "good" until Mother answered the telephone. Quickly, Alicia would initiate a host of "give me's," wants, and demands. When Mother felt annoyed, you can bet that Alicia was into an "I'm going to keep you busy with me" mode that we Adlerians call misguided goal no. 1, *undue attention*. Alicia interprets her situation as she being important in the family only when she is keeping Mother busy with her.

What about the child who argues with his parents at every turn, in essence, saying, "I'm going to be the boss, and I do what I want." Harry's parents reported feeling angry when he plays with them the power game. Inappropriate *power* is misguided goal no. 2. Harry has come to the conclusion that only if he is getting his way, "I do what I want," is he a significant player in his family.

Have you ever known a ten-year-old who lies and steals and whose parents feel hurt by his behavior? Benet was one of those children. After years of losing family power contests, Benet fell into behaviors associated with misguided goal no. 3, *revenge*. Benet's behavior says, "I feel hurt, and I want to hurt back." Lying and stealing are his ways of getting revenge. Benet's interpretation of his family situation was that he belonged and was significant only if he caused trouble and embarrassment to the very people from whom he needed recognition and love.

Every so often one runs across a child who looks and acts defeated. Betty was that girl. Cross-eyed from birth compounded by homely features, Betty looked and enacted the role of the inadequate child, socially introverted and academically poor. Her parents felt as defeated as did Betty. The reality was that Betty, after observing her situation, including how people reacted toward her, chose the defeated or inadequate role in order to become important in her world. Her interpretation of her situation was "I am important only when I show people how *inadequate* I am." This way of behaving we call misguided goal no. 4.

There are excellent solutions to these misinterpretations and misguided goals in the essays of this book, endnotes, and References.

Sometimes, humor is a great way to explain a concept. A friend sent me the following joke (the origin of which I do not know).

One day, eleven-year-old Jane approached her mother and asked, "Mother, how old are you?" Mother looked at her and said, "Jane, that's too personal a question, so I won't answer it." Jane paused and then said, "Well then tell me how tall are you." Again, Mother looked at her daughter and said, "That's a personal question too, so I won't answer it." Without missing a beat, Jane looked at her mother once more and asked, "Tell me then, why did Dad divorce you?" A bit shocked, Mother quickly answered, "Jane, that too is much too personal a question, and I won't answer it either."

The next day, Jane was discussing the incident with her best girlfriend. "Well, Jane," her best friend said, "If your mother won't answer your questions, just look at her driver's license. It gives all that kind of good information."

Early that evening, Jane did look at her mother's driver's license. She then found her mother and said the following. "You are thirty-five years old." Mother looked surprised but answered, "Yes." "You are five feet four inches tall." Again, Mother answered a surprised yes. "And I know why Daddy divorced you." Very surprised, Mother answered "Why?" Jane smugly answered, "Because you got an F in sex."[2]

Summary

Children are great observers but poor interpreters. Perhaps brain immaturity and a lack of real-life experience are the culprit. A baby who has learned to choke in order to be immediately gratified, a child believing that he is the cause of his parents' divorce, or children believing that their only way to belong to the family with significance is through one of the four categories of misbehavers, are all examples of the way children misinterpret their world. The good news is that children's misinterpretations are correctable, and as children grow into adulthood, their ability to better interpret the world grows with them.

The Four Misguided Goals of Children

Misguided Goal	Child Says (Private logic)	Parent Feels (Gut response)	Solution Strategy
1. (undue) Attention	"I'm going to keep you busy with me."	Annoyed	Ignore
2. Power	"I'm going to be the boss and make you do what I want."	Angry	Keep out of the power struggle
3. Revenge	"I feel hurt, and I want to hurt back."	Hurt	Make friends
4. Inadequacy	"I give up."	Defeated	Massive encouragement

Modified from "Children's Mistaken Goals" in Soltz, V. *Articles of Supplementary Reading for Parents.* Chicago: Alfred Adler Institute of Chicago, 1975.

Endnotes

[1]   Parker, "Longitudinal Brain Scan Study."

[2]   I do not know the author of this joke to whom I say, "Thank you for your creativity."

Notes

THE IMPORTANCE OF BIRTH ORDER IN DETERMINING CHARACTER AND BEHAVIOR

Excerpted from
Parent as Consultant[1]

Proponents of Adlerian Individual Psychology have become famous for their groundbreaking observations of the importance of "birth order." Observation and research demonstrates that where a child places in the birth order will have an effect on how the child will view oneself and the world. Differing psychosocial situations and opportunities become available to children depending on their ordinal position in the family structure. For example, *only* children do not have to deal with sibling competition, but do have to deal with being alone as well as living in an adult world. Firstborn children must learn to cope with being dethroned by the next born and, more often than not, are mandated by parents to be the responsible child. Second born children view their family position as the "runner-up" and often work their whole lives to overtake and dethrone their older sibling. Middle children must cope with a feeling of being lost somewhere between older and younger siblings. The youngest child must work hard to find a place in the family and later learn to cope with a world where being cute, irresponsible, and immature is not acceptable.

The following personality characteristics apply to children in general, but not to all children in every family and in every situation. Typical characteristics, however, can be identified.[2]

Only children have been referred to as "onlies" and "firstborns in triplicate." This is due to the fact that they are extreme versions of firstborn children and tend to be extremists in all aspects of life. *Only* children like being the center of adult attention. They often have difficulty sharing with other children. They prefer adult company and use adult language to a greater extent than children of the same age. They mature faster than their peers, are attention seekers, and can be counted on to behave responsibly.

Oldest children begin life as an only child but soon fall into the circumstance of having to deal with one or more siblings. However, other children in the family see their ordinal position as ideal. The oldest child usually has his parents' greatest attention and has been referred to as "king baby." There are two typical types of firstborn children: *compliant* and *aggressive*. The compliant firstborn is often seen as conscientious, reliable, cooperative, a people pleaser, and a team player. The aggressive firstborn is seen as a natural leader, a perfectionist, driven, assertive, and a mover and shaker. Firstborn children share the common traits of being energetic, logical, ambitious, enterprising, and scholarly.

Second children are competitive; they frequently strive to overtake the older sibling. The second child often has the mantra, "If I can't be the best of the best, I'll be the best of the worst." Sibling competition can deteriorate into sibling rivalry.

Middle children often see themselves as being squeezed out of a position of privilege and significance. They feel as though they never have been an older child and soon find themselves no longer the youngest child. However, there appears to be two types of middle born children, often referred to as "middle born no. 1," and "middle born no. 2." Traits of the middle born no. 1 are seen as loner, quiet, shy, impatient, and uptight while that of the middle born no. 2 are outgoing, friendly, loud, laid-back, and patient. Interestingly, middle borns 1 and 2 share the following traits: flexible, rebellious, attention seeking, competitive, and peacemakers.

Youngest children often are considered the baby of the family and frequently live up to that role. Often, their older siblings influence them to act spoiled, manipulative, immature, and self-centered. Last borns are often seen as outgoing, sociable, affectionate, caring, creative, empathetic, and confident.

Endnotes

[1] This chapter is excerpted from "Parent as Consultant" by Drs. Deutch and Martini. This was done in order to allow parents who wish to specifically understand the importance and dynamics of birth order to go directly to the subject.

[2] There are many sources referencing birth order or family constellation. Dreikurs and Soltz, *Children: The Challenge,* chapter 2. Stein, *Birth Order Characteristics.* Witkin, "Birth Order Personality Traits." (Interesting for parents new to Adlerian concepts.) There are also many Internet sources referencing birth order. Three sites that I found useful in writing this section of the essay are Tunde, W., "Are you a First-born Child . . .", http://www.sodahead. com/.living/are-you-a-first-born-child-a-middle-bornchild-or-the-baby-of-the-familylook-at-the-characteris/question-224576/; Child Development Institute, http://www.childdevelopmentinfo.com/ development/birth_order. htm.; and Adlerian Overview of Birth Order Characteristics, http://www. mnstate.edu/kausar/psyc202/Birth%20order%20 Characteristics.htm.

-Note that other variables such as parenting style, physical health, native intelligence, relationships with teachers, grandparents, and others also are powerful determinants of how children will come to see themselves.

Notes

PARENT AS CONSULTANT[1]

Are you stuck in the "my way or the highway" philosophy of child rearing? If so, you are headed for trouble. Our University of Hawai'i students have confirmed what social scientists have said for several decades. Teenagers should be treated as young adults, not as children. The often heard but misguided bellow of many parents, especially the father, seems to be, "That's how I was raised, and I turned out okay." Most often, these statements tell us that the parents are usually unaware of how others see them, have no idea how fortunate they are to have survived their family of origin experience, or are into denial.

What Parents Should Know about Human Behavior

There are some basics of behavior that all parents should understand and which may give meaning to why children behave as they do. Adlerian psychology, also known as Individual Psychology, believes that all behavior is purposeful and goal oriented. This means that children, and parents too, do things for a reason, and that reason is focusing them to reach a personal goal. We believe that children learn through trial and error and that their cognitive skills do not reach maturity until their early twenties. The most important goal of a child is to belong to the family with significance. The best way to belong is by cooperation and contributing to the well-being of the family.

Because children lack worldly experience and cognitive maturity,[2] they often try to belong to the family in mistaken ways. Rudolph Dreikurs, MD, a protégé and colleague of Alfred Adler, found that children have four categories of mistaken goals.[3] Each mistaken goal has the purpose of securing for the child what he regards as his place in the family. These mistaken goals are (1) undue attention, (2) power, (3) revenge, and (4) inadequacy. By understanding the purpose of a child's behavior, a parent is better equipped to understand how to implement the roles of trainer and consultant. See Figure 1 below.

Four Misguided Goals of Children

Misguided Goal	Child Says (Private logic)	Parent Feels (Gut response)	Solution Strategy
1. (undue) Attention	"I'm going to keep you busy with me."	Annoyed	Ignore
2. Power	"I'm going to be the boss and make you do what I want."	Angry	Keep out of the power struggle
3. Revenge	"I feel hurt, and I want to hurt back."	Hurt	Make friends
4. Inadequacy	"I give up."	Defeated	Massive encouragement

Modified from "Children's Mistaken Goals" in V. Soltz, *Articles of Supplementary Reading for Parents* (Chicago: Alfred Adler Institute of Chicago, 1975).

<<FIGURE 1>>

Misguided goal no. 1, undue attention, is exampled by a child who attempts to keep his parent busy with him. A child is playing quietly with his toys until the telephone rings. As soon as his mother picks up the phone, he is demanding a glass of water and is asking questions that do not seem relevant to the events of the moment. If Mother's reaction is to become annoyed, undue attention is the misguided goal.

Misguided goal no. 2, power, is exampled by a child having a temper tantrum. Temper tantrums are pure power and represent the child's attitude of "I'm going to be the boss and make you do what I want" or "I'm the boss, and I do what I want." If the parent feels angry, power is the child's misguided goal.

A child who is stealing or telling lies demonstrates misguided goal no. 3, revenge. This behavior reveals an emotional stance of "I feel hurt, and I want to hurt back." If the parent feels emotionally hurt by the child's behavior, revenge is most likely the misguided goal.

A child who is behaviorally saying, "I give up, I can't do it," represents misguided goal no. 4, inadequacy. If the parents are feeling defeated, misguided goal no. 4, inadequacy, is assumed.

Misguided goals, one to four, each represent a greater degree of discouragement. A child who displays undue attention is a discouraged child; however, the child who displays inadequacy has a significantly greater degree of discouragement. Parents whose child or children demonstrate any of the four misguided goals should seek consultation from a professional or a child guidance organization such as the Family Education Training Center of Hawai'i (FETCH), located at the University of Hawai'i.

Adlerians realize that all movement is from a minus to a plus, from inferior to superior, from incompetence to competence. This means that children are always striving to become better at what they do. Most parents seem to believe that unless they remind and nag their children, they will become lazy and never achieve. This is a false belief. Only those children who are discouraged fail to grow and gain competence.

All human beings, especially children, need encouragement. It is the essential ingredient for growth. Without it, human development, psychological and physical, is retarded. Adlerians differentiate between praise and encouragement. Praise focuses on the individual as a person and comments on his or her worth. This can sound phony and often becomes a discouragement. Encouragement focuses on the behavior, never on the person. We often say, "Focus on the deed, not the dude."

Four-year-old Ben recently had moved to a new home and neighborhood and was now in a new preschool. He was a very verbal and loud child and would often disrupt the class by distracting others with jokes and strange noises. His new teacher began developing a positive relationship with him by mentioning how much she liked it when they were able to have a nice conversation. Ben felt encouraged that his teacher liked talking with him. Soon his need for undue attention gave way to intelligent discussions in the classroom. Ben quickly became a positive leader among his peers.

Children learn respect by watching their parents being respectful to them, others, and themselves. Respect is more than a litany of good words and polite behavior. It is also training a child for responsibility. A parent never should do for a child what a child can do for her or himself. For example, five-year-old Tommy's toys are scattered around the living room, and it is time to pick them up. Tommy is slow to put them away. His mother sighs with exasperation and then says, "Tommy, you go sit on the couch, and I'll pick up your toys, you are too slow." Mother is being disrespectful by assuming Tommy is inadequate to the task of picking up his own toys in a quick and timely manner. She also is teaching her son to be manipulative by allowing him to feign inadequacy.

The Power of Interpretation

Adlerians often say there is no such thing as reality, only *interpretation*. It is not what actually happens to a person but how the experience is viewed. This interpretation is guided by the sum total of the person's life experiences and point of view. For example, a child that has been deprived of food throughout his lifetime will respond differently to an offer of food than a child who never has been similarly deprived. A child who has been physically or emotionally abused or both by his father will act more fearfully toward an angry male than a child who never has been harmed. Likewise, a child whose family background has been one of respect and love and who has been reared having a voice and a choice, in all probability, will seek cooperative and democratic ways to solve problems at school or when confronted by social challenges in other situations.

The Importance of Birth Order in Determining Behavior

Proponents of Adlerian Individual Psychology have become famous for their groundbreaking observations of the importance of "birth order."

Observation and research demonstrates that where a child places in the birth order will have an effect on how the child will view oneself and the world. Differing psychosocial situations and opportunities become available to children depending on their ordinal position in the family structure. For example, *only* children do not have to deal with sibling competition, but do have to deal with being alone as well as living in an adult world. Firstborn children must learn to cope with being dethroned by the next born and, more often than not, are mandated by parents to be the responsible child. Second born children view their family position as the "runner-up" and often work their whole lives to overtake and dethrone their older sibling. Middle children must cope with a feeling of being lost somewhere between older and younger siblings. Youngest children must work hard to find a place in the family, and later they must learn to cope with a world where being cute, irresponsible, and immature is not acceptable.

The following personality characteristics apply to children in general, but not to all children in every family and in every situation. Typical characteristics, however, can be identified.[4]

Only children have been referred to as "onlies" and "firstborns in triplicate." This is due to the fact that they are extreme versions of firstborn children and tend to be an extremist in all aspects of life. *Only* children like being the center of adult attention. They often have difficulty sharing with other children. They prefer adult company and use adult language to a greater extent than children of the same age. They mature faster than their peers, are attention seekers, and can be counted on to behave responsibly.

Oldest children begin life as an *only* child but soon fall into the circumstance of having to deal with one or more siblings. However, other children in the family see their ordinal position as ideal. The oldest child usually has his parents' greatest attention and has been referred to as "king baby." There are two typical types of firstborn children: *compliant* and *aggressive*. The compliant first child is often seen as conscientious, reliable, cooperative, a people pleaser, and a team player. The aggressive firstborn is seen as a natural leader, a perfectionist, driven, assertive, and a mover and shaker. Firstborn children share the common traits of being energetic, logical, ambitious, enterprising, and scholarly.

Second children are competitive; they frequently strive to overtake their older sibling. The second child often has the mantra, "If I can't be the best of the best, I'll be the best of the worst." Sibling competition can deteriorate into sibling rivalry.

Middle children often see themselves as being squeezed out of a position of privilege and significance. They feel as though they never have been an older child and soon find themselves no longer the youngest child. However, there appears to be two types of middle born children, often referred to as "middle born no. 1" and "middle born no. 2." Traits of the middle born no. 1 are seen as loner, quiet, shy, impatient, and uptight while that of the middle born no. 2 are outgoing, friendly, loud, laid-back, and patient. Interestingly, middle borns 1 and 2 share the following traits: flexible, rebellious, attention seeking, competitive, and peacemakers.

Youngest children often are considered the baby of the family and frequently live up to that role. Often, their older siblings influence them to act spoiled, manipulative, immature, and self-centered. Last borns are often seen as outgoing, sociable, affectionate, caring, creative, empathetic, and confident.

Two Possible Parent Roles

As parents, we have two major categories of roles from which to choose: *trainer* and *consultant*. See figure 2 below.

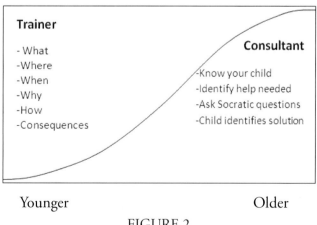

FIGURE 2

Parent as Trainer

From birth to about two years of age, infants and early toddlers need parents who are primarily caretaker-trainers. As the child's cognitive abilities mature, offering him or her a choice of "this or that," is quite appropriate. Soon after this stage of development, the role of parent as trainer begins to grow. We define the role of trainer as the parent advising the child what, where, when, why, how, and the consequences of disobeying. This must be done in a respectful and kind manner. At this level of a child's growth and development, parental leadership can be amazingly exciting and enjoyable for everyone. If parents insist upon a parent dominated dictatorship, then child rearing can be fraught with pain and unhappiness for all involved.

Children need to be able to figure out for themselves the what, where, when, why, how, and consequences of their situation and behavior. This kind of knowledge, especially in the early years, comes through the practice of trial and error. We suggest parents teach using the Socratic method of asking questions that lead their children to intelligent conclusions. "What do you think will happen if you . . . ?" is often a good opening question. We also like a dialogue that eventually asks, "What do you plan to do?"

Parent as Consultant

Adlerian parenting methods provide parents with the opportunity to become their child's consultant from infancy on. We define a consultant as a person regarded as especially knowledgeable in some area of specialization (life and parenting) who may be asked to give an opinion or suggestion about an issue. At a very early age, children begin to become aware of how to use parental consultation. Too many parents attempt to become their child's consultant after the child has reached adolescence. This is far too late in the game to begin a new role. The later in a child's life the parents starts the consultation process, the greater the chances of failure.

To be an effective consultant, the parent needs to understand how a consultant works. A consultant first needs to know and understand his client, in this case the child. Second, the parent needs to obtain information about the child's situation, concern, or problem. Third, the key to effective consultation is identifying what help is needed. Here, modern Adlerians have adopted the technique of active listening, developed by Dr. Thomas Gordon.[5] A good consultant listens liberally and speaks sparingly.

Parents often believe that when their child has a problem, it is their duty to solve it, usually by telling the child what to do and how to do it. This is how parents get themselves fired (or never hired) as consultants, by talking when they should be listening and by denying the child to experience "the thrill of victory and the agony of defeat."

Nine-year-old James saw a toy on a local television show that looked like fun. He had saved his money and was excited when taken by his mother to the toy store. After seeing the toy up close, James felt sad and disappointed. It was a toy for a much younger child, and James knew it. However, he had saved his money and looked forward to buying it. Turning to his mother, he asked her what he should do. Sensing a consulting moment, Mother asked him if he wanted to take a few minutes to think about it. Perhaps they could have a cold drink together and talk. At the table, James again lamented his disappointment and mixed feelings about making the purchase. Mother suggested that James might want to take a piece of paper, draw a line down the middle, on one side write all the reasons why he liked the toy and, on the other, all the reasons for not liking it. James agreed to this task. At the end of his exercise, James looked at the preponderance of reasons for not liking the toy. "Mom," he said, "I think I want to spend my money on something else that I might like better."

Adolescents have (at least) two additional misguided goals, *excitement* and *identity*, in addition to the usual four of childhood. Many teens lust toward the desire for excitement. Fast cars, motorcycles, sex, skydiving, petty theft, and drug experimentation are a few examples. A part of excitement is the misbelief that nothing bad can happen. "It can't happen to me" seems to be an adolescent mantra, whether it is related to an unwanted pregnancy, the result of driving drunk, or the result of soldiering in war. Identity goes to answering the question "Who am I?" and "Where do I belong?" Teens join groups and gangs as well as make decisions about dealing with their sexuality and sexual preferences. Do I belong to a group that serves the useful side of life or the useless? Life is much easier and runs more smoothly when service is to the useful and when one's biological and psychological roles are congruent.

Popular literature relating to adolescents is quite often misleading in that it suggests that parents should enact the role of consultant when a child reaches his or her teens. As mentioned earlier, this is far too late in the game. One of the biggest mistakes parents make is treating their teenage offspring like a child rather than a young adult. If parents are still in the training mode, telling their teen what, where, when, why, how, and the consequences (often punishment) of disobeying, alienation is a significant factor in the existing parent-child relationship. However, we have found that if parents begin their respectful consultation role when their children are young, little or no alienation manifests as their children wander through adolescence.

How Do I Become a Consultant to My Child?

Earlier in this paper, we suggested that to be an effective consultant, a parent first needs to know and understand his child. Second, the parent needs to obtain information about the child's situation, concern, or problem, and third, the parent needs to identify what help is needed. We suggested that an effective parent needs to listen liberally and speak sparingly. Learning "active listening" can be a very powerful tool in every parent's child rearing toolbox.

We believe that for most youth, learning and relationship building are done experientially. Telling a child what to do without the hands-on learning experience is ineffective, just as telling a child that you love him or her without demonstrating love ends up being hollow and fruitless.

We strongly believe that spending fun time and individual special time[6] with your child is a way to grow the relationship. This is best done before the child reaches adolescence, a time when *family* often becomes redefined as buddies and peer group friends rather than mother, father, and siblings. However, if you are behind the power curve in the "spending fun time with your child" department, we believe the following model still can be helpful.

We have borrowed heavily from the Experiential Learning Model used in the 4-H Cooperative Curriculum System, in particular, the experiential cycle.[7] The idea behind all 4-H curricula is to help youth by *doing*. There are three basic concepts in the Experiential Cycle: *do*, *reflect*, and *apply*, and there are five sequential steps in the experiential cycle. See figure 3 below.

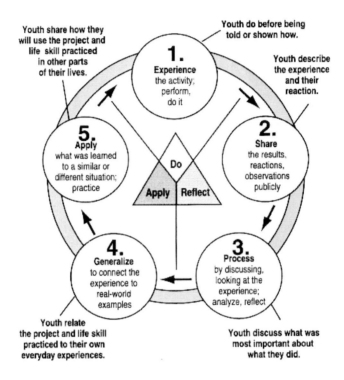

The Experiential Cycle

FIGURE 3

The best way to become your child's consultant in just about everything is to use the experiential concepts model, shown above. Begin by supporting your child in a fun project of his or her own choosing. What the child is doing is called "experiential learning." This will give you, as a parent, a great deal of experience in helping your child grow as a person while simultaneously growing the relationship. As your child shares with you what he or she has done and learned, you will be able to assist him or her in processing the experience, which will lead to ideas on how to apply the learned lesson to the next experience. As you get more experienced, you will find yourself on the way to becoming the best consultant parent you can be. Expect to make mistakes. Remember, mistakes are for learning.

The following steps will be helpful as you work with your child becoming his or her consultant.

Step 1   *The experience.* Allow your child to have a creative experience doing a fun project in which she/he is interested. Allow him or her to "do" before being told or shown how to do it. Allow your child to make mistakes as well as have successes. Be encouraging. Talk about the effort and experience, not about the person.

Step 2   *Share.* Share the adventure. Let your child tell you what she/he thinks was the most important aspect of what was done and why. Let him or her discuss the experience, analyze, and reflect on it. You may want to ask what she/he saw, felt, smelled, and perhaps tasted. You also may want to ask what part of the experience was the easiest and most difficult. Be encouraging by supporting his or her accomplishments. Minimize any mistakes by saying nothing or something like "That's okay, next time you'll naturally do better."

Step 3   *Process.* Processing your child's experience moves it from an activity to a learning experience. Allow your child to discuss, analyze, and reflect on his or her results, reactions, and observations with you. Let him or her discuss what was most important about what she/he did. Ask related questions, listen liberally, and reflect his feelings and experiences by using active listening. Permit your child to be proud of his or her accomplishments. As a parent, you are encouraging when you say, "It looks like you had fun doing it."

Step 4   *Generalize.* Help your child generalize his experiences to real-world everyday experiences. Ask questions whose answers will lead the child to the lesson you want him or her to learn. "What do you think you learned from what you did today?" "How was what you experienced important to you?" "How can you use what you learned?" "Does what you did today remind you of anything? Tell me about it."

Step [5]   *Apply.* Help your child to apply what she/he learned to a similar or different situation or practice. Allow him or her to share what was learned and how she/he will use the project and the life skills practiced in other parts of his or her life. Again, ask questions in a style that will cause the child to think. "What do you think you learned from what you did today?" "How will you use what you learned in the future?" End your consultation adventure on an encouraging note. Your child needs to hear positive words from you. "I'm proud of what you did today. I'm so fortunate to have a hardworking and creative child like you."

Summary

In this article, we described some of the basics of human behavior, which may give insights to parents as to why children behave as they do. We pointed out that all behavior is purposeful and goal oriented. Children learn through trial and error, and their cognitive skills do not reach maturity until their early twenties. The most important goal of a child is to belong to the family with significance, and the best way to belong is by cooperation and contributing to the family's well-being. In their quest to belong to the family, a child may choose a category of behavior that seems inappropriate to the situation. Depending on their degree of discouragement, children will use undue attention, power, revenge, or inadequacy as their solution to the perplexing question, "How do I belong to this family with significance?"

We also learned that there is an innate force that moves children to strive for competence. To help move the child in a positive direction, parents must be encouraging. Adlerians believe that it is not so much what happens to a person, but it is their interpretation of the event that gives meaning to their life.

As children move across the timeline from early toddlerhood to adolescence and beyond, wise parents adjust their methods of parenting to fit the needs of the situation. One of the biggest mistakes parents make in rearing their children is not moving beyond the role of the "trainer." Telling your child what, where, when, why, how, and the consequences of disobeying only goes so far and creates alienation between parent and adolescent. We strongly urge parents to become their child's consultant as soon as possible, not waiting until the teen years. As the years progress, the amount of consultation increases while the degree of training becomes less and less. A major mistake parents make is treating their teenage offspring like a child rather than a young adult.

The Experiential Model used in the 4-H System and a five-step guide for parents who desire to build consultative relationship with their growing child was introduced. The first step of the model requires the child to choose an activity, then experience by doing, before being told or shown how it *should* be done. The second step is to allow the child to share his or her results, reactions, and observations with the parent. The third step is for the parent to listen to the child as he or she processes by discussing, analyzing, and reflecting on the experience. The fourth step is to generalize. The child needs to be guided in order to connect the experience with real-world everyday experiences. Finally, the fifth step is to help the child share how he or she will use the project, what was learned, and how it can be applied to other parts of his or her life. The parent who masters and uses this five-step model will be, to his or her child, a true and valuable consultant.

Seen on a concourse advertising poster at Los Angeles International Airport:

**The smartest consultants don't make
problems go away.
They make sure they never appear.**

Endnotes

[1] This article was coauthored by Dr. Mary I. Martini, a full professor at the College of Tropical Agriculture and Human Resources, Department of Family and Consumer Sciences, University of Hawai'i at Manoa. Dr. Martini is the executive director of Family Education Training Center of Hawai'i and is a founding member and serves on the Board of Directors of the Family Education Centers of Hawai'i, a 501(c)(3) private nonprofit community agency.

[2] Parker, "Longitudinal Brain Scan Study."

[3] Dreikurs, *Challenge of Parenthood*, see chapter 6, "Understanding the Child." Also, see Dreikurs, *Children: The Challenge*. See chart of Children's Mistaken Goals found in Soltz, *Articles for Supplementary Reading for Parents*.

[4] In addition to Dreikurs and Soltz, *Children the Challenge,* pp. 20-35, and Painter and Corsini, *Effective Discipline in the Home and School,* pp. 10-11, there are many Internet sources referencing birth order. Three sites that were found useful in writing this essay are Tunde, W., "Are you a First-born Child . . .", http://www.sodahead.com/.living/are-you-a-first-born-child-a-middle-born-child-or-the-baby-of-the-familylook-at-the-characteris/question-224576/; Child Development Institute, http://www.childdevelopmentinfo.com/development/birth_order.htm.; and Adlerian Overview of Birth Order Characteristics, http://www.mnstate.edu/kausar/psyc202/Birth%20order%20Characteristics.htm. Other variables such as parenting style, physical health, native intelligence, relationships with teachers, grandparents, and others also are powerful determinants of how children will see themselves.

[5] Gordon, *Parent Effectiveness Training. Parent Effectiveness Training* is now in audible format. See www.audible.com. Also see Gordon, *Teacher Effectiveness Training.*

[6] Read "The Gift of Individual Special Time."

[7] Norman and Jordan, *Using an Experiential Model in 4-H.*

Notes

PARENT AS BULLY

Bullying is an assault. Whether it is done by one or more persons in the schoolyard or against another using the Internet and computer, it is, nevertheless, a willful and conscious desire to hurt another human being. The victim is usually an individual who, because of physical or psychological vulnerability, is not able to defend himself or herself.[1]

Although schoolyard and cyber bullies are the types usually mentioned in current popular literature, there is another category of bully that exists, one that most writers ignore: the parent. In no way am I arguing that all parents or even the majority of parents are bullies. Let me ask you a question that I want you to answer truthfully but not out loud. Have you ever yelled at your child to force him or her to do something you wanted done? Have you bellowed your command in a loud, hostile, and threatening voice to make what you wanted to happen happen? If so, at that moment, you were being a bully. I am not referring to the time you yelled at your three-year-old to get out of the street for fear that he would be hit by a car. I am speaking of those times, in the ordinary course of the day, that you behaved in this kind of loud, intimidating, and disrespectful manner.

If I were a gambling man, I would put my money on the idea that very few parents intend to be bullies or intentionally want to harm their children. They are trying to correct situations they find unacceptable and use methods they have learned in the past that seem to work. Unfortunately, whether or not a parent is trying to do the right thing, bullying behavior is still bullying, regardless of the intention.

Adlerian psychology holds *respect* and *cooperation* as two of its key tenets. A parent teaches respect by being respectful and cooperation by modeling cooperative behavior. Bullying your child teaches neither and much of the opposite. Parents who bully, whether by an intimidating tone of voice or through physical force, are teaching their children a myriad of disrespectful lessons, including the one that says, "Power is everything."

I recently had an experience that demonstrates some of the above. I was riding in a car with two parents and their twelve-year-old daughter. The father was seen by the outside world as a friendly and all-around great guy. His wife was a kind, gentle, and intelligent woman. Their daughter appeared to be normal and somewhat assertive. The daughter asked her mother a question. While Mother was replying with what I thought was a very reasonable answer, the father broke into the conversation to disagree. He yelled that his wife was absolutely wrong and that she had no credentials to answer as she did. The tone and timbre of his voice was focused to intimidate and force others to believe his way. This father was enacting the role of a bully. By virtue of his hostile response, the silence in the car became deafening. Perhaps he thought he had won because no one chose to counter his attack. Later, I found that such outbursts were not unusual. To the outside world, he was a "hail-fellow-well met;" to his family, oftentimes, he was regarded as a bully.

Mothers are not immune from the parent-bullying syndrome. To make things happen with their children, yelling in an intimidating voice can often be heard coming from mothers. Mothers are better than fathers at disguising their bullying, perhaps for the same reason that they are more subtle than men in most aspects of life.

A single mother at our Family Education Training Center confessed that the only way to get her four- and six-year-old children out of the house and into the car each morning was to scream, yell, threaten, and intimidate them. Without her bullying actions, she felt impotent to leave the house each morning on time for their appointed destinations. After teaching Mother about the Adlerian concepts of the family council,[2] individual special time,[3] and the morning techniques,[4] she was able to discard the role of the morning mother bully. This mom was very motivated to do better. Within a month's time, she reported a more cooperative, functional, and happy family.

When I was in the military working as a clinical social worker, I often came upon both men and women who used an intimidating voice to bully their children into conformity. They excused their behavior by rationalizing that this is how the world works, and their kids better get used to it. "My father acted this way toward me, and I turned out all right," was their usual rationalizing mantra. What these parents refused to acknowledge was that they didn't turn out "all right." Too many of them had "swiss cheese egos" and damaged self-esteems. Any adult who chronically bullies a child did not turn out "all right."

After leaving the military, I found that civilian parents were equal, if not more ignorant, of family leadership and child-rearing techniques as their brothers and sisters in uniform. Apparently, parental bullying is too universal for the good of humanity.

If you are a parent who chronically uses bullying techniques, you are a bully, and you are hurting your children. You have an opportunity to correct your ways and learn better techniques of managing families and children. I suggest you become a parent of the Adlerian tradition. Consider reading books by Alfred Adler,[5] Rudolph Dreikurs,[6] and others.[7] Better yet, join a family education program such as the Family Education Training Center of Hawai'i. Everyone in your family will benefit from your newfound wisdom. Teaching respect and cooperation shows your child the way to be on a winning team.

Endnotes

[1] Lines, D. *The Bullies.* My university students suggest this is a good book on the general subject of bullying.

[2] Read "The Family Council."

[3] Read "Individual Special Time."

[4] See Painter and Corsini, *Effective Discipline.*

[5] Adler, *What Life Could Mean to You.*

[6] Dreikurs, and Soltz, *Children: The Challenge.*

[7] Nelson and Lott, *Positive Discipline for Teens.* U.S. Department of Health and Human Services. *Stop Bullying Now.* (CD.) For more information, go to http://www.stopbullyingnow.hrsa.gov.

Notes

WHEN A SOLUTION IS NOT A SOLUTION[1]

While being counseled, a FETCH mother lamented about the misbehaviors of her eight-year-old daughter. She said the following.

"Julie regularly acts disrespectful. She is always bothering me for something, and when she doesn't get her way, she has a loud and angry mouth. She has a bloated sense of entitlement, especially of my time and attention. When she acts this way, I feel very annoyed. I believe Julie has become this way because I feel guilty whenever I don't give her our 'together time.'[2] 'Together time' is close to twelve hours a day, which leaves almost no time for my husband and my home consulting business. Yesterday, Julie sassed me and was acting downright disrespectful. I said to her sternly, 'Julie, go to your room and don't come out until you calm down and can be more polite.' She immediately headed for her room, but blurted a few more angry words as she went. An hour later, she came out, and acted as if nothing unpleasant had happened. However, this kind of a problem happens three or four times a day."

After listening to Mother's story, I concluded that Julie's misguided goal was undue attention. My diagnosis was based on Mother's feelings of annoyance and the fact that Julie suspended her misbehavior right after being admonished. I suggested to Mother that instead of scolding with angry words, she should ignore Julie's misbehavior, step away, and do something pleasant for herself.[3] Immediately, Mother's voice changed as she angrily said to me, "I have found something that works for the Miller family, and I don't see why I should change what I do."

The problem here is that Mother's solution is the wrong solution. Unfortunately, she does not know it. Mother believes that because Julie leaves the room after being scolded, Mother has won a victory over Julie's demand for undue attention. If Mother's solution worked as well as she thought, she would not have to scold her child at all. In reality, Mother is causing Julie's repeated annoying behavior by giving it a portly payoff. It is sad that Mother sees her daughter as the enemy who now has to be defeated.

Children who demand undue attention by repeating annoying misbehaviors will repeat those behaviors as long as they are given parental payoffs. When Mother scolds Julie and sends her to her room, Mother is unknowingly giving her daughter a reinforcing payoff through her angry words. Often, kids do not care whether the payoff is positive or negative as long as it gives them the attention they seek, if only for a moment.

Adlerian psychology teaches that one can tell the difference between a child whose goal is undue attention and one whose goal is to ensnare a parent into a power contest.[4] If the goal is undue attention, any attention, whether it be scolding words or a spanking, will give the child the reward she is seeking, and the annoying misbehavior will stop for a while but soon will be repeated. If the child's misguided goal is power, parental words and behavior will feed the argument, and the argument will continue in the current situation. Julie's repeated misbehaviors are definitely symptoms of the misguided goal of undue attention.

The Correct Solution

In this situation, Mother was given permission *not* to feel obligated to spend half the day "entertaining" Julie but divide her time more equitably with her husband, job, and other necessary tasks in her life. Of immediate importance, Mother must learn that the best way to deal with Julie's misbehavior is to walk away silently without displaying signals of annoyance or bitterness, which Julie will see as a reinforcing payoff. At the next family council[5] meeting, Mother should bring up the subject of individual special time.[6] Julie needs to know that she will be guaranteed her share of attention by both parents, but at a specific time and place that is appropriate and agreed upon by everyone.

Summary

A parent can tell that her child is into the misguided goal of undue attention if she feels annoyed, and any reprimand discontinues the child's misbehavior for a while, only to return repeatedly. When this happens, the wise parent stops their reinforcing behavior and changes tactics. Walking away in a neutral and unassuming but positive attitude from the misbehaving child is a very powerful solution. What the parent tells the child through her neutral but positive attitude and action is, "I choose not be mistreated by you. Therefore, I will leave your presence now, and I will choose to return at my convenience."

In the above scenario, Mother did not see Julie's delight in receiving extra attention, even though it was negative. Mother had chosen the wrong solution because as viewed by her, it worked, even if only for a little while. The correct solution when applied appropriately, provides results that last over the long term.

Endnotes

1.   This chapter essay is best understood when a parent is familiar with the concept of the four misguided goals. See "Parent as Consultant," Figure 1.

2.   A dynamic that I chose not to deal with at that moment was the issue of Father not particularly liking daughter Julie and Mother's attempt to compensate for his attitude.

3.   Mother also could use Dr. Dreikurs's famous "bathroom technique." In this technique, the parent leaves the scene of the misconduct and, without words or rancor, locks herself into the bathroom until all is again quiet and civil. When used correctly, it is a very powerful technique for teaching younger children who are misbehaving.

   See Dreikurs and Soltz, *Children: The Challenge.*, p. 158.

4.   Power contests between children and parents eventually can lead to hurt feelings and revenge.

5.   Read "The Family Council." I believe the best book on the family council is by Dreikurs, Gould, and Corsini, *Family Council: The Dreikurs Techniques.* Other good sources are the following: Painter and Corsini, *Effective Discipline,* see chapter 33, "The Family Council," pp. 238-47. Rigney and Corsini, *The Family Council.*

6.   Read "The Gift of Individual Special Time."

Notes

TEACHING RESPECT BY EXAMPLE:
USING THE I-MESSAGE

The other day, I was walking across the local marketplace parking lot with several newly baked breads tucked under my arm when I heard a mother yelling at her preteen boy. "The next time you talk that way, I'm going to hit you one right then and there." Her castigating voice grew even louder. "I don't care what you say happened, the next time I'm going to whack you in the back of the head." The boy, saying nothing and looking straight ahead, continued to walk at his mother's side. His mother continued. "You don't talk to adults that way."

At that moment, I could hear myself thinking, *That woman is really being very disrespectful. How does she expect to teach her son respect when she is treating him with such disrespect? Chipping away at his self-esteem certainly doesn't help in the long run while blaming and provoking feelings of anger only lead to an attitude of "I'm justified in getting revenge."* Mother's "you-messages" never directly told her child how she felt about his behavior or how it affected her. She was trying to discipline with her voice as probably she had done many times in the past . . . without success.

It was then that I had my major insight of the day. *The way that woman is trying to train her son is no different than the way so many other parents try to do it. She is yelling at him to get his attention and to get her point across. She is threatening him with bodily harm to make her point stick, repeating herself to reinforce her message, and being disrespectful while wanting her son to be a respectful young man.*

146

This mother's intentions were good, but her method was misguided. Our children may not always seem to hear us, but you can bet they always see us no matter how we behave. We, as parents, are their role models, and children imitate our behaviors. This young man was behaving just as his mother had taught him; whatever disrespect he committed, he probably learned much of it from her. Children become disrespectful when they are disrespected; children become respectful when treated respectfully.

What's a mother to do? In this case, Mother needed to "cool down" and think the situation through before she acted. Perhaps she could have said to herself, "What is the best way to make this a teaching moment?" Often, it is best to say nothing until one arrives home, having used the driving time to think through the "lesson plan." However, it is also okay as part of a cooling down process to find a private place, such as a corner bench, and apply a respectful teaching moment. A respectful and responsible mother might have begun with an I-message, often called a "responsibility-taking message."

An I-message is a way of telling another person, including one's child, how you *feel* about their behavior and how it *affects* you.[1] It is an appeal to the best part of them. An I-message consists of four parts. Part 1, "when you," is a description of the behavior you would like changed. Part 2, "I feel," is a description of your thoughts or a feeling in your guts about the behavior. Part 3, "because," is a logical reason for your request for a change in behavior. Part 4 is a request: "I would like you to . . ." (action).

Here is an example of what Mother could have said in a calmer, respectful way. "Johnny, when *you* speak disrespectfully to another in my presence, I *feel* humiliated and angry *because* it's like I didn't care enough about you to teach you good manners, and that's not true. *I would like* you to be a gentleman while in my presence and really, at all times. I want to be proud of you because you are my son."

Another example of what this mother could have said is this, but this time reversing parts one and two.[2] "Johnny, I *felt* very angry and embarrassed when *you* talked to that clerk so disrespectfully. [*Because*] I thought I raised you to be a gentleman. I *would like* you to be a gentleman and speak politely to others in the future."

I-messages or "responsibility messages" are far more powerful than you-messages, which are usually seen by the child as put-downs. You-messages are interpreted by the child as negative evaluations of him and are very disheartening and discouraging. A discouraged child is always quite slow to change his behavior. However, I-messages are decoded by the child as statements of fact about the parent. Having been freed of the negative impact of the you-message, the child becomes liberated to act in a more considerate and helpful manner, thus becoming more willing to cooperate and change.

> When discipline is respectful,
> change will come;
> when it is not,
> your child will act like a bum.

Endnotes

1. Dr. Thomas Gordon points out that I-messages put the responsibility for what is happening where it belongs, on the person experiencing the problem, and that "I-messages" are a more effective way to teach than "You-messages." Gordon and Sands, *P.E.T. in Action*. Also see Gordon and Burch, *T.E.T. Teacher Effectiveness Training*.

2. Some parents find it better if they start with a statement of their feelings ("I feel"), then go to a statement of the behavior ("When you").

Notes

THE INCREDIBLY CREDIBLE PARENT
Coauthored by
Sasha Kealoha[1]

We define an incredibly credible parent as a mom or dad who consistently does what they say they are going to do when they say they are going to do it. Is this you? If not, take heart. With a little bit of effort, you can gain that desired commodity, and your children will learn to behave in a very positive and cooperative manner.

Painter and Corsini in their excellent book, *Effective Discipline in the Home and School*, point out the four fundamental rules for disciplining a younger child.[2]

1. Understand exactly what you are supposed to do. Do not tackle a problem until you really grasp the *how* and the *why* of the advice [you are going to follow].
2. Inform the child, explaining clearly what you intend to do about the problem in question. Answer all questions.
3. Act. Silence is necessary during the disciplining. Warnings, reminders, discussions, threats about the problem are unwise.
4. Be consistent during the disciplining. Avoid variations and exceptions. Do not let others sway you. Do not feel sorry for the child; pity will not help to train him.

As Doctors Painter and Corsini say, "So, without nagging, yelling, preaching, threatening or punishing, do exactly what you have told the child you will do, when you said you are going to do it, and do it consistently."[3]

The following story is based on a letter written by the coauthor.

I was in the midst of being tested by my eighteen-month-old daughter at bath time. She would constantly stand up in the tub, dance around, and just laugh at me and at my commands. I realized I had no credibility with her. I don't know how many times I repeated myself with some warning and explanation to her of what would happen if she doesn't follow the rules. However, I never followed through with action on my part. I was all talk and threats, never any action.

Finally, I asked myself, "What is my daughter learning?" I answered myself with the painful insight, "She is learning that 'Mom doesn't really mean it, and I can keep doing what I want because she won't stop me.'"

Of course, the first step in changing a child's behavior is to acknowledge that there is a behavior that needs changing. I decided I needed to earn credibility with her. Instead of repeating my warnings ten times and not getting the results I wanted, I began acting on what I said. I did exactly as I was taught at our FETCH parenting classes.

What I discovered simply amazed me. My eighteen-month-old completely understands me, and can follow the bath rules. Two weeks ago at bath time, I made my move. Kneeling beside the bath tub, I looked straight at her and calmly informed her (for the very last time) of the bath rules, including no standing in the slippery tub. She seemed to understand. I also told her that if she forgot and stood, I would remove her immediately. She could have her regular bath the next day, but not until then.

During the "inaugural" bath, several times she moved as though she were going to stand, each time glancing in my direction as if to see what I was going to do. I said nothing and did my best to keep my body language neutral. Then, all of a sudden she stood up, laughed, and began to dance around.

Without saying a word, I immediately removed her from the bath. As I started to dry her off she protested and began to cry in an angry manner. Still in silence, I carried her to her room and calmly began dressing her for bed. The protesting stopped. I wanted to tell her "I told you so," but I managed to keep my mouth shut with a pleasant look on my face. I felt so proud of myself, I almost burst. I knew she understood the rules and that talking about them would only reward her for misbehaving. That evening she went to bed and quickly fell asleep.

Secretly, I looked forward to the next night's bath. Would my precious baby be cooperative, or would I again have to remove her from the tub? Would what I learned at FETCH work quickly, or was I in for a long fight? My deepest fear was that I might have to give up the pleasure of giving my daughter her bath.

As I helped my child into the bath I could see joy beaming from her face as she splashed around. Several times she moved as though she were going to stand but stopped quickly. It was as though in her head she heard me saying, "You'll have to come out of the bath if you stand." I was prepared to remove her from the tub, but that did not have to happen.

Since that monumental bath, we have had complete success in following the bath rules. No longer does she try to stand up, and I have found joy in bath time, as has she. I am waiting for the "second offensive,"[4] and should it ever happen, I know exactly what to do.

Reminding, nagging, yelling, spanking, preaching, threatening, and other punishments all are ways in which parents lose credibility, fast. Instead, we suggest you use the following rules with younger children to achieve parenting (and bath time) success.

1. Understand what you are supposed to do and have a specific plan in your mind.

2. If your child is under five years of age, kindly inform him or her of what is expected, and what will be the immediate consequence. If your child is older, a discussion and agreement at a family meeting is more effective.

3. Act in silence and without angry body language.

4. Be consistent during disciplining while never feeling sorry for the child.

5. After the consequence has been completed, go on with life, and do not bring up the incident ever again.

6. Should your child several days or weeks later repeat the misbehavior, "the second offensive," repeat your earlier success by immediately removing him or her from the bath without saying a word or a negative body gesture. Your child is normal and is just testing you.

We know by experience and theory that these few simple rules are your key to becoming a successful and incredibly credible parent.

Endnotes

[1] Sasha Kealoha, BA, is coauthor of this paper. She is a wife, mother of two, and a FETCH parent.

[2] Painter and Corsini, *Effective Discipline*, pages 40-41. An earlier version of this book was titled *The Practical Parent*.

[3] Ibid., p.41.

[4] Read "The Second Offensive."

Notes

A DOZEN EASY RULES TO
REAR A DELINQUENT[1]

So you've decided that you want to rear a delinquent. Good. It's important that parents know what kind of a child they want and what must be done to reach that goal.

Rule no. 1   You must begin at infancy to give your child everything he wants. No desire must be delayed or denied. As soon as he indicates a bit of discontent, you must immediately attend to his needs and soothe the situation. For example, should your little one throw his toy onto the floor, you must immediately pick it up and return it. Should he continue, by all means, keep picking it up as it is disrespectful not to allow your child to have fun at your inconvenience. By immediately responding to all his whims, he will grow up to believe the world owes him a living.

Rule no. 2   When your child picks up bad words, laugh at him. This will make him think he's cute. Your reaction will help him learn new bad words that will expand his vocabulary. Children with large vocabularies of bad words receive special recognition by their teachers and become well-known to the school's guidance counselor and vice principal. By doing this, you will find that he will have fun learning new bad words and meeting new adults. All of this recognition will give him a feeling of belonging to the family, the school, and the larger community with significance.

Rule no. 3   Never give your child individual special time as he will come to want or even expect a positive relationship with you. It is better to put your energy into earning a living or keeping the house very clean. Having fun with your child may cause him to like and respect you, which will deny you the opportunity to practice nagging and punishment.

Rule no. 4   Pick up your child's mess. When toys, books, shoes, clothes, and other clutter are left in common areas, always pick them up for him. When doing so, you will be showing him the importance of neatness and an orderly household. In order to make him understand your values, you should always clean up after him while acting mad as hell by raising your voice with threats of punishment and bodily harm. Do everything for him so that he will be experienced in throwing all responsibility on others.

Rule no. 5   You and your spouse should quarrel frequently in your child's presence. This will give him a feeling of power in that he will probably think that he is the cause of your marital troubles. In this way, he will learn to handle guilt associated with a divorce and will not be too shocked later when the home is broken.

Rule no. 6   Give your child all the spending money he wants. Allowances frustrate a child when he runs out of money before the next payday. Our children can wait until they are adults with a family and a mortgage before they need to learn money management.

Rule no. 7   Satisfy your child's every craving for food, drink, and comfort. See that every sensual desire is gratified. Obesity isn't so bad, diabetes can be managed, and accidents can happen when exercising. Parents should be aware that denial of cravings may lead to harmful frustrations.

Rule no. 8   Do not teach your child values. There is no such thing as right and wrong and to teach him otherwise can be very confusing. He should be allowed to do "what feels good."

Rule no. 9   Do not supervise your child's use of the computer. The Internet is safe, and inquiring minds want to know. Allow your child to learn the art of bomb making, view pornography, or indulge on any subject he desires. While you insist that he eats with sterilized utensils, it is all right to allow him to feast his mind on garbage.

Rule no. 10   Take his part against neighbors, relatives, teachers, and law enforcement officials, such as policemen and judges. These people are all prejudiced against your child, and your job is to defend him against society at all costs. He is your child; you must always have faith that he is right and that he cannot, nor will not, make mistakes or do any harm.

Rule no. 11   When your child gets into real trouble, apologize to yourself by saying, "I never could do anything with him no matter how hard I spanked him or how many times I punished him." Parents should never blame themselves for their child's serious misbehaviors as it is always society's or someone else's fault. Above all, do not go for family counseling or to a family education center. You do not have problems, and you do not need help.

Rule no. 12   Prepare yourself for the worst. By following these rules, you will guarantee yourself a life of pain and misery.

Endnotes

[1]   This essay is based on two articles, "How to Ruin Your Child," in Soltz, *Articles of Supplementary Reading for Parents* and "Ten Easy Rules on How to Raise a Delinquent" in Cater, "Parent Work Book for use with The Practical Parent in a Parents Study Group."

Notes

"DO OR DO NOT. THERE IS NO 'TRY'"[1]

Yoda, the Jedi master of *Star Wars* movie fame and mentor to many leaders of the Republic, must have been an Adlerian. I believe this because of the way he treated his students. Yoda encouraged, he never praised; he avoided punishment and reward, using instead natural and logical consequences. His teaching methods avoided criticism, and he minimized students' mistakes. He took time for training, thereby winning students' cooperation. He knew how to withdraw from conflict, be unimpressed by fears, and respectfully talk *with* his students, not *at* them. Yoda was firm without dominating, respectful of others' decisions, and demonstrated a reverence for order and cooperation. These are all masterful traits of a practicing Adlerian parent and teacher.

One of my favorite statements from Episode V, *The Empire Strikes Back*, came from Master Yoda. During his Jedi training, headstrong Luke Skywalker was confronted by many challenges of will and body. However, to date, he had failed to unlearn many of his preconceptions. When asked to raise his sunken starfighter from a Dagobah swamp with the power of his mind alone, he responded he would *try*. "No," scolded Yoda. "Do or do not. There is no 'try.'"

To my Family Education Training Center of Hawai'i (FETCH) parents and anyone reading this book, I implore you not to *try*. The word *try* carries with it doubt and recognition of possible failure. *Try* is one of those words that carry a meaning far beyond its literal and conscious definition.

In our training of parents, we ask them not to change their behavior until they have a sound grasp of what they are to do and the principle behind it. Parents are asked to be consistent in their behavior as individuals and as members of the parenting team. Children, when given conflicting signals or mixed messages, become confused, and in that confusion, they are very likely to act out. Parents are put on notice that they are given our best and most effective correction techniques up front. Thus, if they grossly err when initially carrying out our directions, in the future, they may be forced to use a less effective, second-tier method than originally suggested.

I once had a parent who begged me to help her eliminate her three-and-a-half-year-old daughter's whining and pouting, which Mother found profusely annoying. I gave her several valuable relationship-building techniques and one withdrawal technique to help her avoid further unnecessary power conflicts. For the latter technique, I advised Mother that when her daughter slipped into the whining mode, she was to remove herself, go into the bathroom, and lock herself in. She was to stay there in silence until the child completely quieted down and then in about five more minutes she could come out and act as if nothing had happened. This powerful strategy was developed by Dr. Rudolf Dreikurs and is called the "bathroom technique."[2] The mother thanked me and said that she would "try" what I had proposed.

Three weeks later, the mother visited me again and gave the following story. The next afternoon, she employed the "bathroom technique" as suggested but came out in less than five minutes. Her excuse was that her daughter was making too much noise, and she did not want to bother the neighbors. "And besides, Geraldine seemed so sad that I was not there to be with her." Truly, this was a mother who was not ready to make major changes in her life or her child's life. She did *try* what I had proposed, but she did not *do* it.

Mother continued telling me her story. During the following twenty days, she had used the "bathroom technique" several more times, each time staying in the bathroom longer. However, each time she gave in to the crying child and came out before the crying fully stopped. Since the "bathroom technique" was not working, she wanted another technique to *try* on her child. Certainly, Mother's resolve was lacking. She had forfeited the most effective technique that I had to offer. This time Mother said that she would *do* anything I suggested as she could not stand her daughter's annoying behavior any longer.

I realized that there was a greater problem with the mother than at first I had been led to believe. Psychotherapy was in order. Following several months of therapy, we again focused on the child's behavior that had actually gotten better during the time Mother had been in treatment. However, the best ignoring solution that I could give the mother now seemed impotent as the child knew how to escalate the situation. I had another, but less desirable, technique that Mother could use. As her daughter acted out, Mother could "bear it," that is, she would pretend that nothing was happening and go about her business. Obviously, pretending that your daughter is not annoyingly pouty is immensely difficult to do. The technique did work, but it was not as simple as staying in the bathroom until five minutes after the noise stopped.

Summary

Parents should never change their child-training techniques until they have a sound grasp of what they are to do and the principles behind it. Parents need to be consistent. Children, when given conflicting signals or mixed messages, become confused, and in that confusion, they are very likely to needlessly act out, stressing the parent. When a parent says, or thinks to himself or herself, "I'll try," a "red flag" should go up.

In the above case, when Mother first came to my office, she was not ready in her resolve. She was inconsistent in her application of a very excellent consequence, and later, she had to settle for one that was more difficult for her to perform. *Trying* lacks the resolve and focus of *doing*. Yoda was correct when he gave the reprimand, "Do or do not, there is no 'try.'"

Endnotes

[1]   My appreciation goes to the authors of the website www.starwars.com whose valuable information and quotes from the *Star Wars* movies I freely borrowed.

[2]   Dreikurs and Soltz, *Children: The Challenge.*

Notes

THE PERFECTION SONG

Words by Dr. James A. Deutch
Sung to the tune of "If You're Happy and You Know It."

Oh, perfection is a direction not a goal,
Oh, per-fec-tion is a di-rec-tion not a goal,

Yes, perfection is a direction not a goal,
Yes, per-fec-tion is a di-rec-tion not a goal,

Yes, perfection is a direction,
Yes, per-fec-tion is a di-rec-tion,

So make it your selection,
So make it your se-lec-tion,

Yes, perfection is a direction not a goal.
Yes, per-fec-tion is a di-rec-tion not a goal.

Write your own lyrics here.

SECTION II.
Gifting Your Child

Tom and Zachary Burke, November 2010

A LETTER TO MY SON, ZACHARY*

BY
Tom Burke*

July 4, 2011

Dear Zach,

I love you! I have loved you from the first moment I held you in my arms. From the beginning, I knew you were a very special person. Each day of my life I have become more proud as I watch you achieve and become the man you are becoming. As I observed you jumping into the pool, diving deep, and swimming to the other side, I felt my heart race with pride at your accomplishments. I quietly celebrated your achievements with deep feelings of joy. The talks we had in the car as I drove you to school and the discussions we had while driving home, I saw as your gifts to me, allowing me to peek through your window of tomorrow.

I am so sorry and sad that I will not be at your graduations, your marriage, or will not see and hug your first child. God has seen fit for me to give you a good start, but in his infinite wisdom, he has decided that is only as far as he will let me go. Yet in your heart, I will always be there. When you hear a cheer in

*When my friend Tom learned he had a short time to live, he wrote this letter to his seven-year-old son. Tom asked me to publish it in this book so that all fathers who had similar thoughts and feelings could benefit from his words. Tom passed away August 30, 2011.

the breeze or feel a flush of encouragement, that will be me. You will not see me, but you will know that I am there, just behind you and out of sight.

Every loving daddy has ways he wants his child to be. I call these "goals for my Zach." While I realize that perfection is a direction and not a goal, I want for you to be all you can be. To become the person I want you to be, I offer you four ways of being.

First, have *respect*. I want you to have respect for yourself, for the feelings of others, for your own accomplishments, and for the world and environment in which you will live. I want you always to be respectful to my wife, your mother, and for your ancestors who came before you. Remember, there will always be those around you who would do you harm or no good. Have nothing to do with toxic people. Respect yourself, always do the right thing, and practice love and forgiveness. Remember, everything you do reflects upon your family. When you act with respect, you can never be wholly wrong.

Second, I want you to learn and practice *responsibility*. I want you to gladly contribute to our family's well-being by helping your mother when she asks or requires it. I want you to make a contribution to your family and all those who love you or need your help. My wish is that you will find school a joyous challenge and delight in learning. Build on your strengths, but never fail to work on your challenges.

Third, I want you to be *resourceful*. This means that I want you to be able to take care of yourself, comfortably meet new people, be dignified in each new situation, and be independent as well as self-reliant. Be a leader and rarely a follower. Allow yourself to be creative by allowing yourself to draw outside of the lines. Never fear what anyone has to say about you. Listen to what others have to say, thank them for their interest in you, then accept what is useful and disregard the rest. Allow yourself to feel your feelings; never bury them. Emotions, whether joy or sadness, love or hate, are real and to be valued as momentary beacons along your trail of life. Show other people the way by allowing the light of your goodness to shine through your essence and spirit.

Fourth, I want you to show *responsiveness* to your family, to those around you, and the people who love you. Family is very important; never abandon or deny *ohana*, but allow it to nourish your growth and soul.

These are the important wishes I have for you. Remember them always. And forever know that I love you.

Your proud father,
Tom Burke

Notes

WRITE LOVE LETTERS TO YOUR CHILDREN

Write a love letter to each child in your family. Tell them how you feel about their existence in your life. Be open, honest, and positive, never sarcastic or critical. When you have completed your letter, in private, share it with that child. After sharing and discussing its contents, seal it in an envelope and put it where it will be accessible in ten years or after your death. Your love letter will be a treasure for your child in the years to come.

Use the space below to begin your thinking or to write a first draft.

The Gift of Individual Special Time

THE GIFT OF INDIVIDUAL SPECIAL TIME

If I had a magic wand but could give only one gift to every family, it would be the gift of individual special time. Individual special time, often referred to as "special time", is an Adlerian method guaranteed to make every family member, regardless of status or age, happier, calmer, and more cooperative. It is the most powerful parent educational technique that I know in the art and science of child rearing. When used in conjunction with other Adlerian strategies, such as the family council, encouragement, verbal communication, natural and logical consequences, and of course, respect, the result is a healthy, happy, and productive family.

What Is Individual Special Time, and Why Is It So Powerful?

Individual special time is a *guaranteed* allotment of ten minutes a day, *every day*, which a parent cheerfully gives to his or her child, no matter what.[1] Children need to feel that they belong to the family with significance. If they do not get their basic need to belong with significance met in a useful way, they will misbehave in a useless way to get their desired recognition. Rudolf Dreikurs described children's misbehavior by classifying it as the "four misguided goals."[2] He found that misbehaving children choose one of four dysfunctional behavioral goals: (1) undue attention, (2) power, (3) revenge, and (4) assumed inadequacy. Translated into children's language, undue attention means "I belong only when I'm keeping you busy with me." Power means "I'm the boss, and I make you do what I want," or "I'm the boss, and I do what I want." Revenge means "I feel hurt, and I want to hurt back," and assumed inadequacy means "I give up!"[3]

Parents who spend a few minutes a day of individual special time with their child find that they spend much less time each day in combat operations with a child who is seeking undue attention or another of the four misguided goals. Spending a few minutes each day to play with your child sends the message "You are important to me and to our family. You belong with significance in this household. You are loved and respected." Children who grow up feeling they belong having spent individual special time with each parent become cooperative, respectful, and positive members of the family team. They do not seek attention through disruptive and annoying behaviors. They feel good about themselves, their family, their school, and the world around them. Such children have the courage to try new tasks, are not afraid to fail, and have the courage to be imperfect.

What Individual Special Time Is Not

Individual special time is not a conversation at the dinner table or talking with your child while driving him or her to soccer practice nor is it a pleasant conversation with your child in the living room. It also is not playing with your child while you hold and care for his or her siblings. We use the word *individual* to mean just that—the child alone with your focus, attention, and energy upon him or her.

Individual special time is not a time for teaching. One parent wondered why her middle son was not excited about it as her other two boys. When discussing the situation with her, I discovered that she was using the time to "teach" this boy how to walk the dog. She was violating two principles: teaching when she was supposed to be making the experience a fun-filled time, and dividing her time between the dog and the child. However, the big giveaway was that her son was not enjoying his special time experience with her. It's tough enough to be a middle child, but how do you compete for attention while sharing your time with a four-legged, tail-wagging, face-licking sibling?

Special time is not a reward for "good" behavior. Like food, water, and shelter, individual special time is a right of every child and an obligation of every parent who decides to have and keep their child. Your job as a parent is to deliver your child to adulthood, capable of surviving and thriving, in the world in which they will live.

How Do I Invite My Child to Have Individual Special Time with Me?

First, check your calendar and think long term about your availability, coordinate with your spouse or partner, then be determined to carry out your commitment. Once you and your child start individual special time, your child will love it so much she or he will remind you of your commitment. Never model halfhearted commitment to your child unless you want your child to practice halfhearted commitment toward you.

Second, kneel to the child's height and pleasantly say something like the following. "Now that you're old enough, I would like you and me to have special time together. Special time means that just you and I will play together for ten minutes right after I get home from work (or whatever time is convenient for you both). I'll bring the timer and set it for ten minutes, and you will decide on what we will do. We should do something active like throwing or kicking a ball around. What would you like to do? Do you have any questions? Can we start today?"

The activity depends on the age and experience of the child. Younger children may enjoy chasing the parent and being chased around the yard. A child may want to go to the park and be pushed on the swings. Older children may choose to ride bicycles on the street or play basketball in the driveway. Others may simply like to go on brisk walks or jogging with their mom or dad. What is necessary is that the activity should be active, fun, and never competitive. Muscle memory as well as cognitive memory must be involved. Individual special time does not include computer games, no matter how excited the participants may get. Both child and parent have to agree on the activity. Thus, it is not necessary for the parent to accept the first choice of the child. Young children tend to suggest activities with which they are familiar and may need a parent to broaden their horizon by making suggestions. A teen may choose an activity that is inappropriate for a parent, such as tackle football. Many maturing teens do best when their activity morphs into a once-a-week date such as being an only child for a morning.

While engaged in individual special time, the parent's focus should be on the child. This means no multitasking such as diapering, nursing, or making "nice-nice" to the family baby. Your child needs your undivided, focused attention. Remember to turn off your cell phone!

Individual special time is to have fun and build a special meaningful relationship. When the timer rings announcing that the ten minutes is over, the parent thanks the child for the gift of playing and lets the child know that tomorrow, at the same time and place, they will meet again for more individual special time.

Every so often, a child will balk at having individual special time. Whatever the reason, be it a test or protest, the parent must be at the agreed-upon meeting place, timer in hand, and remain there quietly and wait. At the end of the ten minutes, if the child has not appeared, the parent should quietly leave. Sometimes the child will join the parent a few minutes late. Enjoy the remaining time and quit after the timer rings. Thank him or her in your usual warm manner. Say nothing about the tardiness, now or in the future.

Parents tell me and other Family Education Training Center of Hawai'i counselors that when they give individual special time, the attitude of their children greatly improves, and they become more enjoyable to be with and are less demanding of time and attention. With less demands upon them, parents find that they have more time to accomplish their household duties. Parents also say that their biggest challenge is the pressure to be consistent and give their child individual special time on time seven days a week. Parents are always amazed and pleased at the positive results that individual special time brings to their family.

Endnotes

[1]   While I suggest ten minutes a day as the minimum time to be spent with each child, fifteen or twenty minutes would be even more powerful. However, what is mandatory is that individual special time be the same number of minutes each day, beginning at the same time each day, and that the activity be somewhat vigorous.

[2]   Dreikurs and Soltz, *Children: The Challenge.*

[3]   See "Parent as Consultant," Figure 1.

Notes

THE FAMILY COUNCIL
By
Fay Rawles-Schoch*

Adlerians believe that the primary goal of the human from birth is to belong to the family with significance. Adlerians also know that to have a sense of belonging and significance, a member must make contributions to the family unit.

Parents often err in giving the disciplinary methods of child rearing much more attention than parenting methods that promote and bring about a genuine feeling of belonging and wanting to cooperate. Disciplinary methods are useful when there is no other solution, but they should be at the bottom of the parenting toolbox.

So what is at the top? Adlerians believe that instilling a sense of belonging and significance, getting our children to cooperate and make contributions to the family welfare, teaching them respect, responsibility, resourcefulness, and responsiveness is achieved primarily by giving them relevant platforms through which they can learn life skills in a safe environment. We have found two platforms that serve these goals exceedingly well; to parents they seem like magic. One of these is the practice of individual special time.[1] The other is the family council meeting.[2]

The purpose of the family council is to bring family members together in an open person-to-person dialogue with the result that family members

*Fay Rawles-Schoch, BS, has been a certified Adlerian family counselor for over thirty-five years. She studied and worked with Drs. Genevieve Painter and Raymond Corsini. Ms. Rawles-Schoch is a member of the board of directors of the Family Education Centers of Hawai'i.

enjoy one another as people and gain mutual respect and equality. Our goal as parents is to deliver children who understand what it means to live mature and productive lives to adulthood. Through the family council meeting, children are given weekly practice in cooperation, conflict resolution, negotiating, money management, creative problem solving, presentations, helping others, expressing kindness, communicating, and many other skills.

As children refine their skills, they learn how to contribute in meaningful ways to their families, others, and communities. They believe they belong and are significant because they develop self-confidence through knowing that their opinions and contributions matter. Our children acquire the courage that motivates them to get up each day and do what needs to be done no matter what they face. They learn how to be leaders.

Below are the guidelines of running a family council meeting, including some explanations and clarifications. The first section deals briefly with the first or even the first several family meetings. The second section deals with family meetings in general.

The First Family Council Meeting

1. Prior to the first family council meeting, the parents must get together and find a time when all family members can be present. Then they personally invite each child to the meeting. According to Adlerian rules of order, no child has to attend or stay for the entire meeting. However, family agreements (rules) that are adopted are binding on each member of the family even if that person was not present when the agreement was adopted.

2. An easy way to teach children how to conduct an orderly meeting is by modeling. Many families have Father as the first chairperson and Mother as the first scribe (secretary). At the second family meeting, Mother assumes the role of the chair and Father becomes the scribe. At the third meeting, the oldest child becomes the chairperson and either a volunteer child (who can be helped by a parent) or a parent alone becomes the scribe. Children see the chair as the position they

want most. For some youngsters, keeping the minutes may seem far too difficult a role.

3. The first meeting of the family council should be short, and the discussion should be focused on planning family fun. No problem issues ought to be discussed during the first three meetings. However, if a child brings up the issue of wanting an allowance, a discussion and possibly a decision should be rendered. Unfortunately, parents love to turn the initial council meetings into a "Why aren't your rooms clean?" and "Here are your chores!" sessions. Children are turned off by these kinds of parental power plays and soon lose interest in being a part of any family meeting. The family council is not another form for parents to manipulate their children.

General Rules for the Family Meeting

1. Have the meeting at the same time each week. Select a time when all members can attend.

2. Begin and end each meeting on time. Do not exceed one hour. Use a timer if need be. Items that are not addressed may be brought up at the next meeting.

3. Parents should model and create an atmosphere conducive to success. Most families sit around a large table cleared of clutter and debris. Televisions, computers, cell phones, and all electronic devices must be turned off. Be sure that all family members have been invited, but hold the meeting even if they do not attend. Note that anyone living in the immediate household, grandparents, borders, etc., should be considered "family."

4. Parents are responsible for creating a democratic process and atmosphere at the meeting. Each member may bring up issues, and each must have the opportunity to speak. Encourage your children to offer their ideas. Often, parents know what the solution should be. Be a "cool" parent; make your family meetings a positive learning experience by remaining mostly quiet while the children come up with solutions. Subtly guide them by asking relevant questions, which lead them to find good

solutions. Children value their own solutions more than yours, and they will be more invested in making their ideas a success. Sometimes they surprise us with ideas we had not considered. If you recognize that a solution wanted by the children is a poor one, allow it to happen and live with it until the next family meeting where it can again be discussed and changed. Such mistakes can be great learning moments in your children's lives.

5. Once meetings are established, parents should not be speaking more than children. Have two officers, a chairperson and a scribe. Rotate these positions. It is the job of the chair to make sure everyone has the opportunity to speak and to keep order. The chair is not the boss of the meeting. The scribe's position is to take notes of what was decided at the meeting. Your job as a parent is to model leadership, but in a way that you listen liberally but speak sparingly.

6. Create an agenda. Have an agenda list on the refrigerator so that children can have input prior to the meeting. This agenda list also allows parents to not have to make immediate decision should the child demand one. "Let's put it on the agenda for the next family council meeting," a parent can say.

7. Begin each meeting with appreciations. Each family member says one thing they appreciate about each other family member. Be patient as children go through the thought process of coming up with appreciations. If someone offers a nonappreciation, just smile and say, "Try again." After appreciations, always take up family fun for the week. Once your meetings are going well, introduce other agenda items.

8. The chair needs to prioritize the agenda items at the beginning of the meeting. Though we never exclude appreciations or family fun, we do stop at the end of the one-hour time limit. If an item becomes especially complex or troublesome, it may be best to "table" it until the next meeting, especially if research is needed.

9. Brainstorm problems and encourage each member to offer ideas. No discussion is allowed while the ideas are being offered. Discuss the ideas after all have been presented. Allow the children to do most of the talking. It is the job of the chair to maintain order.

10. Include discussions of relevant family financial matters. This can include financial needs the children might have such as special occasion attire, summer camp attendance, or a new family car. The discussion should be relevant to family matters at hand and not serve to worry the children. Allowances should be passed out at the end of the council meeting, but if someone does not come, he or she still gets his or her allowance. Allowances should be given without any attachment to chores or other conditions. The purpose of allowances is to teach children the art of money management.[3]

11. All family council decisions are made only by *consensus*. Consensus means that everyone must agree on the solution. If there is no consensus, then nothing happens, but the issue may be brought up at the next family council meeting. For example, if the children cannot decide on whether this week's family fun will be to go to the beach or mountains and they refuse to compromise, then family fun for this week does not happen.

12. Handle the "stuff"[4] of the family at the family council meeting. Do *not* handle what you do not need to handle during the week. There is a surprising benefit of this for parents. You are freed from having to make instant decisions. You can relax for the rest of the week; then on family council night, you can turn your full attention to an impartial assessment of what can be done to address the "stuff" situations. In our family, we kept notes from the previous meeting and space for agenda items (including "stuff") for the next meeting in a prominent place. Just writing an item on the agenda would often bring resolution before the next meeting without ever saying a word!

The long-term success of dedication to the family council as a problem-solving process is sometimes only obvious in retrospect.

Some years ago, into our already existing family of four children, we took on one more for a time: a fifteen-year-old nephew who had been out of control for a while and making poor decisions. We gave him the orientation to our family by telling him that he was a member of our family and needed to abide by the decisions of the family made at weekly family council meetings.

We always began our family meetings with appreciations. My nephew was not accustomed to hearing appreciations and had difficulty thinking of what he could say to other family members that expressed appreciation. We waited patiently for him to come up with them. He learned that he too had a say in the affairs of the family. In a moment that was surprising and funny, my husband lapsed and nagged our nephew about something whereupon our nephew told his uncle that he could "bring that up at the family council meeting." During his time with us, our nephew worked three jobs and finished school. Today, he is a successful adult, husband and father of two children. The experience had a successful ending, and based on what our nephew told us and how he responded, we owe it to the family council.

Friends of ours for many years were affected by the recent economic downturn. A year ago, they had to sell their large lavish home and move to a very small condo with two bright adolescent children who were used to a very different lifestyle. In a recent conversation about our families, my friend said that she had been surprised that the children had handled it so well; they remained happy, well-adjusted, and went on with their lives as though there had not been a dramatic change in their situation. They did not complain about anything and continued to be cooperative, participative family members. My friend then added, "It was the family council meetings" (which they had begun some years earlier). She believed that the family meetings helped them care about one another and gave them the courage to go on as a family no matter what they faced.

When our daughter made applications to colleges, each had different essay questions. She gave her responses to me and asked for a final grammar check before sending them off. One of the questions asked her to describe two things that had been meaningful to her in her life. One of the two she described was our family council.

Endnotes

[1] Read "The Gift of Individual Special Time."

[2] Suggested readings. Dreikurs, Gould, and Corsini, *Family Council: The Dreikurs Technique.* Rigney and Corsini, *The Family Council.*

[3] Read "Allowances Teach Money Management."

[4] In this context, I define family "stuff" as the nitty-gritty and often minutia demands of family members upon the time, patience, and sanity of one or both of the parents. Much of the time, decisions that our children want from us are best given after a time of contemplation, planning, and coordination. Demands like "Mommy, can I go to the . . . ?" "Buy me a . . ." "I don't want to . . ." and "I want . . ." are rarely crisis situations that need to be dealt with on the spot. Oftentimes, parents have "stuff" they feel a need to bring up, such as a child not doing the dishes tonight as promised. The parent could get into it with the child, or write the infraction on the family council agenda board and say nothing. By waiting to deal with it as a family issue at the next council meeting, parents are freed from having to nag, remind, complain, or come up with an immediate solution or consequence.

Notes

THE GIFT OF LOVE

One Thanksgiving Day, my wife, Marcia, and I were having a great meal with our dear friend, Ivan. Ivan is a Russian born scholar and mental health therapist who has traveled the world and whose mountain climbing adventures along the Russian-Afghanistan border are right out of an adventure novel. Recently, he spent several weeks meditating at a Buddhist monastery in Thailand. Whenever Ivan speaks, I listen. During our conversation, Ivan made a comment that got my Adlerian attention. *"Love needs to be given in the way it is desired to be received."*

How many of us give love and attention to our children in the way that we would like to receive it? How much does our giving represent our fantasies and needs rather than our children's? These are simple questions, but at the same time, the answers are complicated. What we give to our children represents what we learned as children and what we think is important. As parents, don't we allegedly know what is best for our children? If you think more deeply, your answer may surprise you.

Adlerian psychology teaches us that it is critically important that our children feel respected, loved, and that they believe they belong to the family with significance. Many parents believe that love is shown to their children by putting a roof over their heads, feeding their stomachs, giving them constructive criticism and corporal punishment to make them obey in order to teach self-discipline, and nagging them to do homework to make sure that they do well in school and get into the best college on a fully paid scholarship. And well, you name all the things that you do.

Ask yourself the following questions. When you were a kid and you felt your best, what was going on in your family? Were you thankful for the big or small house that you lived in? Did it give you joy that your parents made enough money to buy you food for your stomach? When you were criticized, how good did it feel that it was "constructive"? When you were nagged about homework, did it motivate you to feel excited about learning and to anticipate the thrill of getting into your dream college on a fully paid scholarship? And when you were hit by a parent for not obeying his or her wish, how many times did you say, "Thank you for hitting me, it will make me a better person in the future." If you are saying yes to any of these statements, my best guess is that you are only fooling yourself in order to make your past more tolerable to your present. But then again, what do I know?

Men, try this. Your wife has her eye on a particular piece of jewelry and has hinted to you that she wants this particular piece on her next birthday. Her birthday arrives, and you give her an expensive five-pound box of chocolates. You are not upset that she is disappointed because you love chocolates. How much love and gratitude do you think you have scored with your gift?

Ladies, your husband has spent the day working on the house and yard, making it look like a team of carpenters and arborists manicured it. He proudly asks you to look at his accomplishments. As you look, you find imperfections in his work and tell him so. After all, he deserves your honest constructive criticisms. How much love and gratitude do you think you have scored with your gift?

When I was a boy of five or six, my father would bring home a shopping bag full of bottles of medicinal rubbing alcohol. I always excitedly asked if there was a present for me somewhere in his grocery bag. He would say yes and then produce a bottle of rubbing alcohol. When each time I looked and felt disappointed, he would proudly say, "Your mother will rub the alcohol on my tired body, and then I will feel better so I can go to work for you in the morning." My father was very proud that he could go to work and support his family. This was his gift of love to me when I was a child. However, sixty-five years later, I can still feel the disappointment in my bones. I bet you have stories of your own to tell.

Adlerian-Oriented Gifts

"What are some Adlerian solutions?" you ask. "What are some of the daily Adlerian gifts we can give to our children voiced in the manner that our kids want to receive them?"

Begin with *you, your time*, and *your attention*. When your child talks to you, listen liberally and speak sparingly. Give him or her your full face and attention. Do not multitask when you are engaged in a conversation. While listening, do not throw roadblocks in the way of your child's communication efforts. Judging, ordering, warning, moralizing, advising, praising, and name-calling are just a few of the roadblocks that turn off your children.[1]

Individual special time is another gift that will be received by your child with enthusiasm. In this book of essays, I have written a special chapter called "The Gift of Individual Special Time"[2] that I urge you to read—twice. To bestow this gift, ask your child if he or she would like to meet with you every day at the same time and place for ten minutes to play together and have fun. She or he should bring the game and you will bring the egg timer. The game should be active so that muscle memory in addition to cognitive memory will be present and stimulated. When the timer goes *ding*, that will be the end of special time for the day, but the two of you will meet every day, guaranteed, from now on. I promise you that once your child believes your word is your bond and that you always will keep your special time appointment, she or he will treasure that time with you. Relationship is the lubrication that makes the gears of family life run smoothly.

Give your child a voice in family affairs. When many of us were growing up, there were child-restricting practices in many households such as "children should be seen and not heard." As democracy has become a way of life in modern Western societies, traditional authoritarian methods of child rearing have become obsolete. Children are no longer raised to bow before the king and emperor. Children in democratic countries are being raised to think and to evaluate and to speak out for justice and freedom. Smart modern parents give their children a voice in the family, which leads to a buy-in of cooperation. This is best done through weekly family meetings that Adlerians call the family council.[3] Get your children's input on family matters such as when and where the family is going to have fun, issues on chores, size of allowances, and issues common to all family members. Adlerians believe that all children should have their say even though they will not always get their way. Children who rightly believe that they are meaningful members of a family will work very hard to be responsible, cooperative, and orderly members of that group.

Show respect. Respect takes many forms. Doing what you said you were going to do, such as showing up on time for the individual special time you promised, using natural and logical consequences rather than punishment as a way of teaching about life,[4] treating your child with dignity as though she or he was an important person in the family. Parents need to consider the feelings of the child and treat him or her fairly.

Parents need to know which of their behaviors are disrespectful. I would like to suggest the following "usual suspects": doing for a child what the child should be doing for himself or herself; telling children how much to eat during mealtimes; scolding, punishing, rewarding or nagging; cautioning repeatedly about the same things. The most usual disrespectful behavior that I have found parents perpetrating is interfering in any way, shape, or form in their child's schoolwork . . . which includes getting overly involved in homework.[5]

Be an encouraging parent. Rudolf Dreikurs wrote, "Encouragement is more important than any other aspect of child rearing. It is so important that the lack of it can be considered the basic cause for misbehavior. A misbehaving child is a discouraged child. Each child needs continuous encouragement just as a plant needs water."[6]

An encouraging parent is guided by three ideas. First, know the difference between encouragement and praise. Encouragement is given for a deed well done; it is also given when the child has failed and needs a boost in courage. Encouragement focuses on the deed while praise focuses on the doer. When a child is discouraged, praise seems phony and increases discouragement. As a New Zealand colleague says, "Encouragement focuses on the deed, not the dude."[7]

Second, accentuate the positive. Years ago, there was a popular song whose opening line was, "You've got to accentuate the positive, eliminate the negative, latch on to the affirmative, don't mess with Mister In-Between."[8] Contrary to popular belief, criticism rarely inspires anyone to higher standards. In my opinion, there is no such thing as constructive criticism. As all competent hypnotherapists know, positive suggestion is more powerful than negative suggestion.

Third, catch your children being good. Reinforcement theory teaches us that when a behavior receives a payoff, positive or negative, you will see that behavior again.[9] So why not choose to reinforce positive and useful behaviors in our children.

In Summary

When a parent gives a gift, she or he should make sure the gift is wanted and can be appreciated by the child. Wanted gifts are always valued beyond the giver's belief. Adlerians know the most wanted and appreciated gifts you can give your child are *you*, *your time*, and *your attention*. This is easily done through individual special time, being respectful, giving your child a voice in family affairs through the family council, accentuating the positive, catching your child being good, and by being an encouraging parent who knows the difference between praise and encouragement. To be the best parent you can be, always remember that your *love needs to be given in the way it is desired to be received.*

Endnotes

1　　Gordon, *P.E.T. in Action.*

2　　Read "The Gift of Individual Special Time."

3　　Read "The Family Council." Also see Dreikurs, Gould, and Corsini, *Family Council: The Dreikurs Technique.* Painter and Corsini, *Effective Discipline.* Rigney and Corisni, *The Family Council.*

4　　Painter and Corsini, *Effective Discipline*, pp. 27-33.

5　　Read "School Homework."

6　　Dreikurs and Soltz, *Children: The Challenge.* p. 36.

7　　Mckimm, *Awesome Parents Handbook.* Read "Words of Encouragement."

8　　Words and music by Johnny Mercer and Harold Arlen. Sung and made famous by Bing Crosby. See http://www.mathematik.uni-ulm.de/paul/lyrics/bingcrosby/accent-1.html.

9　　Read "How Parents Train Children without Knowing It."

Notes

SECTION III.
Role Modeling for Parents

INTERNAL VS. EXTERNAL MOTIVATION: A TRUE STORY ABOUT RON HOWARD AND HIS FATHER

On rainy mornings, I like to lie in bed and absorb the cool Hawai'ian moisture as it wafts through my bedroom. On a June morning, I happened to turn on my bedside radio as visiting host, Clint Howard, began interviewing his father, Rance Howard.[1] The subject was child actors and, in particular, Ron Howard. As you may recall, Ron Howard began his successful acting career as Opie on *The Andy Griffith Show* and later as Richie Cunningham on *Happy Days*. What you may not know is that his father, Rance, himself a successful actor, for many years was present on the set as his son pursued his successful acting career.

Ron's father recalled that one morning there was a stressful kitchen scene where little Opie had many lines and the physical task of handling many cups and dishes. The director, wanting to motivate Ron, said to him, "If we get through this scene fairly quickly, I'll buy you a bicycle." At this juncture, Ron's father, Rance, stepped in and said:

> The only reward Ron needs for a job well done is a pat on the head for what he did, or you can just say, "Cut. Print." Now let's get on to the next challenge. Ron is an actor, and he knows he is an actor. I want him to feel good about what he does. That's what he needs. If Ron gets a bicycle, his mother and I will be the ones to buy it for him.[2]

Rance Howard knew the secret of generating motivation and the energy for lifelong personal growth and success. He realized external rewards, such as a bicycle or other trinkets, soon fade and often lead to a demand for more and greater payoffs from others. He knew that encouragement, a process that generates energy from within by implying faith in another's strengths and accomplishments, is what his son needed to continue his quest for excellence. This father knew that to be successful in the long run, the motivation must come from within. He wanted his son to lead a productive and balanced life.

Today, Ron Howard is a world-class and award-winning film producer, director, and writer. He is an Oscar winner and one of the most sought-after directors in the business. In the June 2006 issue of *Vanity Fair* magazine, Ron Howard was asked, "What do you consider your greatest achievement?" He replied, "Forty-eight consecutive years of steady employment in television and film while preserving a rich family life."[3]

Ron Howard was very fortunate to have a father who knew the value of encouragement and the pitfalls of praise and reward. What Ron has accomplished is an example of the power of internal motivation to carry a person over the long haul.

You, as a parent, can be world class in your endeavor of helping your child to become all that he or she can be. One thing you must always remember and to facilitate is the idea that *to be successful, the motivation must come from inside.*

As Opie Taylor in
The Andy Griffith Show, 1960.

During filming of *Angels & Demons*
in Rome, 2008.

Ronald William "Ron" Howard

Endnotes

[1] KHNR, Honolulu, Westwood One. June 25, 2010.

[2] Although the above quotes are filtered by my memory, I believe them to be an accurate portrayal of what was said.

[3] Wikipedia (Undated). Retrieved July 22, 2011, from http://en.wikipedia. org/ wiki/Ron_Howard.

Notes

BENJAMIN FRANKLIN'S THIRTEEN RULES TO ACHIEVE MORAL PERFECTION

Benjamin Franklin, young America's most versatile Founding Father, cultivated his personal character and integrity to become the man this fledgling nation needed by struggling to adhere to the following thirteen virtues. Franklin's goal was to achieve moral perfection. "I wanted nothing less than to live without committing any fault at any time."[1] Franklin defines each virtue in terms of good and bad behavior. To Franklin, something was virtuous because of the good that came from it. To help implement his quest for moral perfection, each morning upon arising, he would ask himself, "What good shall I do this day?" and each evening upon retiring, "What good have I done today?"[2]

As a wise parent, you may well want to teach Ben Franklin's concepts to your children. Having virtuous offspring is a virtuous goal for all caring parents. Using an Adlerian framework, the following are my suggestions on how to do it.

Ben Franklin's Thirteen Rules to Achieve Moral Perfection with an Adlerian Slant

"*Self-Control:* Avoid dullness from overeating. Avoid drunkenness from overdrinking."[3]

Franklin began his list of virtues with self-control as he believed that its mastery would provide him with the self-discipline he needed to achieve the other twelve.

Adlerians believe that the best way to teach your children to make self-improvements is by being a self-controlled or temperate role model. Your children are watching and learning from you even at those times when it seems they are not. Children who overeat and become obese do so because their parents overindulge them and are fearful of setting limits or being consistent in their use of the word *no*.

Many teens drink because they believe it will make them feel bigger, more important, and happier than they otherwise feel. They often drink excessively because they want the approval of their peer group. Children who are reared in a democratic family where they have a voice and a choice know that they belong with significance and do not have to overindulge or act out in order to believe they are important. These children have internalized feelings of adequacy and do not have to lose self-control in order to feel good about themselves.

"*Silence:* Say only those things that benefit others or yourself. Avoid all petty conversation."

Children learn to speak by being spoken to. The infant learns to recognize a parent's voice as well as cultural speech patterns from birth. When talking to your children, focus on them with your eyes and body and avoid personal multitasking. Children learn communication skills by watching and imitating us. Some children act "parent deaf." When called, they seem not to hear. Parents being inconsistent and not following through on their requests cause this misbehavior. Once a parent acknowledges that he or she is both the cause and cure of the problem, remedial actions are possible.[4]

"*Order:* Keep all your possessions in their proper place. Give each *part* of your business its necessary time."

Ben Franklin, in his essay, "Reflections on the Pursuit of Moral Perfection," at the age of seventy-nine admitted the following: "In the end, I found *order* the hardest to implement in my life." He adds, however, "Now that I am old . . . I wish I had practiced more of it in my youth . . . None the less, I was a better and happier person for making the effort."[5]

A family where parents show leadership and respect for the rights of all its members is a happy family and one that can guide its children to a respect for order. Making a contribution to the family by choosing and doing household chores is an excellent real-life teaching method. Children learn best when they practice by doing, not through parental words. Admonishing children by yelling, threatening, and repeating oneself is an inadequate teaching method. We must supply guidance and utilize life situations to give our children the best training experience.[6]

"*Determination:* Commit to what you ought to do and always carry out your commitments."

Ben Franklin has been hailed as "America's original entrepreneur." His determination to succeed while focused on the public good demonstrates his determination and social interest.

Through their experiences in the real world, parents know the value of determination and tenacity, as well as the worthlessness of procrastination. Our children often procrastinate and give up easily because they fear failure and lack courage. As parents, we need to practice encouragement. We need to teach our children to embrace the concept of "the courage to be imperfect." Adlerian-oriented parents teach their children by their own behavior that failure is not to be feared but respectfully embraced and used as a tool for success.[7]

"*Economy:* Don't waste your money. Let your only expenses be the doing of good to others or yourself."

Benjamin Franklin once said, "A penny saved is a penny earned." He was talking about frugality and the need to spend less than one earns.

In my work with university students, four out of five tell me that it is easy to earn money; their problem lies in money management. Adlerians teach money management using an allowance. Allowances are not tied to work but to family belonging. Through the proper use of allowances, children are taught to live within their means, a virtue that keeps on giving for a lifetime.[8]

"*Productivity:* Don't waste your time. Spend your time on useful matters and refrain from unnecessary activities."

Benjamin Franklin believed in hard work and the entrepreneurial spirit. He did not believe in the "cradle to grave" philosophy of socialism and communism.

Teach your children the value of honest hard work and success by modeling that philosophy. What works to bring meaning to one's life is not what gifts we are born with but how we put our gifts to work. Trying to make a quick buck or doing borderline or illegal activities will teach your children disrespect for self, others, and the law.

"*Truthfulness:* Avoid lies that harm others. Think without prejudice, and if you speak, speak accordingly."

My mother used to say to me, "If you can't say anything good, don't say anything at all. What goes around comes around." I think that she may have been coupling two separate sayings. Nonetheless, I believe her to have been right on the mark. In my work as a psychotherapist, I have learned to be sincere in whatever I say to my patients. In doing so, they have given me the privilege of, from time to time, being wrong in my belief and prediction. In my private life, I do my best to be encouraging and avoid the vices of gossip, sarcasm, and lying. Parents will do well to follow and teach the advice of Franklin and my mother. What did your mother teach you?

"*Justice:* Avoid injuring others by your actions or withdrawing from them the benefits they deserve."

Whom do you want your child to admire or be like? Does this person have the characteristics of fairness, righteousness, honesty, and integrity? Justice carries many images. Most likely, your child wants to be like you or your partner. Be a just person and provide your offspring with a likeness of a "just" person.

"*Moderation:* Avoid extremes. This applies especially to the holding of grudges against those who have harmed you."

Franklin cryptically provides two behavioral definitions to the virtue of moderation. His more general definition is to *avoid extremes*. His second definition speaks specifically about people *holding grudges against those who have harmed you.*

The media sensationalizes the extremes. It tells us that more is better, and perfection is the goal. I believe that there are too many situations where both parents work in order to have more things. We are brainwashed to believe that fulfillment and satisfaction comes from having more—a bigger house, more than one car, a membership in "the club," a more expensive family vacation, a private school for the kids. What your children deserve is not more things, but *more* of you. The concept of perfection is characterized by the importance we as parents put on our children's success rather than on their happiness. We want to brag that our child is valedictorian of her grammar school graduating class. The secret of happiness and internal peace is not more but moderation. Avoid extremes and in all measures be moderate.

Grudge-holding people have the misguided goal of revenge, a feeling of intense retaliation. "I feel very hurt, and I'm going to hurt back no matter what." Between parent and child, revenge is a result of the intensification of the power contest: who is going to be the boss? Parents need to know that "being the boss" is not leadership nor does it generate respect and long-term cooperation on the part of children. Parents need to learn to keep out of the power contest and learn the art of being a parental consultant. Should a revenge situation develop, the parent must become friendlier and let go of hostility, avoid any power contests, and work hard to improve communication.[9]

"*Cleanliness:* Keep body, clothes, and living space clean at all times."

Teaching your children the virtue of cleanliness teaches them about health and develops their attention to detail, discipline, responsibility, and order. Adlerian children have household chores. They learn to belong with significance as they contribute to the family health and welfare. Adlerians believe everyone must give according to their abilities so that they can take according to their needs. Teach your children to be significant members of the family by giving of themselves and their talents. Become their example.

"*Peace:* Don't be overtaken by small irritants or by large troubles that are sure to come."

If you as a parent are not bothered by "little things" or common or unavoidable accidents, neither will your children. However, if every little thing represents to you a catastrophe, most likely you will be rearing an esteem-challenged, neurotic child. Little Johnny spills a glass of milk. You have a choice of telling Johnny how clumsy and stupid he is in your most angry parental voice, or you can calmly say, "There is a clean-up sponge under the sink." Which lesson in self-esteem do you want to teach your child?[10]

"*Chastity:* Indulge your sexual appetites for the sake of health and offspring only. Never indulge to the point of dullness or weakness. Never injure your own or another's peace or reputation."

Chastity, the condition or practice of abstaining from sex on moral grounds, and venery,[11] the pursuit of or indulgence in sexual pleasure, are probably the least popular of all Franklin's thirteen virtues.

As parents of teens, we are very anxious about our offspring's possible sexual exploits and behaviors. Sexual activity is not as benign as most teens and some parents believe. Sexual relations, especially during early adolescence, carry both physical and psychological residual effects on the psyche. As difficult as many parents find it, we need to teach our children about sex and sexuality. Pregnancy, STDs, AIDS, partnering, and love are areas in which our future adult children need to be comfortable and educated.

Young women who are father deprived and want to hear and feel the "love" of a dad are more likely to become sexually involved with a boy than girls whose fathers are present and caring. Children who come from families that are intact, communicate well, and are reasonably involved in their lives are more likely to be responsible in their behavior. Single-mothered families have a greater challenge, but it is very possible to produce a child who values chastity. As an adult, the way you behave will be imprinted on your child's mind. How much chastity and casual venery do you want your children to know?

"*Humility:* Imitate Jesus and Socrates."

Franklin's original list contained only twelve virtues. Then a Quaker friend confided in him that others thought him to be much too overbearing as well as behaving in a superior, condescending and arrogant way. "As a result of his comment, I determined to cure myself of my arrogance by adding Humility to my list of virtues along with a carefully chosen definition of the word."[12]

Franklin, a man of faith who chose not to support organized religion, appreciated the humility, love, and courage of Jesus who he believed was sent to teach the whole human race and who taught his audience using parables. Franklin believed that humility and sacrifice leads the way to wisdom and that it equates with other positive behavior characteristics such as being good, considerate, and caring about all mankind.

A man of great intellect, Benjamin Franklin also greatly admired Socrates and, in many ways, attempted to be like him. He saw Socrates as a man of integrity, abundant with human kindness and an unassuming simplicity that made him a beloved teacher to his students. Socrates wanted his ideas to fit comfortably across every school of social thought. He believed in deeds as being good for community welfare. It was Socrates who first asked, "What is the meaning of virtue?"[13]

As parents, we want our children to be humble, loving, intelligent, courageous, and talented communicators who care about their family and community, as did Jesus and Socrates. One of the major pillars of Adlerian individual psychology is the concept of social interest, often referred to as *gemeinschaftsgefuhl*. This concept suggests that parents are the primary teachers of their children on how to belong to the family, a belonging that eventually embraces relatives, friends, members of the immediate community, and in more advanced people, all humankind. The concept of social interest also suggests that learning and intellectual power should be acquired for the good of everyone and not for selfish purposes. As a parent, when you teach humility and goodness and lay the foundation for learning by modeling these virtues, you teach your child the art of being a loving, caring, and wise human being. Ben Franklin modeled a significant part of himself after Jesus and Socrates. Perhaps these three men might offer your children models for their own lives. Talk with, not at, your children and share with them who you modeled your life after and the good it did you. If you are fortunate, perhaps your children will want to model their lives after you.

Endnotes

[1]   McCormick, *Ben Franklin: America's Original Entrepreneur*. The main chapters utilized in this essay are Franklin's "My Plan to Achieve Moral Perfection," "Reflections on the Pursuit of Moral Perfection," and "Additional Thoughts on Humility."

The word *virtue* has its origin in the concept of what it means to be a true man or woman. Toward the end of his days, Franklin admitted that he had not achieved his goal of "moral perfection." However, he thought that the attempt was well worth the effort and that its pursuit had enriched his life. "Nevertheless, I was a better and happier person for making the effort." McCormick, *Ben Franklin: America's Original Entrepreneur*, p. 124. The reader might be interested to note that Franklin began his quest for moral perfection at the age of twenty-two and last formally reflected upon it at the age of seventy-nine. I wish to acknowledge my use of the scholarship of Brett and Kate McKay whose article first motivated me to look more closely at the personal virtues of Ben Franklin. See McKay and McKay, *The Virtuous Life*.

[2]   Walwik, *Rewarding Virtue* McCormick, *Ben Franklin: America's Original Entrepreneur*.

[3]   For clarity and to enhance the twenty-first-century readers' understanding, I have chosen to use the modern text as presented in McCormick (2005). For example, in the original text, *The Autobiography of Benjamin Franklin*, ed. Labaree, Leonard W., et al., the first moral virtue read, "Temperance: Eat not to dullness; drink not to elevation." McCormick uses a more modern construction, "Self-control: Avoid dullness from overeating. Avoid drunkenness from overdrinking." Franklin stated each principle "and gave each a brief definition that captured the principle I hoped to put into practice." McCormick, *Ben Franklin: America's Original Entrepreneur*, p. 117. The reader is invited to examine the original Franklin text, from Labaree (1964) below.

1.   **Temperance**. Eat not to Dullness. Drink not to Elevation.
2.   **Silence**. Speak not but what may benefit others or yourself. Avoid trifling Conversation.

3. **Order**. Let all your Things have their Places. Let each Part of your Business have its Time.

4. **Resolution**. Resolve to perform what you ought. Perform without fail what you resolve.

5. **Frugality**. Make no Expense but to do good to others or yourself: i.e. Waste nothing.

6. **Industry**. Lose no Time. Be always employ'd in something useful. Cut off all unnecessary Actions.

7. **Sincerity**. Use no hurtful Deceit. Think innocently and justly; and, if you speak, speak accordingly.

8. **Justice**. Wrong none, by doing Injuries or omitting the Benefits that are your Duty.

9. **Moderation**. Avoid Extreams. Forbear resenting Injuries so much as you think they deserve.

10. **Cleanliness**. Tolerate no Uncleanness in Body, Cloaths or Habitation.

11. **Tranquility**. Be not disturbed at Trifles, or at Accidents common or unavoidable.

12. **Chastity.** Rarely use Venery but for Health or Offspring; Never to Dulness, Weakness, or the Injury of your own or another's Peace or Reputation.

13. **Humility**. Imitate Jesus and Socrates.

[4]   Suggested readings from *The Respectful Parent*: "Take Time for Training: Teaching Cooperation to Parent-Deaf Children," "The Art of the Wrist: Conveying Parental Authority through Touch," "How Parents Train Children without Knowing It."

[5]   McCormick, *Ben Franklin: America's Original Entrepreneur*, p. 123. Suggested reading. *The Respectful Parent*: "Creating a Daily Schedule." Rudolf Dreikurs points out that "a child has no respect for order if he is shielded from the results of disorder. He develops a respect for a sharp knife if he cuts himself, a fire that can burn if mishandled, for a bicycle that tips if he doesn't keep it balanced, for a moving baseball if he doesn't duck." Dreikurs and Soltz, *Children: The Challenge*, see chapter 9, "Induce Respect for Order."

6 Read "Parent as Consultant."

7 McCormick, *Ben Franklin: America's Original Entrepreneur,* see "foreword" by John C. Bogle. Franklin, Benjamin, *Poor Richard's Almanack,* p. 4. "Well done is better than well said."

8 Painter and Corsini, *Effective Discipline,* pp. 134-47. Sonstegard and Sonnenshein, *The Allowance.*

9 Painter and Corsini, *Effective Discipline,* pp. 355-60, especially p. 359 on "Revenge." In his book on Franklin's virtues and American presidents, Walwik (2008) suggests President Richard Nixon as the poster child for holding grudges. "Nixon managed to avoid extremes in terms of his personal comportment, but he was never able to forbear, forgive, or forget injuries done to him, both real and imagined . . . . Even at the height of victory Nixon could not escape his fighter's instinct. The morning after his landslide re-election victory in 1972 Nixon met with his senior staff to plot a course for going after his enemies." p. 128.

10 Read "Stress, Cooties, 'n' Ukus: Don't Give 'Em to da Keiki."

11 The word *venery* was used by Franklin in his original writing. It is defined as (1) the pursuit of or indulgence in sexual pleasure, and (2) sexual intercourse. *Merriam-Webster's Medical Dictionary.* I have decided to include the word here as it lends power to Franklin's definition.

12 McCormick, *Ben Franklin: America's Original Entrepreneur,* p. 127.

13 Durant, *The Story of Philosophy,* see Socrates, pp. 7-13.

Notes

SECTION IV.
Improving Routine Living

Colonel Frances A. Deutch

Colonel Deutch began managing money at age 6 with a twenty-five-cents-a-week allowance. Her military history includes the management of very large budgets.

ALLOWANCES TEACH MONEY MANAGEMENT

Do you want your child to understand the value of money and manage it wisely? If you do, then give your child an allowance.

Six-year-old Frances began her money management career when she first began receiving an allowance. It was 1972 and twenty-five cents a week was, for the time and circumstances, reasonable. Frances was instructed that the money was hers to do with what she pleased. She did not have to report her spending actions to anyone, nor did she have to save any of it. It was her money to do with what she wanted, no questions asked. Managing her money was her challenge. The only caveats were that she was not to bother her parents by asking for more money during the week, nor to ask for a loan, or advances on future allowances. The money was to last her all week. At the end of seven days at the next family council meeting, she would be given another twenty-five cents that was to last her for the following week.

Several weeks later, the following story came to light. Near the house was a gasoline station that housed an ice cream bar vending machine. An ice cream bar sold for fifteen cents. The machine took quarters, dispensed a bar, and gave back two nickels in change.

Frances figured out the following. In week 1, she got an ice cream bar and ten cents in change. Week 2, with thirty-five cents in her pocket, she could get two ice cream bars and have a nickel left over. In week 3, she could buy two more ice creams with her money. During week 4, she could purchase one ice cream bar and have a dime leftover, just as in week 1. The joy of the ice cream machine lasted for several months. Frances enjoyed her newfound skills and knack for money management. She kept her word and never bothered her parents for money.

Most parents have been raised to think of an allowance as a reward for work done around the house and yard. They also tell their children, "If you don't work, you don't get any money." Each semester, I ask my students at the University of Hawai'i about their earning and spending habits, and each semester, I consistently am told the same story. Four out of five students have no problem earning money. If they want, there is always a job to be had. What they have difficulty with is managing the money they have and making it last to the end of the week. Most did not receive an allowance when growing up but were given money by their parents when they asked or begged.

In this chapter, I will attempt to introduce the Adlerian perspective of allowances as the medium for children to learn money management . . . a gift to children that pays dividends for a lifetime.

What Allowances Are Not

Let me begin by telling you what allowances are not. Allowances are not to be used as a reward or punishment for chores completed or not. When a job is not done or done poorly, parents should use discussion or logical consequences or both to teach their child about keeping one's word and completing chores. Withholding an allowance, usually seen by children as a punishment, often results in resentments, power struggles, revenge, and manipulations. In the long run, it does not work to parents' advantage.

Money Is Received in Three Forms

Children receive money in three forms: allowances, gifts, and money earned. Allowances should be given to children who are old enough to understand the concept of money. If your youngster believes that a nickel is worth more than a dime because it is bigger or that money is free and all one needs is a credit card, he or she might be a little too young to have an allowance. For this child, a discussion about money from time to time or playing "store" with Mom or Dad might be useful as well as fun. It's up to the parent to decide whether their child is ready or not.

When you decide the time is right, utilize your family council meeting as a platform for discussion. Usually, children of ages 6 or 7 will bring up the subject first. No matter who brings up the subject, the following principles will be useful. The bracketed information following what each party says is presented to help parents understand what is going on during the conversation and the principles involved.

The following is a typical scenario. Kim is seven years old, and her brother, Robert, is five. The family is attending their weekly family council meeting when Kim opens the subject of an allowance.

Kim. Mom, I want an allowance.

Mother. Tell me about that.

[*Mother wants to know more about Kim's request. The more information she knows, the better decision Mother can make.*]

Kim. My friend, Judy, gets an allowance, and she can buy things whenever she wants. I want to be like that.

[*Mother now knows that Kim wants to be more grown up, and at seven, it is time to begin teaching her money management skills.*]

Mother. How much do you think you should get?

[*By allowing the child to name the figure, Mother can see what the child believes is reasonable and her level of maturity.*]

Kim. Ten dollars a week is what I want.

[*Kim shoots high. In this case, she probably does so because at seven years of age, she has only the vaguest knowledge of money and its real value.*]

Mother. I'm glad you want an allowance. It shows me that you are growing up and want to take more responsibility for your life. Let's discuss what is reasonable for a seven-year-old to get and how you are planning to use your money. I also have some ideas about money management and would like to share them with you.

[*Mother shows approval of Kim's idea and suggests to her that having an allowance is a part of growing up and taking more responsibility for one's life. Mother then moves toward helping Kim to think more realistic about what she needs and wants from her allowance as well as to understand the realities of what the family can afford. Mother also opens the door to informing Kim about the rules of allowances, such as making the money last all week long, not asking, borrowing, or begging for money advances.*]

Kim. That's fine, Mom, but I want $10 a week like Judy gets.

[*Children have a right to negotiate their allowances and advocate for their own benefits. However, while respecting this right, parents do not have to cave into their child's demands.*]

Mother. Father, what do you think?

[*Since an allowance for Kim is a family decision, Mother, who was the first to field the request, needs to bring her husband into the discussion. If this were a single-parent family, that parent needs to pursue the conversation. If there was an active father outside of the household, consideration should be given to tabling the discussion and inviting him to the next family council meeting for his input.*]

Father. I think $10 a week is too high for a seven-year-old, but I could be wrong. Kim, what are you planning to do with your money?

[*Typically, fathers lead with their opinion. In this situation, Father wisely wants to "see" Kim's budget. With an older child, the preparation of a budget for a presentation to the parents the following week might be best. For a seven-year-old, talking about their wants and needs while a parent takes notes and adds up numbers is probably best.*]

Father. (After listening to Kim's budget request, which focused on minor casual expenses with no mention of living expenses, Father gives his opinion.) Mother, I would like to suggest an allowance of $3 a week. The family can afford that, and Kim's budget calls for that amount.

Mother (to Father). Three dollars is cutting it awfully close. Do you think Kim should receive more?

    [*Mothers are different from fathers and are often more generous. In this case, Mother is offering her opinion in the form of a discussion.*]

Father. You might be right. But let's try out $3 for this week and have Kim report back to us next week at our family council meeting.

    [*Father knows it is unwise to argue with his spouse about allowances in front of the children. He also knows that when determining the best level of an allowance, it is wiser to pay less money at the beginning and subsequently give the child a raise than to begin too high and have to take away from an ongoing allowance. Before Kim's parents come to a fiscal arrangement with her, they need to let her know the terms and behaviors that go with having an allowance.*]

Mother. As part of receiving an allowance, there are certain ideas that are important to know as well as agreements that we all have to make. Here is how Father and I see things. You will get an allowance because you are a very special part of this family. Allowances are a way for you to learn how to manage your money, something that you will need to do as you grow up. Dad or I will pay allowances at the end of our weekly family council meeting. Your allowance will be the full amount we all have agreed to. We will never deduct money because we are unhappy with the way you do your chores. We will use logical consequences to deal with those situations should they arise. Your money is yours to spend any way you choose. You don't have to tell us how you spend it. If you want to ask our advice, we will give you our opinions, but the final decision will always be yours. You don't have to save your money if you don't want to. However, you are not to ask us for money during the week. We will not give you a loan or an advance on your next week's allowance. Your allowance is to last you for the entire week until the next family council meeting. If you run out of allowance money, you will just have to go without until allowance day. What do you think about what I just said?

[*By being very clear, Mother sets the stage for Kim (and Robert who also is listening) to begin learning how to be financially responsible. As the family discusses the agreement, its terms become clarified for Kim, and the learning process begins.*]

Mother (to Father). I agree with you on a $3-a-week allowance for Kim, and I also agree that we should hear from her at next week's meeting. Kim, will you give us a report on how your money situation went for you?

Kim. I agree.

✂ ✂ ✂ ✂ ✂ ✂ ✂ ✂ ✂ ✂ ✂ ✂ ✂ ✂ ✂ ✂

The odds are ninety-nine to one that five-year-old Robert will be asking for an allowance just as his sister did. Once one child receives an allowance all other children above the age of three will make the same request. I suggest that mothers and fathers, long before the first child brings up the subject, discuss the issue and come to a mutual agreement about how old their children should be before getting an allowance and how much it should be. Questions regarding the rules for gifts and earned money also should be anticipated and discussed. Answers regarding these issues are discussed next.

Gifts of a Significant Amount

Gifts of significant amounts of money are always a challenge for parents. What should parents do, for example, when grandmother gives a birthday gift of a hundred dollars to your child?

I strongly suggest that you head the problem off at the pass. Have a conversation with Grandma and let her know what you are trying to do and why you are doing it. Suggest to her that since it is her money, she should set the rules on how it is to be used. Here is an example. Grandma wants to give $80 to Kim for her eighth birthday. Based on parental suggestion, she tells Kim that she should use $10 to buy herself a toy and save the remaining $70 to go toward buying a bigger gift, "like the fastest bike in the neighborhood."

Sometimes, a present will come from an unexpected source. Second cousin Mabel dies leaving a $500 gift to her cute niece, Kim. No instructions are given, and the estate's check is made out to young Kim. I suggest that parents deal with big gift problems in the following manner. Soon after the new allowance situation has been established, bring up the subject of substantial gifts. If the gift is $300 or less, go to your savings institution and set up a savings account with your child. Allow her to make deposits and learn the joy of saving. If the amount is greater, set up a 529 plan for a college savings program[1] with your favorite mutual fund or other financial institution. Remember to give your child at least $10 to buy a present in the name of the giver. Putting all the gift into savings "for your college education" has little or no impact on a child and throws cold water on the joy of receiving from a significant other. Kids learn and feel by living in the short term; the long term has little meaning for them.

Earned Money

Children should be allowed to use their earned money any way they want. Their allowance should never be reduced because they become ambitious and earn additional money by cutting grass or washing neighbors cars. Ambition should be encouraged rather than discouraged.

Often, children are paid for jobs around the house that their parents do not wish to do. For example, Father does not want to wash and vacuum the family car when it needs cleaning. He can pay an outsider to wash and vacuum the auto for $7.50, or he can pay his son to do the same job. If the son is capable of doing an equivalent quality job, the boy should work for the same price. Children should be paid at the market price for labor. Do not be inequitable to your child because he or she is a vulnerable family member. Teach your child that his or her labor has value and needs to be respectfully compensated.

Families with a teen might consider giving their child an allowance that covers both living and casual expenses. Some teens are readier for financial independence than others. Mercedes was fourteen years old when she came to her parents and requested she be allowed to be more financially independent. She had prepared a budget that she gave to her parents for their inspection. In it, she had budgeted for clothing, personal and hygiene items, as well as casual items. Since she used the bus to commute to school and to other activities, financial challenges related to driving an automobile did not exist. Mercedes told her parents that she was going to get a summer job and requested she not be penalized for having initiative. She also told her parents that if they agreed to the sum she requested, she would not ask them for extra money. After long discussions at two family council meetings and agreeing to have her situation revisited in two months, Mercedes's parents agreed to support her push for greater independence. One year later, Mercedes's parents reported that the "Mercedes money experiment" had been successful, and they were very satisfied with her display of maturity.

Children Are Keen Observers

Children of all ages are keen observers of their parents' behavior. It has been said that a six-month-old baby knows more about the parent than the parent knows about the baby. How a parent manages money is often mirrored by their child. If Mother is a shopaholic, she should not be surprised when her daughter becomes one too. If Father is a tightwad and dislikes spending money, someone in the family, probably the son, will feel and behave the same way. Allowing our children to learn financial responsibility through trial and error as well as to experience his or her choices through natural consequences is a gift we give to our children that will last them a lifetime.

Endnotes

[1] A 529 plan is an education savings plan operated by a state or educational institution designed to help families set aside funds for future college costs. It is named after section 529 of the Internal Revenue Code, which created these types of savings plans in 1996.

Notes

Mrs. Wyatt's Fourth-Grade Class, Central Elementary,
National City, California (1948)

SCHOOL HOMEWORK:
WHO OWNS THE PROBLEM?

"But if I don't keep reminding him to do his homework, he's going to fail the fourth grade!" Many parents believe that it is their responsibility to make sure their child's homework is done correctly and on time. "Do your homework" is the cry of "good parents"[1] everywhere.

During my fifty plus years of helping families, I have found that the most prominent obstacle to being a happy family is the constant fighting that goes on between parents and children over homework. As family counselors at the Family Education Training Center of Hawai'i, we are never surprised when our parents identify homework as one of the major causes of family disharmony. However, family combat operations over homework have become so usual that it seems normal and to be expected as a part of everyday life. Rarely is it recognized as an unnecessary major cause of family discord. Promising, bribing, lecturing, nagging, yelling, begging, bargaining, hitting, and all parental-devised forms of punishment are parental tactics that seriously disrespect the child, the parent, and impair the goal of family happiness.

Parents who have made the completion of homework their responsibility usually use lecturing, nagging, and punishment to motivate their child to complete his work. Forcing your parental will does nothing to motivate your child. Instead of helping your offspring to achieve academic success, parents who use forceful methods have found their power strategies only motivate their child to engage in power struggles and revenge tactics. Lecturing begets deafness, nagging begets stalling, power begets power plays, and punishments of any kind begets revenge. Nothing positive is gained from these well-meaning but misguided parental motivational techniques. They promote family disharmony and create an ever-present, shadowy cloak of family unhappiness.

Parents need to examine three very important and related questions. First, "Whose responsibility is school homework?" Second, "Why is this child resisting doing homework?" And third, "If all else fails, is it all right to let my child fail if he or she doesn't do his homework?"

Whose Responsibility Is School Homework?

Contrary to how most parents act, homework is the responsibility of the child. It is never too early to learn responsibility. Children learn it by first learning how to take care of their own physical needs, then by contributing to the family well-being by being helpful in the home, and then by doing chores willingly, without being asked or reminded. School homework is one of those responsibilities that accompanies a child's growth and development on his winding road to maturity.

Many children do not understand why they must go to school. To them, they are being forced without a good cause or reason. The younger the child, the more blurred his vision of the future. When you explain the need for an education, keep your explanation simple and age appropriate. Make it relevant to a child's current life experiences.

When our children were young, my wife and I explained going to school in the following manner. "In our family, everyone has a job. Daddy's job is to go to work in order to make money so that we can buy things, like a house to live in, food to eat, and clothes to wear. Mama's job is to stay at home, make the meals, and take care of you. Your job is to go to school so that you can learn about things and, in the future, get a good job."

My sister tells the following story. When her youngest son was four years old, the family was driving past a farm field where laborers were bent over, working in the hot son. "What are those people doing, Mama?" he asked. "Those people have to work hard all day long in the hot sun," she replied. "Why, Mama?" he inquired. "Because they never went to school, so they are forced to earn a living by working in the fields, even on hot days." My sister chose to use her "teaching moment" to answer her son's question focusing on his need to obtain an education and not on the plight of migrant farmworkers. What she said turned out to be a shaping moment in my nephew's life. From that trip on, he did well in school and now has a master's degree in education. He is also an entrepreneur and never works outdoors in the noonday sun.

There are other ways to make education, and thus homework, relevant to the child's life. Here are just a few.

— Talk about interesting intellectual subjects around the dinner table. Science, art, music, philosophy, history, politics, and current events can be very stimulating, especially if your children's opinions (without parental comments) are solicited. Include college sports, especially if a child is interested in a specific college or university.[2]

— Subscribe to magazines that are intellectually stimulating for children, such as *National Geographic* or *Scientific American.* Good art and good music seen and heard at home also can be important teaching tools. Watch intellectually stimulating television programs such as those on the History Channel and the National Geographic Channel. There are other channels that stimulate learning.

— Invite your friends over and have stimulating conversations; invite their children and yours to participate.

— Teach your children how to read by reading to them. Reading to your kids should not be just a bedtime gimmick; it is best used to stimulate their minds and imaginations.

There are many ways to stimulate your child's mind and to set the scene for learning, school, and homework. Be creative and have intellectual fun with your children.

Why Is This Child Resisting Doing Homework?

When your child resists doing his or her school homework, ask yourself why. Is your child dreadfully discouraged about his or her abilities? Has he given up trying to keep up with the other children in his class? Does he have a reading problem, which keeps him from achieving his potential? Is there a bully at school who is stealing your child's learning energy by threatening or otherwise distracting him or her? Does your child dislike the teacher and seem to say, "I'm not going to study because I don't like my teacher"? Does your child have attention deficit disorder (ADD), attention-deficit/hyperactivity disorder (ADHD), or dyslexia, all of which make learning difficult, especially in crowded public schools.

We, as parents, don't like to talk about or admit it, but many of our children are not academically minded and should not go to college. Statistically speaking, almost half of the children born will score below the mean average of one hundred on a standard IQ test. Unless otherwise highly motivated to do academic work, these children should be given a superior education in the trades. If your child is great with his hands but poor with abstract concepts, think about changing your goals for him, and build on his strengths, not on his weaknesses.[3]

In order to better understand your child and his school progress, or lack of it, first talk to his or her teacher. Find out her point of view and what behaviors she is observing that lead her to her conclusions. Perhaps psychological testing by the school psychologist will discover the roots of an academic problem. This is often the case of children with dyslexia. Your child's teacher can make this referral. Sometimes a medical examination by a specializing physician also will be helpful. Oftentimes, valid cases of ADD and ADHD can be diagnosed with the help of an electroencephalogram (EEG). You can never go wrong by getting the opinion of a good and caring pediatric physician.[4]

If your child is motivated, a private tutor or a commercial children's learning center might be the right place to send your child for extra help. It may cost you out of your pocket, but if it works, it's worth the expense. To the very limit that it is feasible, I strongly suggest you let the experts work to correct your child's learning problem. Even if you are a teacher, it is far better to let an outsider deal with your child and avoid the emotional hassles and conflicts that correction brings. Remember, surgeons are professionally forbidden to operate on their immediate family members; the same rule should apply to parents.

Is It All Right to Let My Child Fail Because He Doesn't Do His Homework?

The vast majority of families that struggle with homework issues arc familics that do not have children with learning problems. They are normal families with normal parents fighting about school homework with their normal children. Perhaps some relevant Adlerian child psychology perspectives might prove to be useful to parents struggling with the issues about homework.

Parents often do not realize that children want to belong to the family and be seen as significant members. Children quickly learn what behaviors they must exhibit in order to achieve this vital feeling. Parents believe they are teaching their children cooperation when they lecture, nag, beg, bribe, punish, and reward. In reality, they are teaching their children misguided behaviors. Rudolf Dreikurs, MD, found that misbehaving children choose one of four dysfunctional and misguided behavioral goals: (1) undue attention, (2) power, (3) revenge, and (4) displaying inadequacy. Translated into a child's language, undue attention means "I belong only when I'm keeping adults busy with me." Power means "I'm the boss, and I do what I want," or "I won't, and you can't make me do it." Revenge means "I feel hurt, and I want to hurt back." Displaying inadequacy means "I give up. I can't do it. It's too hard."[5]

How does a parent change his child's misguided ("bad," "annoying," or "uncooperative") behavior? The answer is both deceptively simple and hard. A parent must learn that when he changes his own behavior, the child will change his behavior too.

Why doesn't Junior (or Sister) come home and be happily motivated to do homework? Let's put it this way. You, an adult and parent, have just put in a hard eight-hour day at the office, a place where, yes, you have made a decision to work. You have worked diligently to please the boss and ignore his character defects, have put up with interruptions, officemates' bad habits, as well as the office bully, and drove through bumper-to-bumper traffic to get home. You may even have to do office homework in preparation for tomorrow's business. Now you are expected to do more work . . . for your other "boss," your child. How motivated and happily excited are you to do that extra work (the child's homework) though you chose parenthood?

Now let's make a comparison and see the same situation from the child's point of view. You, the child, have just put in a hard six-hour day at school, a place where your parents decided you should go. You have worked diligently to please your teacher and ignore her character defects, have put up with interruptions, classmates' bad habits, school bullies, and came home through bumper-to-bumper traffic. You may have even participated in an after-school activity such as soccer or the "A Plus" after-school program and may even have waited for your parent to pick you up. Once home, you are expected to do more work (for your teacher) called homework whether you need it or not. How motivated and happily excited are you to do this extra work? Then your parents, who are themselves tired, nag and force you to do the extra work, which they say is good for you even though there is research to show that homework in the lower grades does not lead to higher test scores at the end of the semester.[6] Being tired, unmotivated to work extra, you argue with your parents. Everyone becomes angry, and you fight back by doing what you can do, just the opposite of what your parents demand.

When parents act in a repetitively disharmonious way, I am reminded of the old joke about the definition of a neurotic, a person who keeps repeating the same behavior while expecting different results. Many parents practice reminding, nagging, rewarding, punishing, and abusive behaviors because either they do not know what else to do or changing behaviors brings on feelings of fear of the unknown. As one parent put it, "I'm more comfortable with the devil I know than with the angel I don't know."

To bring about new parental behaviors, we strongly suggest that, as a first step, parents ask themselves the "platinum question." "Is what I am doing working for me?" If your answer is no, then the fix is obvious. In the case of homework, get out of the school business and turn over the responsibilities to your child. Yes, you can discuss good study habits, routines, learning strategies, and what kind of equipment and environment your child needs in order to be academically successful. After one discussion, zip it up and get out of there until your child asks for input. When asked, give it to him without preaching or saying, "I told you so." These phrases are definitely a turnoff to your child.

To help your child's teacher understand what you are doing, it is helpful to notify her that you are making homework completion your child's responsibility, and you have withdrawn from the homework struggle. Your child is now primarily responsible for his own school-related behaviors. Tell your child's teacher that she may decide what to do about incomplete homework, and other than corporal punishment, she has your permission to act as she, the educator, deems best. Interestingly, I have found that most teachers understand parental goals and become cooperative and supportive. However, a few teachers will try to bully the parent into continuing their nagging and destructive ways. In this case, the parent must stand up against the teacher's insistence and fight for family harmony. In those situations where the teacher insists that the parent must sign the homework before she will accept it, I suggest the parent affix her signature, but stick to her principles and not check up on her child's work.[6]

Too many parents are fearful that their child will fail. It is as if their child's failure is their own failure, that their child's lack of academic success is their lack of success as both a person and parent. If this is the way a parent truly believes and feels, then he or she needs to change their flawed belief system. Such a parent needs to see their child's school failure not as a defeat but as a much-needed learning opportunity. Without failure, there can be no success. Alfred Adler, MD, points out that as children and youth struggle and build up their skills, they grow and become smarter and more productive family and community members.[7]

As Adlerian counselors, we believe that all movement of mind, body, and spirit within your child is from a minus to a plus, from inferiority toward superiority, from inadequacy toward adequacy, and from incompetence toward competence. If you do not allow your child to fail, he or she will never succeed. If it is your energy that externally powers your child to do his or her studies, that child never will become internally powered and motivated. Children need encouragement in their struggle with the twin issues of failure and success. A child, who is encouraged, rather than praised or threatened, has the courage to succeed even after failures.[8]

To the child, success after failure is empowering. Having your child possess, "the courage to be imperfect," should be the goal of every parent. Having courage will bring about many more successes than failures. The responsible parent allows his or her child to succeed or fail on his or her own efforts and merit.

Samuel Smiles, the nineteenth-century writer and political reformer, was on the mark when, on two separate occasions, he wrote the following on the subject of success and failure.[9]

"It is a mistake to suppose that men succeed through success; they much oftener succeed through failures. Precept, study, advice, and example could never have taught them so well as failure has done."

"We learn wisdom from failure much more than from success. We often discover what will do, by finding out what will not do; and probably he who never made a mistake will never make a discovery."

Let your child be responsible for his or her own homework. He or she will learn how to organize time, thoughts, and priorities. I strongly believe that to be successful, the passion must come from inside. As a parent, it is now time to make your decision. What kind of a parent do you want to be? What kind of a child do you want to lead the next generation?

Endnotes

1 Dr. Genevieve Painter, my friend and Adlerian mentor, would tell her parenting classes that what is needed are not "good parents," but "responsible parents" who have the knowledge to rear responsible children.

2 As your child grows older, you have set the stage for the question, "What kind of grades does this university require for admission? If the child "bites," have him or her research the admission requirements.

3 My friend Jerry tells the following story.

   "In high school, nine of us became friends. We are still friends and have a reunion every year in our home town. What we had in common was that we were all athletes. Eight of us went to college, one did not. I signed a major league contract between my college sophomore and junior year and immediately went to the minors as a pitcher. The other guys did their thing and finished college. The one who did not go to college went into the trades, learned plumbing, and opened his own business. Today, he is a multimillionaire and owns the largest plumbing business in his geographical area. He sponsors and pays the cost of our annual reunions."

4 Lawlis, *The ADD Answer*.

5 Painter and Corsini, *Effective Discipline,* see pages 355-362. Read "Why Children Misbehave."

6 Marzano, Pickering, and Pollock, *Classroom Instruction That Works*. Marzano, et al. also state that many studies show minimal and even negative effects when parents are asked to help students with homework. They suggest that parents must learn to be facilitators and models of scholarship.

7 Adler, *Social Interest*.

8 Adlerians differentiate between encouragement and praise. Encouragement focuses on the child's behavior. "It looks like you really enjoyed drawing this picture." Praise focuses on the child as a person. "How wonderful you are for drawing me such a nice picture." By focusing on the child's behavior, which is usually the issue at hand, a parent can reinforce or change that behavior easily. Praise runs the risk on being insulting and putting down the child as a human being. Praise oftentimes is discouraging, especially when the child is feeling defeated.

9 Brainy Quote.

Notes

EATING SHOULD BE THE CHILD'S BUSINESS

A while back, I was writing a "Dear Dr. Deutch" column for a very fine local health-oriented organization of which I was the vice president at the time. The following question and reply is an edited and expanded version of the original printed article.[1]

Dear Dr. Deutch:

My five-year-old daughter, Lei, would rather play with her food than eat. My husband and I find this behavior very upsetting. Our pediatrician says our daughter is normal and healthy and that there is nothing physically wrong with her. We have been eating in an exceedingly healthy manner for the past two years, and we have worked hard to learn about preparing wholesome plant-based meals. We have done everything to get her to eat. We have played games at the table, bribed her with her favorite desserts, stayed at the table with her until she cleaned her plate, and now we are yelling and punishing her. We don't like how we act, yet we want her to grow up strong and healthy and have a responsible attitude towards healthy food and eating. What should we do?

Humbled by Lei in Lanikai

Dear Humbled:

Many five-year-olds have humbled their parents when it comes to feeding time. Eating problems with children seem to occur when parents openly put great emphasis on nutrition and health. Children pick up on their parents' concern and often use eating as a way of getting undue attention. Dr. Rudolf Dreikurs often said, "There is only one creature on earth that does not want to eat—the American Child."[2]

This does not mean that your daughter has rejected your values of healthy eating. It means that she has learned that your obvious interest in her eating is a way for her to get from you undue attention. As you have found, bribery, yelling, physical punishment, playing games, and staying at the table until she has cleaned her plate does not work in the long run.

Here is a simple strategy you can use to make mealtime more pleasant in your home. At your next family meeting,[3] tell Lei what you are going to do. Explain how the family will continue to eat together at the table, and you will be careful not to overfill her plate and cup. After everyone is done eating, the family will stay and talk for a little while before being excused from the table. When the family leaves, you will take Lei's plate and cup and empty its contents into the garbage. There will be no more food until the next meal.

At the following meal, everyone should be served in the usual manner. Don't overload Lei's plate if you serve her. Let her guide you in the amount as well as her choices of food.[4] Keep the dinner conversation light and pleasant, letting Lei join in the discussion. You might ask her, "What did you do today that you liked the most?" "What did you do today that you liked the least?" If Lei plays with her food, ignore it. After the family has eaten, relax and wait another ten minutes or so. This means that you say nothing positive or negative with regard to how or what Lei is doing with her food. If she is playing with it, it is most likely for the purpose of getting your attention. If you reward her misbehavior by giving it a payoff of either praise or punishment, I guarantee that you'll see that behavior again.[5] When you ignore misguided behaviors, such as playing with food, you allow the behavior to begin to extinguish.

At the end of the meal, clean off the table in your usual manner. This means casually removing Lei's food in a matter-of-fact way without any mention of what you are doing or why. This way, you are saying in a silent and nonverbal way, "When eating time is over, it's over. You'll have to live with the consequences of your behavior (not eating) until the next meal." If Lei protests, do not respond. Explanations at this time only will serve as a payoff and reinforcement for her undesired behavior.

It is important for you to keep in mind that clearing the table and removing the child's remaining food is not a punishment; it's just a way of keeping order in the family. Some parents have a difficult time with the idea of not allowing the child to eat until the next meal. However, I have never known of a child starving by missing one meal. If Lei has special medical needs such as diabetes, of course consult your pediatrician before making any changes. If it's your normal routine to have a healthy snack before bedtime, continue doing this. If it is *not* the norm, *don't* start doing it now.

Three other issues need to be mentioned: dessert, snacks, and eating at the same time every day. Dessert should be a normal part of the meal and should not be used as a reward for eating or a punishment for not eating. Rather than serving junk foods, I suggest you serve freshly sliced fruits, such as pineapples, strawberries, pears, oranges, apples, bananas, or whatever fruit is in season. If Lei wants to eat her dessert first, let her, as this dessert is very healthy and nutritious.

A good friend of mine recently discovered that he was the culprit in his four-year-old son's eating problem. Every day, close to dinner, he and his son would eat a sugary snack. He would then wonder why the boy was not hungry at mealtime. After realizing what he was doing, snacking for both stopped and the boy's eating problem disappeared.

Children need routine; eating at the same time every day with the same people present is important. Eating at irregular times and without key family members present is often upsetting for a child and may interfere with a child's appetite and digestion. As Dr. Rudolf Dreikurs points out, "Irregular feeding schedules show a lack of respect for the [child] and for order."[6]

Here is a tip that I give to all parents. Guarantee Lei and all other children in your family at least ten minutes a day of individual special playtime. Do something active so that muscle memory as well as intellectual memory is involved. Children love having a guaranteed individual special time with their parents. Playing with your child one-on-one for ten minutes a day is a great way to build a positive relationship and help prevent behavioral problems before they start.[7]

Respectfully,

Dr. Jim

Endnotes

[1] The essence of this article was originally published by the author in *The Island Vegetarian*, pp. 183-84.

[2] Dreikurs, Rudolf, quoted in Painter and Corsini, *Effective Discipline.*

[3] Read "The Family Council."

I believe one the best books written on the subject of the family council or family meeting is by Dreikurs, Gould, and Corsini, *Family Council: The Dreikurs Techniques.*

See chapter 33, "The Family Council" in Painter and Corsini.

See Rigney and Corsini, *The Family Council.*

[4] Research has shown that children who are allowed to choose their own foods from the family dinner table will, over the long run, eat a reasonably balanced diet. Many parents pass on their own food issues to their children without knowing it. A classic study in children's self-selection of food is Davis, "Self-Selection of Diet of Newly Weaned Infants," pp. 36, 651-79. Also see Johnson and Birch, "Parents' and Children's Adiposity and Eating Style," pp. 653-61.

[5] Read "How Parents Train Children without Knowing it."

[6] Dreikurs and Soltz, *Children: The Challenge.* p. 92.

[7] Read "The Gift of Individual Special Time."

Notes

YOUR CHILD'S ROOM:
A CASE FOR PROBLEM OWNERSHIP

Children are not naturally neat. They honestly don't care whether or not their rooms meet parental standards. To them, their rooms are a place to sleep, play, or just hang out on a rainy day.

As a long-time family therapist, I have found the demand "Keep your room neat and clean" to be the cause of much family strife and unhappiness. Parents treat their children's rooms as a gift with strings attached. They believe their children need to be grateful and show their deep appreciation by keeping their rooms as near to immaculate as possible. This scenario rarely happens. Thus, parents feel unappreciated, unheard, ignored, and angry about their unrequited sacrifice.

When I say "Children are not naturally neat," I say it with one exception. Twenty years ago, I met a woman who bragged to me that her thirteen-year-old son always kept his room immaculate. Never, she said, was his room less than in perfect order. Suspicious that this really was not going to be the first case in my professional career of an adolescent boy who kept an immaculately clean room and who did not appear to be obsessive-compulsive or neurotically neat, I bit my tongue and smiled a salutation. A week later, I learned that this young man had intentionally shot dead his father the year before. At that moment, I decided that having a young adolescent whose claim to fame was a clean room and a homicide record was not a goal I wanted to set for either of my two children.

As a parent, I found that when my daughter's room was neat, my son's room was messy. And when my son's room was neat, my daughter's room was messy. Rarely were both rooms simultaneously neat or simultaneously messy. I looked at my own standards of room keeping and saw that my behavior was being imitated by my children. Room keeping was not a high priority or value in my life, but love of family, country, healthy relationships, work, play, and honesty were.

Since most parents "give" their child their own room at a young age, by the time parents are annoyed by its messiness, it is usually too late for a quick fix. Retraining your child can take up to a year, and in some cases, it will never happen.

If your child is over three, I suggest you begin by helping him or her to clean up the room using a gentle and calm approach. At this young age, you may have to do most of the work. But that's okay as you are modeling appropriate behavior as well as giving a room-cleaning lesson.

By the time your child is five or six years old and his room still looks like a war zone, you will need to change your tactics. While criticizing, threatening, preaching, bribing, withdrawing privileges, taking away allowances, and other forms of reward and punishment may work temporarily, I guarantee you they won't work for long.

Children often have too many clothes and too many toys. Help your children keep good room order by thinning the clothes in their closet. Ask them which clothes they want to keep and which they want to give to the poor children. Do the same with their games. My son had too many puzzles with many of the pieces missing. He chose which games to keep, which needed to be thrown away, and which games were to go to the poor children. Children get a great deal of satisfaction giving their stuff to the needy, which also cultivates their maturity by developing an awareness and concern for the plight of others.

What Is the Long-Term Solution to the Messy-Room Problem?

The solution is related to the concept of *problem ownership*. If I do not own a problem, I do not have a problem. However, if I choose to own a problem, then I certainly will have one. I suggest that you do not buy, rent, or lease your kid's messy-room problem. Far too often, children intentionally keep their room untidy in order to defeat a parent who tries to control them through their words and a loud voice.

For the best solution, I suggest you simply sit down with your child, preferably at a family council meeting and, in a pleasant and calm voice say, "Now that you are old enough, I am declaring your room your personal property. I will not pick on you for how it looks. You are free to keep it any way you want. There are just two conditions that I need to share with you. First, if your room becomes infested with roaches, ants, mice, and the like, you will have to clean it up immediately, as those vermin will spread to the other parts of the house, and that is unacceptable. Second, so I do not have to see your room if it becomes messy, I may choose to put a spring or other closing device on your door to keep it closed. Is this okay with you?"

Once an agreement has been made between the parent and child, it will be up to the parent to keep his or her word as the parent is the most likely one to break it.

I cannot recall a parent actually finding her child's room to be vermin infested although I have known parents to use this charge as an excuse to break their word when their child's room became messier than their level of comfort.

Wash day is often seen as a problem. Some mothers have solved this problem by telling their child that they will wash only those clothes that are in the dirty clothes hamper. Should the route to the hamper be blocked, I suggest Mother tell her child that she will wash and fold any clothes placed outside the bedroom door in a laundry basket. If the child misses wash day, the parent has two choices. She can let her child know that she will again do washing next week, or she can teach her child to do his own wash. Six—and seven-year-olds are quite capable of learning how to do a light/dark clothes separation, measuring soap, and programming the washing machine and dryer.

Some parents have asked what to do when two children of about the same age share a room. One suggestion is to allow the children to divide their room in half and mark the division with masking tape. Then let them settle any problems without your interference. Parents who try to settle their children's disputes perpetuate the problem. Have faith in the "weakest" child as he or she may be stronger than you suspect. If you need an alternative suggestion on how to best divide the room, ask the children at the next family council meeting. They will have answers that may be helpful.

On house-cleaning day, a parent may want to ask the child if she wants any help in cleaning her room. If the child accepts, the parent may offer help, but should never end up cleaning the room himself or herself. Remember, it's her room. If the room is messy beyond the child's capability, the parent may have to help more than usual. However, the parent should offer services in the form of a room-cleaning lesson while never relieving the child of her responsibility.

A psychologist friend of mine who had learned to ignore her teen son's messiness told me the following story.

> As Matt's messy room was his major fault, I considered myself a successful parent. My husband and I kept Matt's door closed so that we would not have to view how he chose to live. One day Matt came to us and said, "I want a smaller bed and a larger desk so I can make my room into a real pad." We went shopping and got Matt what he wanted. Soon his room became orderly, and he seemed to have gained a real pride of ownership. Thereafter, his room was never dirty or messy. As a parent, I'm still amazed at what happened.

To Summarize

When parents give their child his or her own room, the room and its appearance belong to the child, and its visual condition should not be a concern of the parents. If one gives something away, it is not one's to take back. I advise parents, for family peace and harmony, to get off of the clean room kick and focus their attention on more important life issues such as teaching the child how to make a contribution to the family as a whole.

Keeping one's room clean is not a household chore, but a personal duty to one's self. If parents are uncomfortable looking at a messy room, take the intelligent way out. Keep the child's door shut by attaching a closing device or an inexpensive but strong spring. It will be the best home improvement project you will accomplish all week.

Notes

BEDTIME MADE EASY

Bedtime can be a breeze, or it can be a tornado. By this I mean that parents can accomplish this final task of the day with ease, or they can choose to do it with a great deal of frustration, yelling, and angry words. The choice of how the day ends is completely up to parents, and obtaining a positive bedtime solution is not rocket science.

Recently, a mother who is rather new to our Family Education Training Center of Hawai'i program sent me the following e-mail desperation-gram.

> Dear Dr. Jim:
>
> We are really struggling with bedtime. You might remember, we have a boy, aged three, and a girl, aged five, who share a room. If we ignore them, they get wild, get loud, get out of bed and stay up 'til 10 PM. If we police them, they go to bed faster, but it is a hassle and often leads to a power struggle and open defiance. My husband is concerned that if we do nothing, we send the signal that there is no consequence for not following the rules (stay in bed, stay quiet). What do we do? It seems neither method is really working for us. Thanks for the advice.
>
> Carolynn

✐✐✐✐✐✐✐✐✐✐✐✐✐✐✐✐✐✐✐✐✐✐✐✐✐

The following was my reply.

Dear Carolynn,

Congratulations to you and your husband. You have discovered what so many parents of healthy, active children throughout the years have learned. No matter how determined or forceful you both may get, you cannot *make* a child go to sleep. Sleep is a process of the brain which cannot be forced by an outsider. Literally speaking, like hunger, it is an inside job. Many unproven remedies to get children to go quickly to sleep have been suggested to frustrated parents. Many look like commonsense solutions, and some even may be worth a second look. No sugar in any form after 5:00 PM, no horseplay with parents for one hour prior to bedtime, no exciting or scary TV shows prior to going to bed, warm milk, a warm bath, going to the toilet one last time, all prior to lights out, so forth and so on.

Someone in your family—guess who?—has taught your children that by acting up at bedtime they can get lots of attention.[1] Working moms and single parents often find that their children strive extra hard for attention whenever they think they can get it. Bedtime is one such opportunity. Children of stay-at-home mothers also are prone to bedtime frivolity, particularly if the children feel they are not getting enough individual attention during mommies' day.

What's a Parent to Do?

Let me offer you a simple, commonsense Adlerian answer that has worked for parents over the years. No more "bedtime"! Instead, have "room time." Room time has only one basic rule. Children must stay in their room. I have found that when parents switch from bedtime to room time, the children enjoy their newfound independence so much they become cooperative. Here is a step-by-step method that I want you to follow.

At your next family council meeting,[2] tell your children what you are planning to do.

"Now that you both are old enough, I would like for you to have room time instead of bedtime. What do you think about this? At 7:30 PM you will get ready for bed in the usual manner. At eight o'clock you will go to your bedroom, but you do not have to go to bed or go to sleep. You can stay up as late as you want. However, you must stay in your room and keep the noise down: no radio, TV, playing musical instruments, or electronic games. You may draw pictures with the paper and crayons I will give you or do anything else that you want to do. Your lights can be left on if you want. You may leave your door open or closed, the choice is yours. But remember, you must stay in your room. Every morning we will get up at our regular time. Now please tell me what you think of what I have just said."

If one of your kids wants to go to the toilet, let the child go by himself or herself as long as they immediately return to the room. If you find that a child leaves the room in order to wander the house, without saying a word and with kindness, take the child gently by the wrist and walk him or her back to the bedroom.[3] If the child again leaves the room, you should seat yourself close to the door and each time walk the child back to the room, always without saying a word. If one or both children make noise of any sort, ignore it. The noise is for your benefit so as to get your attention and involvement. Remember, your training must be done in silence and without any display of annoyance or anger; otherwise your behavior will become a reinforcement of the very behavior you are trying to extinguish.

Painter and Corsini[4] and Dreikurs and Soltz[5] offer excellent alternative solutions to the stress of bedtime. I strongly advise all parents, including you and your husband, regularly to have "individual special time."[6] Building a meaningful and trusting relationship with your children is the key to a lifetime of family cooperation and happiness.

Dr. Jim

Endnotes

1.   Read "How Parents Train Children without Knowing It."
2.   Read "The Family Council."

   I suggest that parents also read the following book if they can find it. *Family Council: The Dreikurs Techniques for Putting an End to War Between Parents and Children (and Between Children and Children)* by Dreikurs, Gould, and Corsini.

   See chapter 33 in Painter and Corsini, *Effective Discipline in the Home and School.*

   See Rigney and Corsini, *The Family Council.*
3.   Read: "The Art of the Wrist."
4.   Painter and Corsini, *Effective Discipline*, chapter 13.
5.   Dreikurs and Soltz, *Children: The Challenge,* pp. 155-58.
6.   Read "The Gift of Individual Special Time."

Notes

THE ART OF THE WRIST:
CONVEYING PARENTAL AUTHORITY
THROUGH TOUCH

Recently, I was spending a morning sharing Adlerian parenting principles and strategies with a mothers' study group. Through the efforts and zeal of a mother who had attended our Family Education Training Center, these young mothers had been exposed to Adlerian psychology through the works of Rudolf Dreikurs[1] and Painter and Corsini.[2] The group's enthusiasm and openness was delightfully contagious.

While talking about the issue of "room time—not bedtime,"[3] the subject of returning a roaming child to his room arose. "How can I do this without it ending in a power contest?" one mother asked.

I explained to her that prior to using any consequence, it first should be discussed at a family meeting.[4] A consequence "requires an understanding, preferably expressed or implied, between a parent and the child as to what is expected from the child and what is to happen if the child does not perform as expected or misbehaves."[5] I have found when consequences are discussed at family meetings and the children willingly agree, when a consequence is applied, the children usually go along with their agreements. When the parent applies the consequence, such as walking the child back to his room, it should be done in silence and without negative body language. Mother talking to little Johnny, whether her words or tone of voice be positive or negative, is giving him the undue attention he wants. If Mother shows her annoyed or angry feelings by stomping or other body language, little Johnny will perceive her behavior as a positive reinforcement for future misbehaviors.

"But what do I do?" another mother questioned, "Take him by the ear and hope the rest of his body calmly follows?" At that point, I realized that a demonstration was in order. Standing up, I asked the nearest mom if I could demonstrate on her; she agreed.

Instinctively, I gently but firmly took her by the wrist and tucked her forearm and elbow between my forearm and elbow and my body. Focusing my mental energy on lightly guiding her wrist, I walked her around the room. She yielded to my nonverbal parental authority without resistance or a struggle.

"What did that feel like?" another mother asked my subject. She explained as follows. "When Dr. Jim took me by the wrist, it was different than if he would have taken me by the hand. Hand-holding is cooperative, it's fun, and it's like skipping down the street with my five-year-old. His hand holding my wrist was firm, it didn't hurt, but it said to me, 'I am the parent, I have authority, and you will come with me.'"

Sometimes a parent cannot tuck the child's forearm near hers. It's okay to take the child's wrist and physically move in the desired direction. Sometimes a resistant child will fall to the floor and struggle or become deadweight. Should this happen, it is best to continue with the exercise all the way to the child's room, lest the child learns to control the parent with defiant behavior or a deadweight response. Unless the child has a bone and tendon medical problem, no damage is likely to be done. Let me remind parents, again, this drill must be done in silence and without anger, otherwise it loses its power as a teaching tool.

The mother whom I chose as my subject was correct in her verbal response. Being taken firmly by the wrist offers a different feeling to the child than holding his hand. It is meant to convey that parental authority is now in action. Yet, in my opinion, it does not violate any of the tenets of Adlerian psychology. Parents will find this training technique to be most effective when it is part of the explanation given to a child when discussing the new behavioral scenarios, such as moving from bedtime to room time. A wise parent never surprises a child with a new and unexplained logical consequence as it lowers the probability of long-term success. That is why it and all parental consequences ought to be done in conjunction with a family meeting.

Endnotes

1. Dreikurs and Soltz, *Children: The Challenge.*
2. Painter and Corsini, *Effective Discipline.*
3. Read "Bedtime Made Easy."
4. Read "The Family Council"
5. Painter and Corsini, *Effective Discipline.*

Notes

THE SECOND OFFENSIVE:
OR
"WHY IS SHE DOING THAT AGAIN?"

Just when you thought you had corrected your daughter's annoying behavior, *bam*, it starts all over again. "What the heck is going on?" you ask yourself. "I did exactly as Dr. Jim told me, and sure enough, she stopped doing it. And now, it's come back. What happened? Where did I go wrong?"

The odds are you did nothing wrong. What happened is what my mentor, Dr. Genevieve Painter, referred to as "the second offensive." Children do not give up easily on behaviors that once got them a handsome payoff. In a way, they say to themselves, "It worked once, maybe it will work again. I think I will give it a try and see what happens."

What your child doesn't realize is that you have become smarter than the average parent. You know exactly what to do to counter her second offensive. Your first thought is to go back to what you did to extinguish the behavior the first time. Once you clearly remember what you did or did not do, you repeat that behavior. Trust me; if it worked well once, it will work well for you again.

Here are two examples. You "cured" little Susan from dawdling and playing with her food at the dinner meal by silently removing her plate a few minutes after the meal was over.[1] Do it again! Use the same technique with the same spirit, silence, and elegance.

Three-year-old Karla used to come out of her room every evening and prowl the house, looking to keep you busy with her. You took care of the problem by gently and firmly taking her by the wrist and, without a word, escorting her back to her room.[2] Your consequence worked then; it will work now. Karla is doing nothing more than being a normal three-year-old on the prowl for undue attention. That's what three-year-olds do.

I have been asked about a third or fourth offensive. My advice is to treat any recurring offensive as though it was a second offensive.

Parents, take heart,
your children are smart,
just don't let them outsmart you.
When they do it again,
calmly whisper, "Amen,"
and do what you know you must do.

Endnotes

1.   Read "Eating Should Be the Child's Business."
2.   Read "Bedtime Made Easy" and "The Art of the Wrist."

Notes

TEACHING COOPERATION TO
PARENT-DEAF CHILDREN:
TAKE TIME FOR TRAINING

On a beautiful Father's Day weekend, FETCH went to camp. Forty-five parents and their children, university student-volunteer counselors, and FETCH professionals spent three days having fun at Camp Erdman on the beautiful and pristine North Shore of Oahu, Hawai'i. It was an experience to remember.

The focus of our summer program is on family strengthening. At camp, parents are in charge of their children, not the staff. As the senior counselor at FETCH, one of my duties is to observe and make mental notes of parent-child interactions. My ability to be an "on the mark" consultant is always enhanced when I observe family interactions firsthand. These observations also add relevance to our FETCH Friday night counseling sessions.

While the examples and solutions described in this paper are focused on children aged eight and under, parents of older children may find the information very useful.

We parents are creatures of habit, whether at home or elsewhere. Once we begin treating our children in a certain way, we continue the pattern, even when it doesn't work. We frustrate and overwhelm ourselves by trying to control our children by being inconsistent with warnings, threats, nagging, random punishment, too much talk, and without a scrap of sturdy follow-up action. We often say to ourselves, "This is the way my parents treated me, so it must be right." Or, "All I have to do to make it work is do it harder." Many parents' behaviors also seem to say, "If I yell enough times, maybe the kids will finally catch on." I have no doubt there are probably as many reasons for parental behaviors as there were people who parented us.

I have concluded that most misbehaving children under age 8 have only a few patterns of misbehavior. The cure to rid these annoying "I'm going to keep you busy with me" and "I do what I want" behaviors is quite simple—if only parents would consistently carry out what Adlerian psychology teaches. Here are some of my observations from our camping experience.

Mr. Castle loves his two boys, Tony, aged seven, and Tom, aged five. However, he talks too much, makes needless threats, and does not follow through on his words. Consequently, both of his boys have become "father deaf." While on a camp nature hike, the group was exploring an ancient Hawai'ian habitat located high on a cliff overlooking a North Shore valley. The guide gave orders to keep away from the edge as the ground could give way. Soon, Tony and Tom were near the dangerous edge. "Get away from the edge," Father told the boys. Tony and Tom did not budge. Mr. Castle did nothing. Soon the boys moved closer to the rim. "It's dangerous near the edge," he again warned. The boys continued to ignore him. Mr. Castle allowed himself to be dismissed. A few minutes later, I heard a now angry father threatening one of his boys, "If you do that again, I am not going to bring you to camp next year." Throughout the nature hike, the boys continued to ignore their father's words, without any follow-up on his part. Father has trained his sons to ignore him and to be father deaf.

Mr. Yamane also has taught his two boys, Leo, aged eight, and Tad, aged six, to be father deaf. While watching our talented FETCH counselors perform musically, the two boys became fidgety. Soon they were wrestling on the floor. "Stop that," Mr. Yamane whispered loudly. The boys continued their annoying play fighting. "If you don't stop now, I'm going to put you to bed." Nothing changed. Finally, the older boy decided to do something else and began crawling around the floor. The younger brother rolled over and sat quietly, then attentively began listening to the music. After a while, Mr. Yamane rose from his chair, grabbed the younger child who was behaving appropriately, and marched him out of the room, leaving the older boy crawling annoyingly in front of everyone.

Mrs. Townie is the mother of four-year-old fraternal twin girls. During an evening slide presentation, one of the twins, Lisa, decided to run back and forth across the room. When Mother said nothing, Lisa added a loud voice to her antics. Mrs. Townie responded to the misbehavior with dirty looks that only served to heighten the girl's volume. Finally, Mother got up, chased Lisa down, and made threats. "We're not coming back to camp next year if you do that again," she scowled while marching Lisa back to their seats. A few minutes later, Lisa was running and screaming again.

There are several principles that help us understand why children behave as they do. Knowing these principles and their application helps us effectively intervene and correct our children's misguided behaviors.[1]

All children want to belong to the family with significance. Cooperation should be their goal as it will get them the belonging and significance they want. However, through a system of trial and error, mishaps, and inconsistent parenting techniques, children come to believe that they belong with significance only if they are behaving in one of four misguided or useless ways: seeking *undue attention*, inappropriate *power*, *revenge*, and assumed *inadequacy*.

Children, up to the age of about eight, when manifesting a misguided goal, usually will use undue attention or power. Rarely is revenge or inadequacy in evidence. Undue attention is portrayed by a child wanting to keep everyone busy with him or her, requesting special services, clowning, or otherwise being a nuisance. Power is seen when a child is openly defiant, significantly resistant, or when he or she will not do what is asked. Older children who are significantly more discouraged will manifest either revenge or display inadequacy. Revenge is a hurting back behavior that may be vicious, violent, or destructive. It often includes violent sibling rivalry and bullying others at school. Revenge includes delinquent and illegal activities. A child displaying inadequacy is a child who is so discouraged he no longer hopes to find significance in any productive way. He may assume the role of the helpless baby or incapable child.

What's a Parent to Do? What Are Some Good Solutions? The Castles

Tony and Tom Castle have been taught to ignore their father. Their father deafness began long before they came to FETCH camp. They have come to realize that their dad is a lot of talk, some threats, no consistency, and a man who can be counted on not to follow through on discipline. They have little respect for him. Mr. Castle is responsible for not sending clear messages to his sons. Perhaps Mrs. Castle plays a significant role in this family's substandard communication, in that a spouse who does not support a partner's efforts contributes royally to family dysfunction.

Mr. Castle must stop talking so much, quit making empty threats, and follow through on his words. He needs to deliver clear messages and be consistent in order to be seen by his boys as credible. For a long-term solution, specifically, here is what he should do.

1. Think through his plans on what changes he is going to make with himself and his children.
2. Discuss his plans with his wife; get her buy-in and cooperation.
3. Call a family meeting where every member will be present.
4. At the family meeting, he should tell his boys what he is going to do, using a calm and kind tone of voice. For example:

> Boys, I find that I have been doing a lot of yelling, and I don't like myself when I do that. How about from now on, I tell you just once what I am going to do. For instance, if we are eating at Queen Burger and you decide to make a scene, how about if we just go home. What do you think of what I have just said?

A discussion with the boys needs to be encouraged. Father, and Mother, should do more listening than talking. Both parents should answer the boys' questions, but be brief. It is best if the parents and children came to agreements on what the consequences for certain misbehaviors will be. The entire interaction needs to be done in a friendly, cooperative, respectful, and unemotional manner.

Right after the restaurant discussion, Father might want to discuss another challenging situation, such as a family outing to the beach.

> When we go to the beach, we like to have fun. I like it when we throw the football around. I am very proud to have two athletic boys. However, we need to remember that there are families there who also like to have fun. When you deliberately run through their picnic area, kick up sand, or deliberately annoy other people, what do you say that we immediately leave and go home? What do you think of what I just said?

As before, Father should allow, for respectful discussion, listening liberally, speaking sparingly, and answering the boy's questions briefly. In both the restaurant and beach examples, Father's goal is to gain both boys' agreement by being reasonable in his expectations and consequence. Trying to make the boys agree will not work.

I strongly suggest that the entire family go on one of the two discussed outings that day. For example, if the family goes to the restaurant and the boys do well, Father should reinforce their behavior by saying something encouraging like "I enjoyed being with my two boys today, you were such gentlemen." If one or both of the boys begin misbehaving, the family must immediately leave the restaurant and go home. This must be done in silence and without angry body language. Words and body language are payoffs to children and will reinforce misbehaviors. If the boys resist leaving, in silence, use "the art of the wrist" technique[2] while removing them to the family vehicle. The above suggestions hold true for behaviors at the beach. If the children do well, encourage their useful behaviors by focusing on the deed, not the child: "I like the way you helped me, I am very proud of your behavior." If one or more of the children misbehave, as a logical consequence, in silence, immediately remove them from the beach and go home. As a rule of thumb, put all the children "in the same boat." A parent rarely can be sure which child is the perpetrator of misbehaviors.

In the situation of Tony and Tom deliberately going too close to the edge, it would have been best if Mr. Castle would have calmly and silently removed the boys by their wrists and taken them to the level below. If Father could manage only one boy at a time due to the difficult terrain, he should choose first the older boy as the younger son most likely would follow on his own volition.

Mr. Yamane

In the case of Mr. Yamane, the same long-term training principles presented above apply. Tell the children what you are going to do, followed by a brief discussion for clarification and reinforcement. As soon as possible, put your plan into action and follow through with consistent behavior. Long-term credibility is the goal.

When the Yamane boys began wrestling during the musical performance, Mr. Yamane talked too much, threatened without an immediate follow-up, and in the end, removed the nearest, but by that time, the wrong child. Removing the fighting boys should have been done the moment their bodies hit the floor. Removal is best done in silence and without acting angry or frustrated.

Mrs. Townie

In the case of Mrs. Townie and twin Lisa, Mother would have been more effective if she would have retrieved Lisa by the wrist, in silence and without showing anger. If Lisa runs again, the above retrieval method must be repeated. Mother must be sure not to make her retrieval a fun-and-games situation.[3]

At another time and place, Mrs. Townie needs to use the long-term training principle of telling the child what she is going to do, followed by a brief family discussion for clarification, agreement, and reinforcement. Mrs. Townie needs to develop credibility in the eyes of her girls.

In Summary

Your children want to belong to the family with significance. The problem comes when children choose behaviors that are other than cooperative. Most children under the age of eight select forms of *undue attention* (I'm going to keep you busy with me) or *power* (I'm the boss, and I do what I want) when they misbehave. Only a few children this age choose the more serious misguided goals of *revenge* or *inadequacy.* Unfortunately, the way parents correct their children's misbehavior is usually off the mark and does not change even when they come to realize that it isn't working. The usual parent errors are excessive talking, empty threats, inconsistent parenting behaviors, and no follow-through actions. The corrections suggested in this chapter must be done in silence or, when speaking is necessary, in a calm and soft voice, without any signs of anger. Moms and dads need to realize that they must *take time for training* and be *consistent* in their parenting behaviors. Parents need to be viewed by their children as *credible* in order to get the cooperation they want.

Endnotes

1 Read "Why Do Children Misbehave?"
   Read "How Parents Train Children Without Knowing It."

2 Read "The Art of the Wrist: Conveying Parental Authority through Touch."

3 The reader will note that one twin has chosen to belong to the family with significance by pursuing the cooperative role while the other, Lisa, has chosen the misbehaving role. Often, the "good" child and the "bad" child become trapped in their respective roles. This is an unhealthy situation as neither child has an opportunity to learn new roles.

Notes

ADAM AND EVE:
THE FIRST DYSFUNCTIONAL FAMILY

The other day while preparing a lecture on the subject of sibling rivalry, questions began hitting me like a biblical stoning. Were Adam and Eve responsible parents, or did they create the world's first dysfunctional family? What caused Cain to murder Abel, his younger and only sibling? What was it in the child-rearing process that caused this tragedy? Was sibling rivalry a chronic problem in this household? Is a struggle between siblings inevitable? What are the implications of this story for modern families?

Since I was not present those thousands of years ago, I can only look at biblical, historical evidence, ask questions, make assumptions, use logic, and apply Adlerian principles before coming to conclusions. With due respect to all biblical scholars, past, present, and future, the following is my interpretation of the *sibling rivalry* issues embedded in the family history of Adam and Eve.[1] Simply put, this paper is an analysis about a well-known family whose ways of interacting led to an intensive sibling rivalry that ended up as a high-profile murder. By examining what happened, my hope is that modern families will work to promote family and sibling harmony and avoid needless similar tragedies.

A Social History

To understand better the dynamics of this family and the roots of their sons' intensive sibling rivalry, a family social history, with commentary, is offered.

Adam, born an adult, lacked real-life experiences in interpersonal and family relationships. He knew not the joy of being nurtured by a warm and caring mother, nor the experience of feeling the supportive strength of a loving, supportive, and encouraging dad. Adam also was void of all childhood family experiences that could have served to help him understand and deal with sibling rivalry and help each son to find his significant place in the family. Adam's experiences with women were limited, and he had no role model to show him how to deal with the challenges of marriage.

Characterlogically, Adam, the man, was flawed. He was less than truthful when it came to accepting responsibility for his own decisions and behavior. For example, in the Garden of Eden when the Lord questioned him, Adam replied, "The woman You put at my side—she gave me of the tree, and I ate."[2] Truly, Adam was not the man, husband, and father that he could have been. It appears that Adam was naive about life and did not know how to be supportive and encouraging. Like so many of his descendents, Adam's marital and parental style was authoritarian, perhaps even dictatorial.

Eve, also born an adult, had similar problems. She had no childhood experiences to help her learn what healthy family life was like. She was unable to understand the meaning of encouragement and its art of separating the deed from the doer. She had no role models to help her understand how to rear children. Eve accepted Adam's authoritarian ways, and as a discouraged wife, she was ineffective at helping her two energetic boys with their sibling rivalry.

Cain and Abel probably were born close in time. Cain, as many firstborn sons, identified with his father and became a "tiller of the soil." Abel chose to make his contribution to the family by becoming a "keeper of sheep." Based upon results, sibling rivalry between the brothers must have been a chronic problem. Sibling rivalry does not have to be overt in order to exist, and quiet and subtle pathology also is dangerous.

Discussion of Family Dynamics

Authoritarian leaders, such as Adam, do not lead by consensus; they lead through power, fiat, and intimidation. As parents, they ignore consensus, that is, a buy-in by all family members. Their children have no voice. Authoritarian parents use reward and punishment as consequences, and they use praise instead of encouragement. Children reared under these circumstances crave external approval. They lack an internal reward system and the courage and self-esteem that come with the internal satisfaction of knowing that they did their best and made a significant contribution to the family's welfare.

Women who marry authoritarian men, even while acting submissively, often harbor a deep-seated, unspoken rage against their husbands. They often seek revenge by sabotaging his efforts. In the case of Eve, one has to wonder if eating the apple was her way at getting back at an authoritarian, controlling Adam. Eve also had a personality problem. She had difficulty accepting personal responsibility for her actions. As she said in response to the Lord, it wasn't her fault. "The serpent duped me, and I ate."[3] Could it be that as a couple, Adam and Eve had little to offer each other and their children in the way of a strong, nurturing, and healthy family life?

Children, like Cain and Abel, often obey their authoritarian parents until they are strong enough to rebel. They rarely respect rules thrust upon them, and they resent not being allowed a voice or an opportunity to have a say in family matters. Children from authoritarian-dominated families often find themselves enmeshed in intensive sibling rivalry.

Birth Order and Sibling Rivalry

In the following discussion, the dynamics between the first—and second-born child are discussed. When both children are boys, the intensity of the rivalry may become very pronounced.

Children in the same family are different from each other and see all the circumstances and happenings of their life differently. While most parents want to believe that they treat all their children alike, in reality, parents never treat two children the same. There may be differences in the affection parents hold for each child, as well as in their opinions about each. The eldest child is a novelty in the new family. For a limited time, he is king baby, the center of his parents' attention and the only object of their care. He may be spoiled with unlimited attention and his every move noted and recorded. Having little experience and great expectations of their firstborn, these parents may subject their child to greater scrutiny, demand, correction, criticism, and spoiling.[4]

Suddenly, after the birth of a second child, the first child experiences a great change in the family's routine; things are different.

> A brother or sister is thrust upon him. Even if the first child is already a few years old he is hardly ever able to gauge the situation correctly. He notices only that another child now monopolizes his parents, especially the mother, who devotes herself to him, and lavishes any amount of time and care on him. He readily believes that the newcomer will rob him of her love . . . . Feeling that he has been set aside, the eldest child frequently shows understandable jealousy when another child is born, even if before the birth of this child he longed for a brother or sister.[5]

In a mature and insightful family, the parents will make known to the eldest child his undiminished value and his importance to the family group as the more advanced child. His cooperation in helping his parents to care for the younger baby will be elicited and encouraged. By using this strategy, parents find that children will adapt to the new situation with relative ease.

However, many parents, especially those who are authoritarian or dictatorial in their parenting methods, may not understand or even care what is going on in the older child's mind. They may punish him for what they label as unfounded jealousies and misbehaviors.

Rudolf Dreikurs has pointed out that even in the most favorable circumstances, two siblings who grow up together and seem to live in harmony may become intensely involved in a competition, which, though not always openly declared, is nonetheless deadly. The oldest child, unless early on defeated, will always try to keep his superior position as the eldest and most advanced child. The older the second child becomes, the more worried about being overtaken the first child feels. A determined younger sibling enjoys the chase and deliberately dogs the heels of his older sibling. This is true, even if the younger sibling chooses a different talent to become significant. The older child regards anything and everything the younger child can do better than he as a sign of his own inferiority.[6]

The Murder

According to biblical history,[7] both Cain and Abel brought their best work offerings to the Lord. The Lord examined the offerings, and in doing so, he paid close attention to Abel's offering but ignored the offering of Cain. Cain did not receive from the Lord the payoff of attention and adoration he craved and thought he rightly deserved. This rejection so discouraged Cain that he felt it to the very foundation of his being. Seeing his pain, the Lord then asked Cain about his feelings. "Why are you distressed, and why is your face fallen?"[8] Cain did not have a chance to answer before the Lord continued, "Surely, if you do right, there is uplift. But if you do not do right sin couches at the door: its urge is toward you, yet you can be its master."[9] The Lord's words that internal rewards are preferable to external rewards did not have an enlightening or transforming effect on Cain. Soon thereafter, a discouraged Cain invited Abel to the fields where he murdered him in cold blood.[10]

Why did Cain kill Abel? In my opinion, Cain killed Abel because Adam and Eve were ineffective in helping Cain to deal with his jealousy in a healthy and constructive manner. Cain's parents did not train him to take responsibility for his own feelings and behaviors. They did not teach their eldest son that the locus of responsibility for all actions comes from within, not from without; the greatest satisfaction for achievement is internal, not external.

Dreikurs makes an observation about parents who are impatient or punitive toward their older child's jealousies. "If, as is most probable, they then take the younger child under their protection in order to defend him against the elder child's overbearing conduct, the elder child may easily give up trying to win good opinions by making himself useful, as he probably could do, but become obstinate and try to take up his parents' attention by resorting to every possible trick that naughtiness can suggest to him," even murder.[11] It becomes obvious then that children who grow up with reward and punishment as their motivational force have a difficult time internalizing any excellence in their achievements. They have been trained to need others to give them a payoff of attention for their accomplishments. For Cain, only external rewards and adorations from on high had great value.

A closer examination of Cain's behavior reveals that he had a personality flaw similar to that of his parents. He was unwilling to accept the responsibility for his own decisions and behaviors. When questioned by the Lord as to the whereabouts of his brother Abel, he replied, "I do not know, am I my brother's keeper?"[12] Even after being caught in a lie by the Lord, Cain was not remorseful for his behavior. His greatest worry was that he would be harmed by others for the sin he committed against his brother. This egocentric, immature, and fearful behavior was the consequence of being reared in an authoritarian household. Cain did not realize that in all situations he had a choice in how he thinks, feels, and behaves and that angry impulses are under his control and use. Knowing that his offering was the best he could do and that it was his contribution to the welfare of the family should have been enough.

A Contemporary Lesson to Be Learned

Are the roots of what happened to this family still happening in today's society? Are parents today still as inept at dealing with sibling rivalry as were Adam and Eve? For far too many parents, the answer is yes. Many parents still practice an authoritarian style of parenting, commanding, using rewards and punishment as well as praise. These methods teach children that only power and external payoff count; rewards are to be expected, even demanded.

Effective parenting follows the democratic way of child rearing where each child has a voice in family matters, and encouragement is a way of family life. Many people, even so-called experts, confuse democratic parenting with permissive parenting. Democratic parenting is not permissive, because a child having his say does not mean he will get his way. In democratic parenting, parents are expected to practice leadership and keep order in a functioning family. Parent-child channels of communication are kept positive and open, and communication roadblocks such as yelling, preaching, threatening, and ordering are avoided. Adlerians believe that talking should be for communication, not for punishment. Natural and logical consequences, as a correction method, work better than punishment without imposing pain and discomfort on the child.[13] Respecting a child teaches that child respect of self and others.

After a half century of clinical practice and parenting, I have concluded that sibling rivalry is a given, even in the most encouraging and harmonious families. However, of importance is not the presence of sibling rivalry, but the degree to which it exists. Children do not have to fight. However, when they do, they are gaining satisfaction from the encounter, not so much in the fight as from the results. In the usual family, the bottom line is that children fight for the misguided goal of their parents' attention and to keep Mom and Dad busy with them.

If sibling fighting has escalated to a level where parents say in jest that they are ready to give their children away if only someone would take them or has reached a level where parents are seriously worried about one child physically harming another, be assured that the parents are doing something wrong.

I suggest three fixes that are available to all parents who are willing to grow and do things differently.

First, keep out of your children's arguments. Becoming involved only increases the probability of it happening again.

Second, give each child the gift of individual special time. Regularly schedule ten minutes a day to play with each child individually.[14]

Third, start a family council[15] and stay with it religiously.

Couples wanting at least two children should ask the following question as a prophylaxis strategy. "What should we do when a second child comes along?" Dreikurs suggests the solution. "If a mother can make the elder child aware of his undiminished value by pointing out to him his importance as the elder and therefore more advanced child, and so enlist his will to cooperate, he will adapt himself to the new situation with comparative ease."[16]

In Summary

With due respect to biblical scholars, in this essay, we looked at the biblical history of the Adam and Eve's family. We found that Adam and Eve had no experience with family relationships or child rearing. Their relationship was hierarchical with Adam the superior and Eve the inferior. Both Adam and Eve had characterlogical problems; neither was willing to take responsibility for their own misguided behaviors.

Adam ruled his family in an authoritarian and perhaps dictatorial manner. Based upon results, it appears that Adam and Eve disregarded Cain's feelings and used reward and punishment as well as praise to control both children. Such children learn to respond to the world by believing that only external payoffs are acceptable and that doing one's best and contributing to the welfare of the family is not good enough. Thus, when the Lord ignored Cain's offering but paid close attention to Abel's, even though he had done his best, Cain saw himself as the loser. Again, the discouragement of perceived failure drove Cain to rage and then to murder.

Unfortunately, the legacy of Cain and Abel still lives on in modern families. Parents need to be more respectful of their children's feelings, give them a voice, and be generous with their time and encouragement. Three basic ideas on how to deal with sibling rivalry are suggested, including helping the displaced first child to feel he belongs to the family with significance.

The answer to the question, "Why do siblings fight?" is deceptively simple. While children do have disagreements, the bottom line is that they fight for their parents' attention and to keep their parents busy with them. Children who chronically fight are discouraged and believe fighting is the way to belong to the family with significance.

What should parents do when children fight? Parents should keep out of their kid's squabbles. Parents rarely know who actually started the fight; the innocent-looking child is not always the victim. When parents interfere, they reinforce each child's self-concept of his mistaken opinion of his own value. Rather than teaching the children to stop fighting, parents end up showing children how profitable fighting can be. Parents who rule their families as authoritarians and those moms and dads who try to referee and settle their children's fights inadvertently may be setting up a Cain-and-Abel situation in their own home.

Endnotes

1   All biblical references and quotations are from *The Torah: The Five Books of Moses.*

Much background thought for this essay was gathered from Plaut, *Torah.*

2   Genesis 3:12

3   Genesis 3:13

4   Dreikurs, *Fundamentals of Adlerian Psychology*, see "The Family Constellation," pp. 37-42.

Providing background thought and material: Dreikurs and Soltz, *Children: The Challenge.*

5   Dreikurs, *Fundamentals of Adlerian Psychology*, pp. 37-38.

6   Ibid., pp. 37-42.

7   Genesis 4:1-5

8   Genesis 4:6

9   Genesis 4:7

10 Genesis 4:8

11 Dreikurs, *Fundamentals of Adlerian Psychology*, p. 38.

12 Genesis 4:9

13 Painter and Corsini, *Effective Discipline.*

14 Read "The Gift of Individual Special Time."

15 I strongly suggest that parents read the following book if they can obtain it. Dreikurs, Gould, and Corsini, *Family Council: The Dreikurs Techniques.*

If not available, read chapter 33, "The Family Council," in Painter and Corsini, *Effective Discipline.*

Rigney and Corsini, *The Family Council.*

Read "The Family Council."

16 Dreikurs, *Fundamentals of Adlerian Psychology*, p. 38.

Notes

SECTION V.
Unique Solutions to Unique Problems

CREATE ORDER:
MAKE A FAMILY DAILY SCHEDULE

Is your family chaotic? In the morning, do your children seem not to know what happens next? Do family members fight over the use of the bathroom? Is breakfast often missed because people are late? Do you have trouble getting the kids off to school in the morning, or are you too often late for work? Is suppertime a mess with members eating at all times of the evening? Is getting the kids to bed a major hassle? Do you often wish you could find a way to stop nagging and reminding? At the end of the day, do you feel exhausted as if you had run around in circles all day long? If any of these situations are yours, your problem may be as simple as *a need for a family daily schedule to create order.*

Having a schedule of daily events brings order and respect to a family. For any family, it moves them from the frustration of chaos to the calm of order. Children need to know what is to happen next in order to feel safe. For them, order is calming while chaos brings out feelings of anxiety and moments of hyperactivity and disrespect.

Parents too need a schedule of order. Parents need to know what time to get up in the morning in order to attend to the needs of the family. Working parents need a schedule of order to plan on how to arrive at work on time. A schedule helps both parents and children plan for contingencies when things don't go as planned. Order is an important function for acquiring success at home, at school, and at work.

To have a smooth-running and happy family, every member of the family must participate in the creation of a coherent family daily schedule.

This means that your children must have an input. When kids have a say, even though they may not always get their way, they become part of the creation process. Their buy-in makes them far more likely to participate in the new scheduling process.

I suggest each family develop their functional schedule at a family council meeting.[1] This formal meeting will give this event a place and time for all members to gather and participate, as well as provide them a structure for future daily schedule reviews.

At the scheduling meeting, parents must be careful not to dominate the process. I have found during family problem-solving sessions, many parents want to dominate and thus fight over who is right and who is wrong. Their real issue is to win, not to create consensus. Forcing your child to give in is humiliating and destroys the creative problem-solving process. In the discussion, parents should focus on the situation, not the people involved. They should avoid roadblocks such as put-downs, sarcasm, criticism, blaming, labeling, or ridiculing.

Listening to what your children have to say is vital to making the daily schedule work. Cooperatively creating a daily schedule can be like magic in creating a quality relationship between you and your children. It will also enhance the creative spirit within your kids.

Families need to be creative in their own process and be guided by the Adlerian principle of *respect*.

How to Create a Schedule

Step 1. The parent should own the problem. Be specific when you share your ideas.

"I have a problem, and I need your help to solve it. I don't want to live this way anymore. Our mornings are chaotic. It's as if nobody knows what to do and when to do it. We get into each other's way, and I end up yelling at you. I see my children's feelings being hurt, and this makes me feel sad. After school, supper, and bedtime are the same. We have no schedule, I see no order, and I yell more. I feel like a bad parent. We are a special family, and I want to do better."

Step 2. Invite discussion and ask for help in resolving the problem. "What do you think?"

At this point, the children will begin to brainstorm and answers will flow. A parent should write their answers down, preferably where everyone can see them. Do not evaluate the quality or practicality of each suggestion at this time. You are allowing each child to contribute to the family welfare; you are developing cooperation among family members.

Step 3. Help the children organize their ideas on a personal basis. A parent might say the following. "I have an idea. Let's each of us write our moment-by-moment schedule of what we need to do in the morning before we leave for school or work. We can use some of the ideas that we just thought of." Supply each of the children with a pencil and paper, and let them personalize their schedule. Do the same for the time after school, supper, and bedtime. The parent also needs to have the family develop a weekend schedule, which includes fun and play, not just work. If a child is not able to write, a parent or older sibling should help him or her.

Step 4. The parent needs to collect all the schedules and coordinate them to create an orderly and readable document. The plan can be as specific or general as the family needs. Some families or members need a minute-by-minute calendar while others need only a general guide. The creative parent will know what to do in the creation of the family schedule and the timing of its presentation to all. Any last-minute problems can be worked out at this or subsequent meetings. The schedule is then presented to the family for an agreement by consensus. What is important is not the creation of a perfectly ordered blueprint for lockstep behavior, but the creation of a beginning blueprint for family cooperation. The more cooperative and coordinated the family, the happier are its members.

Parents and children need to know that with the development of the family schedule, everyone becomes responsible for following their own personal to-do list. Only very young children are to get personal attention during family routines. Parents no longer are to remind, repeat, pester, badger, or nag. Should difficulties subsequently arise, these issues are to be brought up and resolved at the next family council meeting. Some parents may well benefit from further reading on the use of natural and logical consequences.[2]

Having a schedule
Will make all able
To accomplish what they need to do.
With everything done,
There's more time for fun,
Like paddling an outrigger canoe.

Endnotes

[1]   Read "The Family Council."
        Read Chapter 33, "The Family Council," in *Effective Discipline*.
        Rigney and Corsini, *The Family Council*.
        Dreikurs, et al. *Family Counsel: The Dreikurs Techniques*.
[2]   Painter and Corsini, *Effective Discipline*, pp. 27-33.

Notes

THE FROG PRINCESS

Once upon a time in the Kingdom of Wish, a beautiful girl was born to a yuppie knight and his loving royal wife. They had many dreams for their young child. They longed for the day when they could play tickle on the royal floor, hear their baby's joyous laughter, watch her chase a magical glass ball, share loving hugs, take her to the castle preschool, and then one day wave good-bye to her at the front door of the royal kindergarten. Their dream was to have the perfect child, a princess who they could brag was far and away above average.

As the princess grew, her royal parents noticed that there was something wrong. Each day their beautiful princess looked and acted more and more like a frog. She often ignored her parents when they all played on the royal floor. It was as though she lived in a land of her own. There was no joyous laughter, only annoying and sometimes angry screams. She chased the magical glass ball only when she wanted, and often she would hurl it at her parents in an angry manner. There were no loving hugs shared between parents and child, only heated, insensitive, and hurtful behaviors. The young princess ran around the castle like she was training to become the king's royal runner. She seemed to treat her parents like they did not belong in her life; she acted detached and indifferent. By the time the princess entered the castle preschool, her teachers reported that she was acting much like a frog. Later, at the royal kindergarten, her teachers sadly reported that the princess truly had taken the form of a frog. How sad the knight and his loving royal wife felt. Their beautiful baby princess had become an ugly frog.

The knight and his wife brought their frog princess to the royal physician. He examined the child thoroughly and diagnosed that the child must have been hexed by a mean and vengeful ogre. There was nothing he could do but give her toxic potions from his royal garden. And in any case, they should take the frog princess home and take good care of her.

The royal couple felt depressed, and sadness covered the land. What could they do? Could they trade the frog princess in on a better model? Should they have another child to replace this faulty one? Could they purchase a real princess from another kingdom to replace their frog? What could they do? Then like magic from the universe, the couple heard about a wise wizard from the Kingdom of Fetch. Could the wise wizard turn their frog back into a princess?

The knight, his royal wife, and the frog princess soon found themselves at the entrance to the cave of the wise wizard. He was an old man, with a long white beard and flowing white hair. He wore a tall hat as wizards do and a traditional wise-wizard robe embroidered with scenes of stars and moons and flashes of shooting white light.

"I was expecting you," the wise wizard said. "Come in and learn." The knight and his royal wife told their story, and the wise wizard agreed to examine their child. Soon the wise wizard and the frog princess emerged from the examination room. "Can you save our princess from the spell of the mean and vengeful ogre?" the parents asked. The wise wizard, stroking his long white beard looked at the couple for a few moments and then spoke.

> You have been thinking about trading your frog daughter in for a better model, wanting to replace her because of her faults. You also have secretly been planning to purchase a real princess from another kingdom as a replacement. All of these ideas are because of your sadness and disappointment with your imperfect child. She has not met your expectations and dreams of being the perfect child. I do not know if she will ever be an above-average princess. I do know that if she will ever become a princess who is respectful, responsible, resourceful, and responsive, it will be because you have taught her in a loving, warm, and accepting environment. Any child who receives a message from her parents that she is not good enough, not pretty enough, not smart

enough, not loving enough, not talented enough, or does not try hard enough will soon come to believe that she is damaged goods and not enough. Such a discouraged child will never believe that she can belong to the royal family with significance. Such a child will forever be doomed to be a frog.

"What can we do?" the royal couple asked. The wise wizard spoke again.

You must take your frog daughter home and treat her with respect so that she can become respectful. You must help her choose age and temperament-appropriate responsibilities so that she will become responsible. You must permit her to solve life's problems so that she will become resourceful. You must treat her with love and respect so that she may become responsive. Your princess must learn courage so that she will no longer be discouraged. She will develop courage when you, as her parents, become encouraging, speaking and acting in an encouraging manner. You must focus on her behavior, not on her as a person. Her frog-like behaviors are her solutions to problems that the mean and vengeful ogre and you have put upon her.

The parents looked surprised and became angry. "What do you mean we are a part of the cause of our daughter's frog behavior?"

Again the wise wizard spoke.

By not accepting your daughter as the person she is, with all her warts and bumps on her green skin, you have unknowingly strengthened the curse of the ogre. Your daughter knows of your disappointment with her and your secret wish to replace her. This knowledge has only made the curse worse. Go now and accept your child as the princess she is. She will change as much as her creative self, time, and private logic will allow. Your job is to accept, respect, and love her for the child she is and to never dislike her because she does not fulfill your fantasy. She needs your support and encouragement if she is ever to become a productive member of the royal family.

Then in a flash of glowing light, the wise wizard disappeared.

History does not tell us what happened to the frog princess. I have it on good authority that after her parents got over their anger, they realized that the wise wizard was, as ever, correct. They became accepting of their daughter's warts and bumps and green skin, and with time, these imperfections faded.

Legend has it that many years later, the knight, who had become king, had the following inscription written on his grave.

> Open the door, my princess dear,
> Open the door, thy parents are here.
> And mind the words that we say this day,
> We are proud of your deeds, in every way.

"Did the princess ever become an above-average child?" you ask. "Why not?" is my answer. Doesn't every loved child seem to be above average in the eyes of his or her parents? And tell me, what could be more important than that?

Notes

STEPPARENTING HAILEY AND HUGH

Stepparenting is never easy. Ask any adult who elected themselves to this position, and they will tell you tales that seem to come from a *Friday the Thirteenth* look-alike horror show or a classic "Laurel and Hardy" comedy. Give them a chance, and they also will tell you about sweet and wonderful moments from their new life. The best overall advice that I can give any potential or new stepparent is to enter the new family as an *explorer*. Steppers need to ask themselves, "How does this family work, and what are the rules and processes that help it to work?" Too many new parents step into a family and, like a drill sergeant, attempt to "shape up the troops." From the children's point of view, the new intruder has not earned the right to boss them around. Many children still have the hope that their biological mom and dad will eventually get back together.

Knowing what to do at the right time can make all the difference in the world to succeed at stepparenting. At a recent FETCH parenting class, a new stepfather, Dan, asked for help, describing the following scenario. He has been a stepfather for six months. His new wife is the mother of two children, a girl, Hailey age six, and a boy, Hugh age three. When Dan comes home from work each evening, his new six-year-old daughter is all over him. "Hailey hugs me, kisses me, sits on my lap, and is so affectionate that I feel embarrassed. It lasts for ten minutes or so and then she is gone." In a more powerful but anxious voice, he continued by saying, "I think I need to set boundaries. Maybe I need to show Hailey more discipline."

Dan was about to make the greatest mistake of his short stepparenting career. Words like "set boundaries" and "more discipline" are red flags to the cause of a good stepparent-child relationship. Hailey is a six-year-old girl who is starved for the love of a daddy. She has learned from life that she can get a quick fill of Dan's attention by being a loving, snuggly cutie-pie, and then be gone.

When parents talk at our family education training center, we view what we do as education, not psychotherapy. The information gathered is considered family interpersonal dynamics, not psychopathology. We make known to all the universality of problems experienced by families. We emphasize that what is common to one family is, in all likelihood, common to most families. When we offer solutions, we tailor them to the dynamics of the family, make them easy, never complicated, and always obtainable.

Dan was given the following tailored solution.

"When you come home at night and you are about to be set upon by Hailey, immediately head for the couch and sit in the middle. When Hailey comes close to you, gently pull her in with your arm around her shoulder. Hug her, give her a kiss on the cheek, tell her how much you love her, how proud you are of her, and how glad you are that she is your daughter. If her three-year-old brother comes to you, do the same with him; both are your children. The trick is to hold your children tight. Not so tight that you hurt them, but just tight enough that they can barely wiggle. Children love to be held tight, but only for a minute or so; then they have to wiggle or otherwise they become uncomfortable. I guarantee you that after five minutes of being barely able to wiggle, Hailey and Hugh will be gone to do their thing. The rest of the evening will be yours without too much more in the way of onslaughts of attention."

Two weeks later, Dan came up to me at the FETCH parents' class. His smile was wide and there was joy in his eyes.

"Dr. Jim, your hugging technique worked like a charm. Five minutes on the couch and the kids are happy and gone. I see a great improvement in Hailey, and I no longer feel embarrassed by her behavior. I guess the problem was mine. However, until you told me what to do, I didn't have a clue. Dr. Jim, you were right; the best answers are always the simplest."

Notes

STRESS, COOTIES, 'N' 'UKUS:
DON'T GIVE 'EM TO DA KEIKI[1]

It only seems like yesterday when my friend Donna called to apologize for missing the first two weeks of the new Family Education Training Center of Hawai'i (FETCH) semester. "I have been so busy at work that the time got away from me," she lamented. Hearing the disappointment in her voice, I quickly pointed out to her that FETCH was to begin next Friday, not two weeks ago. Donna's voice immediately calmed after hearing my words. I knew that she wanted to come to our parenting classes and learn our methods. Donna was one of the first persons to read all my parenting essays. I felt privileged that this highly intelligent professional and ethical woman appreciated my writing.

As I listened, Donna's conversation quickly turned to what was happening at work. Donna, who works for a large service company, had been told that she was not a "team player" because she had refused to do an act which she deemed highly questionable and borderline ethical. She had become so disturbed by the situation, she said, that she was having sleepless and restless nights.

Then came the bomb. Her eight-year-old daughter, Judy, suddenly began having problems at school. The teacher reported that she had become anxious, was unable to concentrate on simple learning tasks, and for some unknown reason, had become a "nervous child."

"When did Judy change from being a happy child to a nervous one?" I asked. There was a long pause as silence filled the air. "Now that I think about it," Donna said slowly, "Judy changed right after my problems at

302 DR. JAMES A. DEUTCH

work began." "Do you think there is any connection?" I inquired, knowing what was to come next. After another pause, I heard the voice at the other end say, "Oh my god, that's the connection." Without skipping a beat came the predictable next question, "What do I do about it?"

Parents may not always realize it, but children pick up on their energy and react to it. Our problems cause our children to behave in unusual ways even to the extent of misbehaving. Adlerian psychology teaches us that all behavior serves a purpose and is a result of private logic, the way we believe and think about things. Students of Adlerian psychology are taught that it is not what happens but our interpretation of it.

Children are great observers, but they are poor interpreters.[2] Because of their lack of life experiences and belief that the world revolves around them, children often believe that they are the cause of parental or family misfortunes. In my practice, I have seen this most often in cases of divorce. Children usually blame themselves when parents divorce. "If only I had minded better . . . If only I had made better grades at school . . . If only I would have kept my room clean" is not unusual child thinking.

I had little doubt that Judy had observed her mother's apprehensions and concerns even though Donna thought she was hiding them. The child interpreted the situation as she had caused Mother's troubles. She did not want to test her hypothesis by asking Mother directly as it might prove to be true. The result for Judy, in her eight-year-old mind, became an unsure world, filled with worries and impending disasters. Who can think creatively at school when the mind is troubled?

Knowing that Donna had "gotten it," I said to her the following.

"When you do what I am about to tell you, keep it simple and communicate to Judy at her level. At your next family council meeting, look into her eyes and say, 'I want to tell you about something that is happening at my work. There has been a lot of pressure at work, nothing I can't handle, but pressure nonetheless. Lately, I have been reacting to the pressure by thinking too much about it and even finding myself staying awake at night. My big concern today is that you might be worried about me worrying. Sometimes when children do not know what is going on with their parents, they start worrying too. Oftentimes, children think that they are the cause of the parents' worry, as if it's their fault. Do you ever feel that way about me?'"

At this point, I wanted Donna to stop and wait for Judy to enter the dialogue. Judy is a very verbal child, and I knew she would begin participating and gain understanding when given the chance. It is important children have a voice in family matters, especially when what is happening affects them.

Often, parents believe just by giving children information, it will cause them to have insights and relieve them of stress. This is not necessarily true. Children, as do adults, need to process information in order to gain a firm understanding of the material. When people begin to understand at a deeper level, they feel empowered and less vulnerable.

As a final step in the dialogue, Donna needed to reinforce Judy's (hopefully correct) conclusion. "I want you to know, Judy, that Mama's worry has nothing to do with you. You didn't cause it, you don't have anything to do with it. It is caused by my work situation and the way I am looking at it."

Usually, it is good to ask your child what she just heard you say. If you can get her to repeat the context of what was said, you have good communication. Sometimes, when repeating your statements back, the child will get it wrong. Take the opportunity to kindly and gently say, "Not quite, let me say it again." Respectfully repeat this until the child understands what you thought you just said to her.

One week later, at the first FETCH meeting of the semester, I had a chance to talk with Donna in private.

"I did exactly what you said. Judy and I talked like grownups. I really enjoyed sharing with her and hearing what she was thinking. You were right on. Even in this short amount of time, she looks and acts as relaxed as she ever was."

Later in the semester, Donna told me that her household was back in order, her work situation had worked itself out, and she was her old self.

In Summary

Much of the time, parents are not aware of their impact on their children. Like cooties and ukus, problems are passed on without ever knowing it. This is especially true when parents are under stress caused by outside forces such as work. It is important that children know, by parental sharing, that they are not at fault for the parent's problem and that sometimes bad things happen to good people. As children, it is not their place to fix it. Fixing parental problems is the job of the adult.

Endnotes

[1] In Hawai'i, a child is called a "keiki," and head lice are known as cooties and "'ukus."

[2] Read "Children Are Great Observers but Poor Interpreters."

Notes

"IT'S NOT YOUR FAULT!"
MITIGATING CHILDHOOD GUILT

Are you training your children to believe that when things go wrong, it's their fault? If you are like most parents, you probably do.

Let's take the case of two-year-old Ben. The toddler goes to the refrigerator with his cup in hand and says, "Milch." This smart little guy is asking for a cold glass of milk. Mother obliges him by pouring milk from the carton into his outstretched cup. As soon as Ben's cup approaches full, he takes it away, and Mother ends up pouring milk onto the kitchen floor. Mother's first response is to yell at Ben. "Damn it, Ben, look at what you made me do. You're a bad boy. Never do that again, you're bad." Ben may not understand all of Mother's words, but her meaning is clear to him. He has displeased the person whom he is most dependent upon, and a certain terrible bad feeling clutches his body. He did something wrong, it is his fault; he is bad because Mother said so. Ben is learning the pain of guilt.

While some guilt, or the potential of it, seems to keep some humans from engaging in destructive behaviors, teaching children it is their fault when things go wrong is a very poor parenting technique. For two-year-old Ben, it is his mother's obligation to anticipate his behavior and try to understanding his private logic, the biased way he sees the world based on his interpretation of his experiences. Ben believes that when his cup is full enough, "Mother, my all-powerful and all-knowing caretaker will realize that I have enough milk in my cup and will stop pouring." Add this to the fact that Ben's brain is developing, and he will not master "cause and effect" relationships until he is in his early twenties. Mother should be the one who feels guilty for yelling and using her power destructively. Of course, the smart thing for Mother to have done after she realized her error of not anticipating the behavior of her two-year-old is to either have said nothing or ask Ben to get a sponge and help her clean up the mess.

Eight-year-old Tiffany has watched her mother and father bicker and yell at each other for many years. Recently, their fighting had become worse. One day, Mother informed Tiffany, "Your father and I are going to get a divorce." Tiffany felt devastated, and questions of self-preservation tore through her mind. "What will become of me? Where will I live? Who will take care of me?" After the initial shock, her questions expand. "Why are my parents getting a divorce?" Children of divorcing parents struggle to find an answer and make sense of the baffling situation. Because children tend to see themselves as omnipotent and are trained by parents to blame themselves when things go wrong, they quite easily accept the blame for their parents' misery. "It must be my fault that my parents are going to get a divorce" is a usual answer. In their search for answers, many children follow the "if only" line of reasoning. "If only I had . . . tried harder to stop them from fighting . . . cleaned my room when my mother told me to . . . not fought with my brother . . . made better grades in school."

Divorce is never the fault of the child. Adults create their own misery and problematic situations. As in the case of Tiffany and other children victimized by parental mistakes, the message "It's not your fault" must be emphasized. Parents and counselors must repeat this idea until the child realizes and accepts the fact, "It wasn't my fault." Only after the self-imposed guilt is lifted can the child return to a healthy state of mind.

Many years ago, ten-year-old Terry was referred to me by his pediatrician who knew that I used hypnosis in my clinical practice.[1] Terry's body had been covered with weeping hives for the past half year. When I looked at Terry, I saw a sad little boy who was feeling miserable, in mind, body, and spirit. His social history revealed the following facts. Terry was the second of two boys. His older brother, Jack, had fought leukemia, starting when Terry was aged five. From the moment of the diagnosis, the parents' energy was vested in Jack. His life was their number 1 priority, and other people and issues had become secondary. To young Terry, it felt as though he was no longer worthy of parental attention. He began hating his older brother whom he saw as siphoning away parental love and attention. During the past five years, this hate turned into wishing his brother were dead. Six months earlier, Brother Jack died. Within weeks, ten-year-old Terry had broken out with hives. Home and pharmaceutical remedies did no good; Terry's skin continued to weep for his brother and his own guilt.

The answer to this mystery was all too obvious. Terry's weeping skin was symbolic of his feelings of sadness and guilt that he was holding inside. Because he had wished his brother's death, in his mind, he made it happen. Terry believed himself guilty of murdering his brother. Children do this to themselves due to their beliefs, perceptions, and private logic; so did Terry.

Hypnosis allows the therapist a gateway into the mind. I put Terry into a trance and gave him new information. I told him that he was not responsible for Jack's death. It was not his fault; it was the fault of the disease of leukemia. I said it was usual and all right to be angry with his brother as their parents spent an enormous amount of time tending to Jack's needs. During the trance, I emphasized to Terry that Jack's death was not his fault and it was now all right to stop punishing himself by having weepy and uncomfortable skin.

Terry returned to see me in one week. His skin was clearing of hives. Using hypnosis, I reinforced the suggestions of the prior week. Two weeks later, a happy and cheerful Terry visited me. The hives were completely gone as was the sad and miserable boy that I had first seen three weeks before. I spoke briefly with his parents who now understood their part in Terry's situation and were giving him healthy attention and encouragement. I discharged Terry back to the pediatrician with the comment Terry might never have had this problem had his parents merely said, "Terry, your brother's death is not your fault!"

Children are trained to believe when things go wrong, it is their fault. The results are often dreadful. I do not believe that we, as parents, are willfully bad; it's that we naively repeat the mistakes of our parents. We all need to think about what we say to our children before we act. The next time you are about to fault your child, take a moment to think the situation through. Perhaps the most truthful words are "It's not your fault, let's fix this situation, together."

Endnote

1   Dr. Deutch is a diplomate in clinical hypnosis and is a past president of the American Hypnosis Board for Clinical Social Work.

Notes

ROBBING KYLE TO PAY LAUREN
By
Sasha Kealoha*

I rejoined FETCH after a semester's absence and quickly requested a recounseling. As I was signing up, I informed Dr. Jim that I would not be bringing four-and-a-half-year-old Kyle to the toddler class that date. I explained that my husband would not be able to watch our two-year-old daughter, Lauren, so I was hiring a babysitter. I planned to have Kyle stay home with Lauren and the sitter.

Dr. Jim quickly took me aside, away from Kyle, and asked if I thought Kyle enjoyed attending FETCH. I answered yes. Dr. Jim explained the importance of Kyle's participation with his FETCH peers and his opportunity to learn in the social group environment. It was best for Kyle to continue attending FETCH rather than sit at home with his sister. Dr. Jim then asked Kyle, "Do you like coming to FETCH?" Timidly he answered, "Yes." Dr. Jim then asked Kyle if he was learning anything. His eyes sparkled as he again answered yes. Dr. Jim pointed out to me how unfair it was to make Kyle stay home with Lauren and spy on the sitter as he loved the program and was benefitting from his participation and involvement. Pausing to think, I then realized how unfair I was being to Kyle. I agreed to bring him to his next class and leave Lauren with the sitter.

---

*Sasha Kealoha, B.A., is a wife, mother of two, and a FETCH parent.

As a mother, I still had my concerns, such as I know if Kyle is with Lauren when I have a stranger (sitter) there, he is a huge help with his baby sister. Lauren loves her older brother so much that I believe she is much more comfortable in strange situations when Kyle is with her. In all honesty, I just feel more comfortable with Kyle at home with her as I know he will watch over her and tell me everything that happened.

Really, I was not thinking at all about what Kyle might want to do but just doing what makes me more comfortable. I realized how unfair I was being to Kyle. I was being unfair to Lauren too by not giving her the chance to be more independent from both Kyle and me. Kyle was not an object to be discounted for my convenience or to allay my fears as a mother. He was a growing young boy who loved his FETCH experiences and felt disappointment when they were denied.

The night arrived for Kyle and me to attend FETCH while leaving Lauren by herself with a sitter for the first time. It was not easy leaving Lauren as she cried for us as we departed home. I kept my phone in sight throughout class in case she needed me. I didn't get one phone call. Upon returning home, Lauren was in bed, and the sitter said Lauren only cried for a few minutes after we left and then they played. The sitter had worked with Lauren to make a picture for us.

The evening was a success! Kyle and I attended our respective classes, I was counseled, and Lauren was fine at home. In the morning, Lauren proudly showed off her picture to everyone.

I invite all mothers and fathers to look deeply into their reasons for denying one child a growth experience for the benefit of another. A deeper self-question to be asked is "Am I really doing this for the benefit of both children, a more favored child, or am I motivated to make my own self feel better or perhaps less inconvenienced?" Should you find yourself being less of the parent you want to be, change your decision, even apologize to the offended child. Children learn when their parents openly do a course correction. They learn that the world is changeable, and being flexible has great merit.

By way of summary, I want to tell parents that robbing one child for the convenience of another or for your peace of mind is wrong and a misdemeanor that no parent should commit.

Notes

BARBER COLLEGE BOUND

One of the joys of being a twenty-first century FETCH counselor is to be able to help parents immediately and thereby prevent further crises. I love e-mail and tell my FETCH parents that I am always available to them. So far, no one has abused the privilege, and I have derived much joy out of responding to desperation-grams like the following.

> Hi, Dr. Jim,
>
> This is Stacey from FETCH with the four-year-old twins, Nikki and Heather. My daughter Nikki, while on my husband's watch, took a child's scissors and cut her hair. She did a pretty good job of it. I had to take her to a beauty parlor, and they literally had to give her a boy's cut. Well, with the holidays here, we had a big party with family, and the family was giving her a lot of undue attention. "Oh, you look so cute"; "Don't worry, your hair will grow back"; and "Why did you cut your hair?" Now that I think of it, Heather, who was with me and doesn't usually do things to that extreme, didn't get any attention. Should I reward her? What should I do? Thanks for your advice.

$\mathscr{r}\ \mathscr{r}\ \mathscr{r}\ \mathscr{r}\ \mathscr{r}\ \mathscr{r}\ \mathscr{r}\ \mathscr{r}\ \mathscr{r}\ \mathscr{r}\ \mathscr{r}\ \mathscr{r}\ \mathscr{r}\ \mathscr{r}\ \mathscr{r}\ \mathscr{r}\ \mathscr{r}\ \mathscr{r}$

> Dear Stacey,
>
> Welcome to the club. Frustrating, isn't it? Forty years ago, when my daughter was Nikki's age, she took a pair of scissors to her hair for whatever reason I do not remember. The big difference

is that her behavior was not reinforced by well-meaning friends nor did we have a second daughter waiting in the wings to get her fair share of undue attention through similar misbehavior. When my wife discovered what Frances had done, she merely said, "Oh, that's too bad," and never said a word thereafter. My wife gave me a heads-up, and when I came home from work, I said nothing. Adlerian psychology must have worked because Frances never did that again.

As your desperation-gram indicates, you know the "damage" already has been done and what remains is how to mitigate the fallout. I suggest you do the following. Say nothing more about the incident to Nikki. By you bringing it up in any form, the behavior will be reinforced, which may cause her to do it again. If Nikki brings up the subject, listen liberally and speak sparingly. My best guess is that she already knows of your disapproval. This is where you actively listen and use those listening grunts I taught you. This incident is never again to be spoken of, at least on your and Dad's part.

Next, at a quiet and neutral time when you and Heather are comfortably alone, I want you to one time, and one time only, say to her, "I like your hair just as it is," while for just a moment lovingly stroking it. If you do this more than one time, you could be opening the door for Heather to become the family goody-goody and possibly locking Nikki into the role of the family baddy-baddy. I want your small gesture to be an encouragement to Heather so she does not have to replicate Nikki's behavior to feel significant in the family. As I said above, this incident is never again to be spoken of by you or Dad. If it is brought up by family or friends, quietly say, "We don't talk about that anymore," and immediately change the subject. If your friends and family are cool, they will get the hint and change the conversation with you.

As for your husband, I gather that you are miffed at him since the incident happened, as you say, "on his watch." May I remind you that this could have happened on your watch! It is near impossible to keep an eye on two healthy and active girls every second. Love and forgiveness go together in a marriage. And please remember the words to my song, "Perfection is a direction, not a goal."

With much aloha and respect,

Dr. Jim

Notes

HUSBAND OR CHILD?
HOW TO HELP YOUR MAN GROW INTO FATHERHOOD

One day, I was about to give a talk at a mothers' parenting support group when a young woman approached me with a neatly folded piece of paper in her outstretched hand. "Here," she said, "I wrote you a letter because I don't want to talk about this to my girlfriends." I put the letter in my pocket and thanked her for her confidence in me. The following is what she wrote.

Dear Dr. Deutch:

Please help me to understand, and tell me what I can do. Here is the situation. My husband fights with our son. The scenes remind me of sibling rivalry between an older and younger child, each competing for mommy's attention. They are not playing, they really are fighting. The battles usually end with little Bobbie crying and me yelling at my husband, Robert, to stop the nonsense. I don't think these fights are good for three-year-old Bobbie as I see him becoming more and more aggressive with his playmates. I don't believe in fighting, and these scenes really annoy me.

Here is some background that might be helpful. Robert is 25, and I am 23 years old. Bobbie is our first and only child. Robert is an only child, and we live with his parents, but in a separate part of the house. Robert is a good and honest man and is not otherwise prone to violence; he treats his mother and me respectfully. However, his mother still babies him, and he likes it. Robert earns a good living as an engineer for the city and is an honest and faithful partner. He does not drink or do drugs. I want our son to grow up as a strong and kind human being who treats others in a respectful manner.

Again, please tell me what's going on, and what can I do to stop this silly behavior on my husband's part?

Sincerely,

Annoyed Mother of Two

〃〃〃〃〃〃〃〃〃〃〃〃〃〃〃〃〃〃〃〃〃〃〃

I wrote back the following letter.

Dear Annoyed Mother of Two:

I think you've hit the nail on the head. From what you describe, Robert, on an emotional level, sees himself as a competitor with Bobbie for your attention. As an only child, Robert was pampered by his mother and did not have the chance to learn the art of sharing love, time, and attention with others. Nor did he learn much in the way of self-sufficiency and self-soothing. He learned that to belong to the family with significance, he had to assume the misguided goal of undue attention. His mother probably liked that attention and thus reinforced his "I'm going to keep you busy with me" behaviors. Now that Robert is married, you have become his new mommy figure. With the advent of baby Bobbie, the competition for your time, attention, and maybe even love has grown. Robert's fisticuffs with Bobbie are his way of "beating the competition."

How do you help your husband become a father to his son and not act like a competitive older sibling? Believe it or not, you have the power to help your husband become the father he wants to be but doesn't know how. Focus on his strengths, what he does right, not on his weaknesses, which will get you resistance and oppositional defiance.

I suggest the first thing you need to do is to make more time for your husband. What did you do when you and Robert were first dating and enjoying each other's company? Think back and remember why you married him. Ask him out on dates. Get Grandma, or even a babysitter, to come and free you so that you both can go out and be with each other at least one night a week. Try to find ways to make him feel important, even if it's as simple as making toast for him in the morning or pouring him a cup of coffee. It's amazing how those little things can add up.

A three-year-old should have room time by eight o'clock.[1] You can't make a child go to sleep, but you can have him in his room where he can play or have the opportunity to go to sleep when he is ready. Room time is a way for parents to enjoy each other and nurture the love that brought them together. Too much "baby and me and husband makes three" is a way to burn out and KO your marriage.

Look for ways to encourage your husband's fathering behaviors.[2] Hand him Bobbie when you are doing minor tasks and ask hubby to help. Your husband does not believe in his ability to do child care. And why should he? He has no experience in that line of work. Thank him for his help and never criticize. Criticism is a turnoff, and at this stage of his fatherly development, he needs much encouragement. Catch Robert doing things right and acknowledge his achievements by talking about his deeds and how they affect you or Bobbie. Focus on the deed, not the dude. "I really like the way you help me with Bobbie, it makes my life easier." "I love it when you take Bobbie to the park, he enjoys your company so much." "I like the way you answered Bobbie's question, you are teaching him how to be respectful."

At a neutral and quiet time, sit down with Robert and let him know that while he is a great husband and father, fighting with Bobbie in the manner that he does is not dignified and teaches his son the wrong way to settle disputes. Then ask him how he otherwise might do it.

During your conversation, tell Robert one time, and one time only, that the next time he fights with Bobbie, you are going to walk out of the room and go elsewhere. This will serve as a reminder that Robert is the father, and it is his responsibility to care and mentor his son. Should they fight again, immediately leave the room without saying a word and without any angry body language. Silently leaving the field of battle is a nonverbal way of letting your boys know their misbehavior will not get them your attention. When you follow-up by doing what you said you were going to do when you said you were going to do it, you earn credibility.

If you find that there are classes in democratic parenting in your area, such as the Family Education Training Center of Hawai'i, ask your husband to accompany you. If he refuses, go anyway. Moms have reported that even when their husband does not accompany them, they continue to educate him by sharing what they are learning in class. Many husbands eventually attend class, and the results are always positive.

Since you know your husband better than I do, continue this list of ways that you can be an encouraging partner. Then act upon your insights. You both are young and you have the time and talent to become awesome parents. I am reminded of an old Greek saying that while the husband is the head of the family, the wife is the neck. So tell me, who in the family really has the power to change views? To paraphrase Rudolf Dreikurs, children and husbands need encouragement like plants need water.[3]

Respectfully,

Dr. Jim

Endnotes

1   Read "Bedtime Made Easy."

2   Read "Words of Encouragement."

Encouragement is one of the most powerful interpersonal tools I know. "Encouragement is the nourishment of the soul just as food is the nourishment of the body. Any uncooperative child [or husband] is likely to be a discouraged one." Painter and Corsini, *Effective Discipline*, p. 34. Also read pp. 34-39.

3   Dreikurs and Soltz, *Children: The Challenge*.

Notes

SECTION VI.
About Teenagers

Frances Deutch

AFROTC Cadet James A. Deutch

Jimmy Deutch
Libby Jo Davidson

Ella Svet Prager-Cashuk
Jimmy Deutch

PEER POWER IN TEEN LIFE

The other day I was talking with my friend Dennis in his office. Dennis is one of those rare persons with multiple qualities. He is a handsome, soft-spoken, warm, intelligent, insightful, and tall Hawai'ian man, whose ancestors must have been aliis to the great Hawai'i ruler, King Kamehameha I. When Dennis speaks, intelligent and learned men and women listen. This is what Dennis said.

"You know, Jim, my son is now six foot two inches and weighs 195 pounds. Even though he is only a sophomore, he plays varsity basketball at Kamehameha [a private school for children of Hawai'ian ancestry]. He wants to play football next year and play as a free safety. I have worked with him in sports all his life, but now he is working out every day at the gym and has become dedicated to his athletic goals. He is studying on the Internet which food supplements will work the best to make him stronger and healthier. His positive attitude has transferred to his studies. I have never seen him so dedicated. What I have observed is that his motivation and dedication comes from his association with his friends. They are all working toward healthy bodies and minds. It's not me anymore, but his relationship with his friends, his peers, that now seems to count most for him."

Dennis's observations are astute. A goal of every child is to belong to the family with significance. As a child approaches adolescence, the feeling of wanting to belong refocuses from the immediate family to a chosen peer group. Although at times it seems like our children want to divorce us, in reality their preference is to add a peer group to their definition of family. This process of widening the meaning of family is natural and usual. All children in our Western culture go through this step on their way to becoming an adult.

Adlerian philosophy teaches that respectful parents allow their children to choose their own friends. If this process is ongoing since toddlerhood and communication between parents and child has been open, then selecting close friends during adolescence is usually smooth. If communication has been blocked or poor, then your teen's choice of friends will likely be peers whose behavior is on the useless side of life. The influence exerted by parents on their adolescent's choice of friends begins many years before the child reaches adolescence. If a child and parent have been involved in a power contest throughout the growing years, you can bet the type of peer chosen will never meet the expectations and hopes of the parent. Additionally, girls who did not receive the encouragement and attention of a strong father figure will find teen boys who will give them that attention, usually at the price of sexual favors.

What is a parent to do? What influences do we, as parents, have over our teens? How can we guide them to the useful side of life and away from the useless?

In my many years of professional life, I have found that the family is, and always will be, the most powerful influence, for good or for evil, as your child travels through the life cycle.

When dealing with teens, punishment is useless; yelling, screaming, threatening, grounding, and taking away privileges works poorly. Parents need to treat their young adults with the same respect they give their friends and colleagues. Would any of us treat our peers in the same manner as we often treat our teens? Whereas logical consequences work well with younger children, they do not work well with adolescents. Logical consequences are often interpreted by teens as parental power plays. Parents need to hold respectful conversations with their teen, listening liberally and speaking sparingly. Most parents who have used power to control their children find that when a child reaches adolescence, the will to assert themselves grows stronger, and parental power tactics no longer work. In fact, power often produces the opposite of the desired result, escalating conflict and increasing misguided behaviors. However, when children are young and parents consistently practice Adlerian democratic parenting, their children's teen years will be filled with cooperation, goodwill, joy, and respect. The *family council* [1] and *individual special time* [2] are proven effective tools in preparing children to be cooperative teenagers.

When your child reaches his teenage years, there are behaviors you can do to make life more satisfying for you both.

The first thing you need to consider is whether to change your parenting style. If you have been using punishment and control, you need to change tactics so that your child will become a responsible listener. The more rigid your role, the less responsible your teen will be. The more real you become, the more responsive your teen becomes. From your teen's point of view, *real* is better than *perfect*.

Be a role model for your teen. As with the ideal child, if you want your teen to be *respectful, responsible, resourceful,* and *responsive,* you need to model these behaviors in your own life. [3] Teens become *respectful* when you treat them with respect. Yelling, screaming, bossing, put-downs, and punishments are disrespectful. Treat your teen as you would a respected friend, neighbor, or relative. Be *responsible* in your own life. Your contribution to your family's well-being teaches your teen that his actions affect everyone in the family and that his behavior is not performed in isolation. When your behavior is *resourceful,* you are teaching your teen independence and self-reliance. You are teaching him to meet new people and the world with courage. Model for your teen the courage to be imperfect. As in the old saying, "It matters not how many times you are knocked down; what matters is how many times you get up." When you, as a parent, are *responsive,* you are teaching your teen the art of treating you and others with love, respect, and kindness.

Be your teen's consultant, not his boss. When you play boss, your child hears your behavior as "I'm going to *make* you do what I want." This is a guaranteed setup for a power struggle that, in the long run, you cannot win and whose residuals are resentment and more conflict. A consultant is a respected person who is regarded as especially knowledgeable in some area of specialization who may be asked to give an opinion or suggestion about an issue. Your teen will more readily listen to a consultant than to a boss. [4]

Talking with your teen should be for communication, not for punishment. I suggest that parents of teens listen liberally and speak sparingly in order to get their message across. As you listen, give feedback to what you think you have heard. If your teen says you misheard, ask him to repeat what he said, and repeat again what you heard until agreement is achieved. Allow for differences of opinion. Don't cram your belief down the throat of your teen; it will not work. If there is a wide difference between ideas, ask for an opinion of a mutually respected third party. Keep a calm friendly voice, and allow for a "cooling off" break if necessary.

As a psychotherapist and counselor, I have found it very useful to ask questions rather than make statements. Here, in no particular order, are a few questions over the years I have found useful. There are others.

— Tell me more about that.
— How does that make you feel?
— When that happened, what did you do?
— And what else?
— Is that how you want to be treated?
— Is this how you want to be remembered?
— If you did this, would your grandmother be proud of you?
— Are you sure this is the right thing to do?
— Would you advise your daughter to behave like that?
— What do you need from me?
— How can I help you?
— Thank you for sharing your thoughts with me.

A wise parent will provide room in their home for their children's friends to gather and play. When our children were adolescents, my wife and I made room on the back porch for the teens to play and socialize. Thus, we always knew where our children were, what they were doing, and how they were doing it. Cookies, milk, juice, an occasional picnic meal, and respect were always available for our children and their friends. Today, over thirty years later, several of these teens and my children are still in contact.

My friend Dennis must be doing a great deal right. To have a son who cares about his family, friends, self, and community, is a parenting achievement greatly to be admired. Our job as parents is to prepare our children to live and prosper in the world as it exists and to move that world to a place that nurtures everyone. Our job does not stop when our kids become adolescents. It is only the manner of our tasks that change as our children move through the lifecycle.[5]

Endnotes

[1]   Read "The Family Council."

   Read Chapter 33, "The Family Council," in *Effective Discipline*.

   Rigney and Corsini, *The Family Council*.

   Dreikurs, et al. *Family Counsel: The Dreikurs Techniques*.

[2]   Read "Individual Special Time."

[3]   Painter and Corsini suggest a model for the ideal child. See pages 8-9.

4. I strongly recommend that parents begin their preparation for parenting an adolescent when their child reaches toddlerhood. Read "Parent as Consultant."

[5]   Three additional books parents of preadolescents and teens will find helpful.

   Cassel and Corsini, *Coping with Teenagers*.

   Gordon and Sands, *P.E.T. in Action*.

   Nelson and Lott, *Positive Discipline*.

Notes

TOWARD A BETTER UNDERSTANDING OF TEENAGE REBELLION AND WAYS TO DEAL WITH IT

Are you worried that your newly adolescent child will soon defy your advice and authority? If your style of parenting has been one of authoritarian command and control, you probably have a right to worry. Children who have been under the thumb of a strict parent, if their spirit has not been broken, will find rebellion a very seductive tool to use in their new status as an adolescent. However, parents who have been democratic in their style of child rearing, having given their children a voice and a choice, will find their continuing role as a consultant very productive as well as enjoyable.[1] Having a cooperative teenager is fun and an adventure for both parent and child.

For those parents who find themselves behind the power curve of parenting an adolescent, the following information will be of value. The key to dealing with a rebellious teenager is to avoid confrontation, learn to be a consultant, practice patience, and recognize that you have a unique person called a teenager. You need to remember that your child eventually will pass through this phase and, one day, become a normal adult.

The major reason for teenage rebellion is for the child to find his or her place in an adult world where he or she can belong with significance. Teenagers cannot know the limits of their newly expanded world without first exploring its edges. Human beings are not born with an innate sense of right and wrong, good and bad, usefulness and uselessness, but learn these differences through trial and error as they mature through life. Teenagers need time and life's lessons to learn and internalize what their society and culture deem proper and useful behaviors.

There was a time in the Western world when there were no "teenagers." Adulthood came with the passage of time and the awakening of the teen body. Boys were expected to become men and labor equally with adult males. Girls were expected to become women and labor equally with adult women. Both were expected to marry and rear children. Society provided rites of passage to mark this transition. Today, there are no such rites nor are there similar expectations for young people of this age. The teenage years offer a decade of ambiguous roles and little expectation, the one exception being to obtain a formal education.

Confronting teenagers with your power using punishments and imposing logical consequences almost never works. It only gives them an opportunity to test their will and strength against yours. A calm and sincere discussion about behavior will help a teen begin to think about his or her impact on the entire family. Most teenagers, like other children, do not believe that their behavior has any impact on family members at all. When discussing behavior, the wise parent will talk about behavior in general, not the teen's behavior in particular. An indirect approach will allow a teen more room to be objective and avoid the need to protect his or her position at any cost.

When discussing issues with teenagers, be prepared for an argument as they may question every point you make. Your children do not have the years of experience you have accumulated to find wisdom. What you know may not match what they believe. Do not just impart wisdom, also ask questions that lead them to wisdom. Be like Socrates, the philosopher whose questions focused on helping his students find correct answers. Wise parents talk *with* teens, not *at* them. During your interaction, be prepared to listen liberally and speak sparingly.

Another aspect to handling teenage rebellion is for parents to keep in mind the issue of "harm." When dealing with behavior, think about how important the behavior really is. Does an ankle tattoo really announce slutty behavior? Is a navel ring really immoral? Is a red or green Mohawk haircut the end of the world? The reality is, the stronger you denounce these behaviors, the stronger your rebellious teen desires to do them. Although you may deplore these and similar behaviors, before committing to combat, you need to ask yourself the ultimate question, "What is the real level of harm being done?"

If the teenager is behaving dangerously toward oneself or others, it is necessary for a parent to take some sort of action, but not angry confrontation. A parent who has become his or her teen's consultant is in a stronger position to be heard than a parent who is yelling and threatening.

Patience and forgiveness is vital to the parenting process as is being fair and firm. I strongly suggest parents treat all their school-age children as adults, but protect them as well, and be there for them when they need you. Never talk to your child disrespectfully, no matter what their age. It is often wise to ignore annoying but harmless behavior at the moment of crisis. Ignoring means *not* showing emotions such as anger, annoyance, disgust, or hurt. I suggest at those potentially angry and disrespectful moments, a parent calmly and respectfully say, "Let's talk about this later," and walk away in a neutral, respectful manner. This may be difficult for some parents to do as they want retribution and correction then and there. However, at the moment of conflict, who is listening? Adlerians refer to calmly walking away as "fighting with your feet." Later, at a more neutral time when everyone has calmed down and able to listen, the parent can discuss the incident using I-messages.[2] An I-message is a way of telling another person, including one's teen, how you feel about his or her behavior and how it affects you. After giving the I-message, the wise parent takes the time to focus on listening to what the teen has to say.

Consistency in parental behavior also is an important concept as it helps parents gain credibility.[3] Yelling, threatening, bargaining, and pleading with teens does not work because, most likely, getting you upset is the teen's current goal. When a misguided child believes he or she has the power to determine the parent's behavior, the child will use their misguided power to control their parent over and over again.

A lack of consistency also trains your child to be angry and lose trust in your word. When you make a promise, keep it. When you tell your child the choice is his, going back on your word teaches that you, the parent, cannot be trusted.

To the once small child with feelings of inferiority, the now bigger and stronger newly adolescent sees the world differently. People who were once large now seem smaller. Parents who were omnipotent are now viewed with their flaws. The child is turning into a preadult. Parents need to change with the times. The old method of being the boss needs to change to being the consultant. Telling the teen what to do and when to do it will no longer work.

Parent and family-life educators strongly recommend parents have talks with their children about respect, friends, sex, drugs, computer safety, driving habits, the relationship between school and career goals, and other "what life could mean to you"[4] issues, long before they reach their teens. The discussion and information needs to be delivered at the age level of the child. Teenagers will listen to parents who have, for a lifetime, listened to them.

There was a time in the Western world when there were no "teenagers."

Endnotes

1. Read "Parent as Consultant."
2. Read "Teaching Respect by Example: Using the I-Message." Gordon and Sands, *P.E.T. in Action.*
3. Read "The Incredibly Credible Parent."
4. Read Adler, Alfred, *What Life Could Mean to You.*

Notes

SECTION VII.
In Memory

REMEMBERING OUR TEACHER, RAYMOND J. CORSINI, PHD

Dr. James Deutch, Dr. Frank Dumont, Mr. Tom Burke, Dr. Mary Martini, and
Dr. Raymond Corsini at age 94

OBITUARY

By
Danny Wedding
American Psychologist 65,
No. 1 (January 2010).

Raymond J. Corsini, PhD
(1914-2008)

Raymond J. Corsini, one of the great psychologists of this era, passed away on November 8, 2008, at the age of 94 in Honolulu, Hawai'i. With his accomplished wife, Kleona, a medical doctor, he was a resident of Hawai'i since 1966 and contributed widely to the welfare of Honolulu and its environs through his *pro bono* services to various school and church organizations. Dr. Corsini pioneered radical innovations in school psychology, prison psychology, community psychology, psychodrama, and clinical psychology, and he published widely in these various domains. In his own words, he sought to " . . . afflict the comfortable, and comfort the afflicted." More remarkable still is that in his 70s and 80s he developed world-class reference works as an encyclopedist (*The Corsini Encyclopedia of Psychology*) and lexicographer (*Corsini Dictionary of Psychology*). His textbook, *Current Psychotherapies,* co-edited with Danny Wedding, is considered the best textbook in psychotherapy education and supervision.

Dr. Corsini was born in Vermont to impoverished Italian immigrant parents, and spent much of his youth in New York City before accepting professional positions in California and Illinois. He received his doctorate in clinical psychology from the University of Chicago and subsequently trained at the Alfred Adler Institute in Chicago.

Dr. Corsini was an indefatigable scholar and continued to work daily in the last months of his life, when he was overcome with crippling back and pulmonary problems. His encyclopedias, handbooks, dictionary of psychology and other reference works, textbooks, and specialized books number more than 40, and many are now being digitized as an enduring part of his legacy to psychology and related mental health and educational fields.

But he was not just a scholar. He worked for much of his life as a prison psychologist, a clinical psychologist, teacher, and community organizer. These signal contributions to the larger community were consistent with his profound Adlerian conviction that an individual's primary responsibility was to actively contribute to the health, integrity, and well-being of their community—they must demonstrate "social interest."

In 2003, the Hawai'i Psychological Association honored Dr. Corsini with its Lifetime Achievement Award, the highest honor the Association can bestow. Finally, it must be noted that he considered his development of "Individual Education," (also known as the Corsini 4-R System), an educational and school administration system that has now taken root in various parts of the world, as the most important intellectual achievement of his life. This system is rooted in democratic principles of interaction between teacher, pupil, and family.

Raymond Corsini is survived by his wife, Dr. Kleona Rigney, his daughter Evelyn Anne Corsini, and three stepchildren, Michael Rigney, Roberta Rigney, and Jon Rigney.

REFERENCES

Adler, A. (1931). (1992). (1998). *What Life Could Mean to You.* Center City, Minnesota, Hazelden Foundation. United States of America.

Adler, A. (1998). *Social Interest: Adler's Key to the Meaning of Life.* Boston: Oneworld Publications.

American Psychological Association (2002). Is Corporal Punishment an Effective Means of Discipline? *American Psychological Association.* Website: http://www.apa.org/news/press/releases/2002/06/spanking.aspx.

Ansbacher, H. and Ansbacher, R. (1956). *The Individual Psychology of Alfred Adler.* New York: Basic Books, Inc.

Ansbacher, H. and Ansbacher, R. (1973, 1964). *Superiority and Social Interest.* New York: The Viking Press.

Bahr, S. J., Hoffman, J. P. (2010). Parenting Style, Religiosity, Peers, and Adolescent Heavy Drinking. *Journal of Studies on Alcohol and Drugs,* 71(4), 539-543.

Bakan, D. (1971). *Slaughter of the Innocents.* San Francisco: Jossey-Bass Publishers.

Barber, Jim. (2004 February 6). Does Spanking Work? *Toronto Star.* Website: http://www.nospank.net.

Berlin et al. (2009). Correlates and Consequences of Spanking and Verbal Punishment for Low-Income White, African American, and Mexican American Toddlers. *Child Development, 2009; 80(5): 1403DOI: 10.1111/j 1467-8624.2009.01341.x.*

Bettner, B. and Lew, A. (1998). *Leader's Guide: Raising Kids Who Can Series Parent Study Group*. Newton Centre, Mass: Connexions Press.

Blumenthal, N. (2009). *Be the Hero*. San Francisco: Berrett-Koehler Publishers, Inc.

Boyle, L. (2011 June 4). Corporal Punishment in American Schools—Teaching Tough Terror? *Huffingpost.com*. Retrieved June 24, 2011 from http://nospank.net/n-u53.htm.

Bradshaw, J. (1996 November 22). *The Bradshaw Connection*. Broadcast on November 22, 1996. Website: http:/www.nospand.net/bradshaw.htm.

Bradshaw, J. (1996 November 22). "The Bradshaw Connection" broadcast on November 22, 1996, WOR-TV. Website: http://www.nospank.net/bradshaw.htm.

Brigham Young University (2011 June 13). Fathers Still Matter to Kids Who Have Moved Out. *ScienceDaily*. Website: http:/www.sciencedaily.com /release/2011/06/110613122529.htm.

Buddha. (Undated). (a.k.a. Siddhartha Gautama.) Website: http://www.quotationsbook.com/quote/38840/.

Cassel, P. and Corsini, R. (1990). *Coping with Teenagers in a Democracy*. Toronto, Canada. Lugus Productions Ltd.

Cater, M. (1979). *Ten Easy Rules on How to Raise a Delinquent. Parent Work Book for use with The Practical Parent in a Parents Study Group*. Unpublished manuscript.

Child Development Institute. (Undated). http://www. childdevelopmentinfo.com/development/birth_order.shtml.

Child Trends Databank (2008). Attitudes towards Spanking. *Child Trends*. Website: http://www.childhoodtrendsdatabamk.org/?q=node/187.

Child Welfare Information Gateway (2008). Long-Term Consequences of Child Abuse and Neglect. *U.S. Department of Health & Human Services*. Website: http://www.childwelfare.gov/pubs/factsheets/long_term_consequences.cfm.

Coghlan, A., Le Page, M. (2001 June 16). Babies Might Be Killed by Even Mild Shaking. *New Scientist*. Website: http://www.nospank.net/shake.htm.

Collins, R. (2009 October). James Dobson Just Has to be Responsible for Many Psychopaths in America. *End Heredity Religion.com. Website*: http://www. endheredityreligion.com/2009/10/james-dobson-just-has-to-be-responsible-f . . .

Corsini, R. and Painter, G. (1984). *The Practical Parent*. New York: Simon & Schuster, Inc.

Deutch, J. (2000). Eating Should Be the Child's Problem. In *The IslandVegetarian: Vegetarian Society of Hawai'i Quarterly Publication*, Volume 11, Issue 1, March 2000, pp. 183-84.

Dreikurs, R. and Soltz V. (1964). *Children: The Challenge*. New York: Hawthorn Books.

Dreikurs, R. (1953). *Fundamentals of Adlerian Psychology*. Chicago, Illinois. Alfred Adler Institute.

Dreikurs, R. (1958). *The Challenge of Parenthood*. New York: Meredith Press.

Dreikurs, R., Gould, S., and Corsini, R. (1974). Chicago. *Family Council: The Dreikurs Techniques for Putting an End to War between Parents and Children (and between Children and Children)*. Chicago, Illinois: Henry Regnery Company.

Durant, W. (2008). *The Story of Philosophy: The Lives and Opinions of the Great Philosophers*. New York: Simon & Schuster.

Dyer, Wayne. (Undated). http://en.thinkexist.com/quotes/Wayne _ Dyer/.

Ellenberger, H. (1970). *The Discovery of the Unconscious: The History and Evolution of Dynamic Psychiatry*. New York: Basic Books, Inc.

Ellis, A. and Dryden, W. (1997). *The Practice of Rational-Emotive Behavior Therapy*. New York: Springer.

Everyday Health (Undated). Shaken Baby Syndrome Causes, Symptoms, and Treatment. *Everyday Health*. Website: http://www.everydayhealth.com/health-center/shaken-baby-syndrome.aspx.

Franklin, B. (Undated). *Poor Richard's Almanack*. Mount Vernon, New York: Peter Pauper Press.

Furtmuller, C. (1979). In Hooper, A. and Holford, J. (1998). *Adler for Beginners*. New York: Writers and Readers Publishing, Inc.

Gershoff, E. T. (2002). Parental Corporal Punishment and Associated Child Behaviors and Experiences. A Meta-Analytic and Theoretical Review. *Psychological Bulletin*, 128(4), 539-579.

Gershoff, E. T. (2008*). Report on Physical Punishment in the United States: What Research Tells Us about Its Effects on Children*. Columbus, Ohio: Center for Effective Discipline.

Glueck, S. and Glueck, E. (1940) *Juvenile Delinquents Grown Up*. New York: Commonwealth Fund.

Glueck, S. and Glueck, E. (2011). In *Encyclopedia Britannica*. Website: http://www.britannica.com/EBchecked/topic/1353094/Glueck-Sheldon-and-Blueck-Eleanor.

Goodmama, Tammy (2005 August 30). The Statistics on Spanking. Website: http://www.epinions.com/content 4499546244.

Gordon, T. and Sands, J. (1976). *P.E.T. in Action*. New York: Wyden Books.

Gordon, T. (1970). *P.E.T.: Parent Effectiveness Training*. New York: Wyden Books.

Gordon, T. and Burch, N. (1974). *Teacher Effectiveness Training*. New York: Peter H. Wyden.

Gordon, T. (2009). *P.E.T.: Parent Effectiveness Training: Audiotape. http://www.audible.com*.

Guthrow, J. (2002 December). Correlation between High Rates of Corporal Punishment in Public Schools and Social Pathologies. *Parents and Teachers against Violence in Education*. Website: http://www.nospank.net.

Holden, G. W. (2002). Perspectives on the Effects of Corporal Punishment: Comment on Gershoff (2002). *Psychological Bulletin*, 128(4), 590-595.

Kobayashi, K. (2011 June 20). Judges Split on Ruling on Parental Discipline. *Star Advertiser* (Honolulu, Hawai'i). Website: http://www.staradvertiser.com/news /20110620.

Kohn, Alfie. (2005) *Unconditional Parenting: Moving from Rewards and Punishments to Love and Reason.* New York: Astra Books.

Labaree, L., and others. (Eds.) (1964). *The Autobiography of Benjamin Franklin.* New Haven: The Yale Press.

Lawlis, F. (2004). *The ADD Answer: How to Help Your Child Now.* New York: Penguin Group.

Legacy.com (2011 March). Dr. Benjamin Spock: Child Care and Controversy. The Obit Report. *Legacy.com.* Website: http://www.legacy.com/ns/news-story.aspx?t=dr-benjamin-spock-child-care-and-controversy&id=278.

Lehigh University (2001 February 1). Lehigh Researchers Examine Link between Abusive Child-Rearing, Overly Aggressive Behavior. *Lehigh University.* Website: http://www.eurekalert.org/pub_releases/2001-01/LU-Lrel-3101101.php—8.1KB—Public Press Releases. Also found on http://www.nospank.net.

Lines, D. (2008). *The Bullies: Understanding Bullies and Bullying.* Philadelphia: Jessica Kingsley Publishers.

Lombardo, L. (2002 November 17) Our Child Don't Deserve to Be Beaten. Website: http//: nospank.net/lombardo.htm.

Marlin, K. (Undated). Words That Encourage. In Cater, M. (1979). *Parent Work Book for Use with the Practical Parent.* Unpublished manuscript.

Martini, M. (2009). *Syllabus for Family Resources, Course FamR 341, Parenting.* (Unpublished document.)

Marzano, R., Pickering, D., and Pollock, J. (2001). *Classroom Instruction That Works: Research-Based Strategies for Increasing Student Achievement.* Alexandria, Virginia: ASCD Publications.

McCormick, Blaine. (2005). *Ben Franklin: America's Original Entrepreneur. (Franklin's autobiography adapted for modern times.)* Canada: Entrepreneur Press.

McKay, B. and McKay, K. (2008). *The Virtuous Life: Wrap Up, June 1, 2008.* Website: http://artofmanliness.com 2008/ 06/01/the-virtuous-life-wrap-up/.

Mckimm, Lisa. (Undated). *The Awesome Parents Handbook.* Waikato River, New Zealand: Parenting Worx.

Miller, A. (1998). *Every Smack Is a Humiliation.* Written for *Project NoSpank.* Website: http://nospank.net/miller3.htm.

Miller, A. (1999, June). Spanking Is Counterproductive and Dangerous. *Parents and Teachers against Violence in Education.* Website: http://www.nospank.net/miller10.htm.

Miller, A. (2001). *The Truth Will Set You Free.* New York: Basic Books.

Miller, A. (2002, 4th Edition). *For Your Own Good.* New York: Farrar-Straus-Geroux. Retrieved June 23, 2011 from NoSpank.net. [Free download.]

Miller, A. (2008 September) *The Roots of Violence Are Not Unknown: The Misled Brain and the Banned Emotions.* Website: http://.www.nospank. net/miller33pdf.

Miller, A. *Truth of Illusion? Afterwards to the Second Edition (1984) of For Your Own Good.* Website: *http://www.nos*pank.net.

Miller, A. (1998). *Paths of Life.* New York: Pantheon.

Mister In-Between. (Undated). Website: http://www.mathematik. uni-ulm. de/paul/lyrics/ bingcrosby/ accent-1.html.

MyDr.com (Undated). Sciatica: Symptoms, Causes, and Diagnosis. *MyDr.com.* Website: http://www.mydr.com.au/sports-fitness/sciatica-symptoms-causes-and-diagnosis.

Nelson, J. and Lott, L. (2000). *Positive Discipline for Teenagers.* New York. Random House, Inc.

Nelson, J. (1996). *Positive Discipline.* New York: Ballantine Books.

Newman, D. (2009). Families: A Sociological Perspective. New York: McGraw-Hill.

Norman, M. and Jordan, J. (Undated). *Using an Experiential Model in 4-H.* Website: http://edis.ifas.ufl.edu.4H243.

NoSpank.net (2009 April). Corporal Punishment to Children's Hands: A Statement by Medical Authorities as to the Risks. Website: http://nospank.net /hands.htm.

NoSpank.net (Undated). Psychological Evaluation of a Child Abused at School. *NoSpan.net.* Website: http://www.nospank.net.

Ohio State University (2009 August 12). Mothers, but Not Fathers, Follow Their Own Moms' Parenting Practices. *Science Daily.* Website: http://www.sciencedaily .com /releases/2009/08/090810024827.htm

Olson, D., DeFrain, J., and Skogrand, L. (2011). *Marriages and Families: Intimacy, Diversity, and Strengths, Seventh Edition.* New York: McGraw-Hill.

Painter, G. and Corsini, R. (1990). *Effective Discipline in the Home and School.* Muncie, Indiana: Accelerated Development, Inc.

Parents and Teachers against Violence in Education. www.nospank.net/violatn.htm.

Parents and Teachers against Violence in Education. *Quintilian's Observation on the Smacking of Children.* Institutes of Oratory, Rome, circa 88 CE. Website: http://www.nospank.net/quint.htm.

Parker, R. (2004 May 17). *Longitudinal Brain Scan Study Shows How Brain Matures.* Website: http://www.futurepundit .com/archives/002116. html).

Patten-Hitt, E. (2000 December 29). Child Abuse Changes in Developing Brain. *Reuters Health*, Yahoo! News. Website: http://www.nospank.net/teicher.htm.

Pepper, F. (Undated). *The Characteristics of the Family Constellation.* In Soltz, V. (Ed.) (1975). *Articles of Supplementary Reading for Parents.* Chicago: Alfred Adler Institute of Chicago.

Physorg.com (2008 February 18). Children's IQ Go Up When Parents Learn [Parenting Techniques]. *United Press International.* Website: http://www.physorg .com/news122545602.html

Pitten-Hitt, E. (2000 December 29) Childhood Abuse Changes the Developing Brain. *Yahoo! News.* Website: http://nospank.net/tericher.htm.

Plaut, W. (Ed.). (1981). *The Torah: A Modern Commentary.* New York: Union of American Hebrew Congregations.

Reimer, C. (Undated). In Soltz, V. (Ed). *Articles of Supplementary Reading for Parents.* (1975). Chicago: Alfred Adler Institute of Chicago.

Reuters (1998 August 3). Want Smarter Kids? Don't Spank Them. *Reuters.* Website: http://www.nospank.net/straus4.htm

Riak, J. (2006, April). Ask Ten Spankers. *Nospank.net.* Website: http://nospank.net /askten.htm.

Riak, J. (2009 Edition). *Plain Talk about Spanking.* Parents and Teachers against Violence in Education. Read online. Website: http://www.nospank.net/ pt2009.htm.

Rigney, K. and Corsini, R. (1970). *The Family Council.* [Booklet]. Chicago: North Side Unit of the Family Education Association.

Ron Howard. (Undated). Website: http://en.wikipedia.org/wiki /Ron_Howard.

Sagan, G. (2010 July 6). *Spanking Can Turn Easily into Abuse.* Website: http://nospank.net/sagan-1.htm.

Satten, Dorothy B. (2006). *Real Is Better than Perfect.* La Verne, California: Hopedancing Publishing.

Shakespeare. W. (Undated). Website: http://www.enotes.com/shakespeare-quotes/nothing-either-good-bad-but-thinking-makes.

Smiles, S. (Undated). http://www.brainyquote.com/quotes/ authors/s/samuel_smiles.html.

Society for Research in Child Development (2009 September 15) Spanking Found to Have Negative Effects on Low-Income Toddlers. *ScienceDaily.* Website: http://www.sciencedaily.com/releases/2009/09/090915/100941. htm

Soltz, V. (Ed.). (1970). *Articles of Supplementary Reading for Teachers and Counselors.* Chicago: Alfred Adler Institute of Chicago.

Soltz, V. (1975). *Articles of Supplementary Reading for Parents.* Chicago: Alfred Adler Institute of Chicago.

Sonstegard, M., and Sonnenshein, M. (1977). *The Allowance: Wages for Wee Folks.* Chicago: Adams Press.

Spock, B., Needleman, R. (2004). Baby and Child Care. 8th Edition. New York: Pocket Books.

St. Joseph's Hospital and Medical Center. Pudendal Neuralgia. Website: http:www.stjosephs-phx.org/Medical Services/Center for Women's Health/196316.

Stein, H. (Undated). *Adlerian Overview of Birth Order Characteristics.* Website: http://pws.cablespeed.com/~htstein/birthord.htm.

Straus, M. and Paschall, M. (2009). Corporal Punishment by Mothers and Development of Children's Cognitive Ability: A Longitudinal Study of Two Nationally Representative Age Cohorts. *Journal of Aggression Maltreatment & Trauma,* 2009; 18 (5): 459 DOI: 10.1080/10926770903035168.

Straus, M. (1997 August 13). Spanking Makes Children Violent, Antisocial: Effects Same Regardless of Parenting Style, Socioeconomic Status, Sex of Child or Ethnic Background. *American Medical Association News, Update.* Website: http://nospank. net /straus.htm.

Straus, M. (1999 July 24). Spanking Teaches Short-Term Lessons, but Long-Term Violence. *Forkidsake.org.* Website: http://forkidsake.org/spanking.html.

Straus, M. (2001). 2nd Edition. *Beating the Devil Out of Them: Corporal Punishment in American Families and Its Effects on Children.* New Jersey: Transaction Publishers.

Teicher, M. (2002 March). The Neurobiology of Child Abuse. *Scientific American*, pp.68-75. Website: http://nospank.net/teicher2.htm.

Teicher, M. (2010 October 18). *The Pierre Janet Memorial Lecture: Does Child Abuse Permanently Alter the Human Brain?* Website: https://www. softconference.com /isstd/itin.asp.

Terner, Janet and Pew, W. L. (1978). *The Courage to Be Imperfect: The Life and Work of Rudolf Dreikurs.* New York: Hawthorn Books, Inc.

Torah. (1974). *The Torah: The Five Books of Moses. A New Translation of the Holy Scriptures according to the Masoretic Text.* Philadelphia: The Jewish Publication Society of America.

Tunde, W. (2009 January 3). *Are You a First-Born Child, a Middle-Born Child, or the Baby of the Family?* http://www.sodahead.com/.living/are-you-a-first-born-child-a-middle-born-child-or-the-baby-of-the-familylook-at-the-characteris/question-224576/

U.S. Department of Health and Human Services. (Undated). *Stop Bullying Now.* (CD) Website: http://www.stopbullyingnow.hrsa.gov.

University of Chicago. (2011 June 19). Fathers Benefit from Seeking Help as Parents. *ScientificDaily.* Website: http://www.sciencedaily.com/ releases/ 2011/06110615103222htm.

University of Illinois at Urbana-Champaign (2009 August 13). Parental Influences Differ in Determining Later Latter Academic Success. *ScienceDaily.* Website: http://sciencedaily.com/releases/2009/08/0908111443htm.

University of Michigan Health System (2011 March 18). Sad Dads Spank More, Read Less, Study Finds. *ScientificDaily.* Website: http:// scientificdaily. com /releases/2011/03/110318121905.htm.

University of New Hampshire. (2008 March 2). Spanking Kids Increases Risk of Sexual Problems as Adult. *ScienceDaily.* Website: http://www. sciencedaily.com /release/2008/08/080228220451.htm.

University of North Carolina School of Medicine (2010 August 9). Corporal punishment of children remains common worldwide, studies find. *ScienceDaily.* Website: http://www.sciencedaily.com / releases/2010/08/100809111232.htm.

Walwik, J. A. (2008). Rewarding Virtue: The Presidency and Benjamin Franklin's Plan for Moral Perfection. New York: Hamilton Books.

Weber, G. (Undated). Grooming Children for Sexual Molestation. *The Zero 5.Olaf-The official website of Andrew Vachss.* Website: http://www. vachss.com/guest _dispatches/grooming.html.

WebMD (Undated). Results for: *Sacrum.* Website: http://www.webmd. com/ search/search_results/default .aspx?query=sacrum&sourceType= undefined.

Wedding, D. (2010 January). Corsini Obituary. *American Psychologist, Volume 65, Issue 1, January 2010, 54. doi: 10.1037/a0017770.*

Whitehurst, T., Haskins, D., Crowell, Al. (Undated). *The Nonviolent Christian Parent.* Christian Nonviolent Parenting. (Read online at http://www.nospank .net/ cnpindex.htm).

Wikipedia (Undated). *Child Grooming.* Website: http://ne.wikipedia.org/ wiki/ child grooming.

Wikipedia (undated). Corporal Punishment in the Home. Website: http:// en. wikipedia.org/wiki/Domestic_corporal_punishment.

Witkin, G. (2010). *Birth Order Personality Traits.* YouTube. Website: http://www.youtube.com/watch?v=YstSLxQQqDw&feature=fvw.

Yoda. (Undated). Website: http://www.starwars.com/databank /character / yoda/.

PHOTO CREDITS

Cover.   Clipart copyright GraphicsFactory.com
with adaptations by Eumir Carlo Fernandez.

Section I.   Page 20, William B. Pierce; p. 46 (upper) Widelec.org, (lower) Design Pix.

Section II.   Page 170, Monica Lau; p. 176, Elaine French.

Section III. Page 202, left and right pictures, Wikipedia.

Section IV.   Page 218, courtesy of United States Air Force; p. 229, courtesy of Marcia Ellis Deutch.

Section VI.   Page 327, upper and lower pictures courtesy of Marcia Ellis Deutch; p. 328, all pictures courtesy of Dorothy L. Deutch; p. 336, KMDN Daily PikDump; p. 340, Widelec.org;

Section VII. Page 344, courtesy of James A. Deutch.

INDEX

A

B

R

S

U

V

W

T

Y

Edwards Brothers Malloy
Thorofare, NJ USA
August 2, 2013